The Critic
Examinati

The Critical Examination

An Approach to Literary Appreciation at an Advanced Level

MALCOLM PEET
&
DAVID ROBINSON

Nelson

Thomas Nelson and Sons Ltd
Nelson House   Mayfield Road
Walton-on-Thames   Surrey
KT12 5PL   UK

51 York Place
Edinburgh
EH1 3JD   UK

Thomas Nelson (Hong Kong) Ltd
Toppan Building 10/F
22A Westlands Road
Quarry Bay   Hong Kong

Thomas Nelson Australia
102 Dodds Street
South Melbourne
Victoria 3205   Australia

Nelson Canada
1120 Birchmount Road
Scarborough   Ontario
M1K 5G4   Canada

© Malcom Peet and David Robinson 1977
First published by Arnold Wheaton (a division of Pergamon Press) 1977
(under ISBN 0-0-08-021099-6)

This edition published by Thomas Nelson and Sons Ltd 1989

ISBN 0-17-432261-5
NPN 9 8 7 6 5 4 3 2

Printed in Hong Kong.

Preface

The Critical Examination is written to and for Advanced Level students of literature who will sit an unseen paper in 'critical appreciation' as part of their final examination. It is not another work of 'Lit. Crit.' because our aim is modest and practical— namely, to enable students of English literature to survive an outmoded form of examination. We have tried to do three things: to discuss and apply the critical methods encouraged by Examiners; to write introductory studies of some topics in criticism which, in our experience, students have found difficult; and to compile materials which candidates and teachers may find useful in preparing for examinations. This book is not conceived as the kind of thing one reads through quickly as 'background'. We have tried to produce a volume best used as a reference or text-book. The essays on such matters as 'Form', 'Meaning', 'Irony' and 'Tone' and so forth are intended to raise issues for discussion; they struggle with problems that are complex and slippery, and for which there are no simple answers.

ACKNOWLEDGEMENTS

Thanks are due for the use of the following material:

Wild Swans at Coole by W. B. Yeats to M. B. Yeats, Miss Anne Yeats & The Macmillan Company of London & Basingstoke.

A Singular Metamorphosis by Howard Nemerov from MIRRORS & WINDOWS, University of Chicago Press, 1958. Copyright 1958 by Howard Nemerov.

The Heron by Vernon Watkins from THE DEATH BELL, Faber and Faber Ltd., to Gwen Watkins.

White Christmas by W. R. Rodgers from COLLECTED POEMS, © Oxford University Press 1971, by permission of the Oxford University Press, Oxford.

The Visitant by Theodore Roethke from COLLECTED POEMS, Faber and Faber Ltd., to the publishers.

Avenue by Michael Gibbs.

An Elementary School Classroom in a Slum by Stephen Spender from COLLECTED POEMS, Faber and Faber Ltd., to the publishers.

The Survivor by R. S. Thomas from TARES, Rupert Hart-Davis, to the publishers.

Low Barometer by Robert Bridges, to Oxford University Press.

First Snow in Alsace by Richard Wilbur from POEMS 1943–56, Faber and Faber Ltd., to the publishers.

An Open Air Performance of 'As You Like It' by E. J. Scovell, Barrie & Jenkins, to the publishers.

The Statesman by Hilaire Belloc from CAUTIONARY VERSES, Gerald Duckworth & Company Ltd., to the publishers.

Red Wheelbarrow by William Carlos Williams, COLLECTED EARLIER POEMS. Copyright 1938 by New Directions Publishing Corporation. Reprinted by permission of New Directions Publishing Corporation, New York.

Wind and Silver by Amy Lowell from THE COMPLETE POETICAL WORKS OF AMY LOWELL, Houghton Mifflin Company, to the publishers.

In Memory of W. B. Yeats by W. H. Auden, from COLLECTED SHORTER POEMS, Faber and Faber Ltd., to the publishers.

In a Station of the Metro and *Alba* by Ezra Pound, from COLLECTED SHORTER POEMS, Faber and Faber Ltd., to the publishers.

Low Barometer and *Nightingales* by Robert Bridges from THE POETICAL WORKS OF ROBERT BRIDGES, by permission of the Oxford University Press, Oxford.

White Christmas, W. R. Rodgers: COLLECTED POEMS 1971, by permission of the Oxford University Press, Oxford.

Attempts to trace the copyright holder of *The Woman at Washington Zoo* by Randall Jarrell, have been unsuccessful.

Contents

Introduction

I THE MYSTIQUE OF THE UNSEEN

The only end of writing is to enable readers better
to enjoy life or better to endure it.

Dr. Johnson

A poem . . . ends in a clarification of life—not
necessarily a great clarification, such as sects
and cults are founded on, but in a momentary stay
against confusion.

Robert Frost

The article of faith which underlies these two statements—that
literature actually improves the quality of the reader's life—is,
presumably, that which justifies the teaching of literature in
schools. It is an idea which is, of course, strictly a matter of faith,
since, as numerous writers have pointed out, the empirical,
historical evidence for its validity is most ambiguous. I cannot be
certain that any of my students have become in some way 'better'
people for having studied *King Lear*, say, or *Pride and Prejudice*.
Nevertheless, most writers, teachers and examiners, would, I feel,
agree in general terms with Johnson and Frost.

Criticism (which we understand to mean the three interrelated
activities of scrutiny, interpretation and evaluation), is, or should
be, a means of facilitating the communication between a writer and
ourselves. 'The whole apparatus of critical rules and principles is
a means to the attainment of finer, more precise, more discriminat-
ing communication.'* To read critically is to seek to understand
and appreciate more fully the writer's attempt to help us enjoy,
endure or clarify life. Criticism is thus an essentially creative and

*I. A. Richards: *Practical Criticism* (1929), Introduction.

ix

personal activity. It is in sympathy with imaginative literature and in a number of fundamental respects resembles it.

This being so, the way in which we assess, at Advanced Level, a student's critical sensitivity is curious, to say the least. After some two years of study, he is confined in a heavily-populated room, where he is asked to demonstrate his abilities in two and a half hours; during this time he is not allowed to move about, read verse aloud or otherwise speak, nor refer to the texts under discussion. For a large number of the victims the shape of the immediate future depends upon the outcome. It is difficult to think of any worthwhile work of literature or criticism which has been written under similar circumstances. On the other hand, it might just possibly be the best method yet devised for instilling into people a deep-seated aversion to literature. Yet this current mode of examination is not in itself the greatest disservice we do either literature or our students.

Since it is part and parcel of a teacher's job to get his or her students through the examination, that teacher's approach to literature must inevitably be shaped not only by the criteria of the examiners (which may not in themselves be bad) but also by the conditions of the examination itself, and these *are* completely irrelevant to a true appreciation of literature. We refer, of course, to such things as the mechanical efficiency in writing demanded by the time limitation, the memorization of 'strategic' quotations, the learning of convenient essay structures. (The kind of thing, in short, that we deal with in this book). While the talented minority of students will perhaps not need instruction in these matters, the fact is that the majority do. This means that teachers spend time teaching their students how to pass examinations when they could be doing creative things, such as encouraging and developing critical approaches to literature. The examinations that deal with prescribed texts have little or no relevance to a student's personal critical awareness. Since the A-Level examiners do not expect originality from their candidates, and since they do not encourage writing which shows a subjective response to, or deep engagement with, the works under study, a student who has (a) familiarized himself thoroughly with a handful of texts, (b) a good collection of notes from class, (c) an acquaintance with a small body of critical opinions about the various texts in question, (d) a reasonably polished 'A-Level style' and (e) an ounce of wit and general good sense can, and usually does, pass the 'set author' papers quite handsomely. In honest or unguarded moments, teachers will admit that they have known many students, thus suitably equipped, obtain high A-Level grades, even though some of them demonstrate no more real critical awareness of, or personal reaction to, literature than does an IBM computer. And of course, experienced teachers can and will predict, if not the actual phraseology of the exam questions, then the topics they are likely to involve. (I once taught in a college where the English staff bet hard cash on their predictions. One or two members regularly did quite well out of it.)

That the present A-Level examination system still prevails does not necessarily mean that the examiners are unaware of its inherent absurdities. The fact that students of literature can and do scientifically 'swot' their way to examination success is one reason why a number of Boards set unseen practical criticism papers (variously called 'Critical Appreciation and Comment', 'Comprehension and Appreciation', etc. For brevity we shall call them collectively 'The Unseen'). As one Examiners' Report puts it: 'The kind of reading the paper is trying to encourage is one that is not aimed simply at the external features of, say, a poem, but one that attempts to involve the reader's sensibility as a whole.' We might view The Unseen, then, as an attempt by the examiners to bring the A-Level study of literature closer to the function of criticism as it is understood by I. A. Richards (for example), and thus more in touch with what we could loosely term the moral dimension of literature as expressed by Dr. Johnson and Robert Frost. The Unseen also requires that examinees have some ability to handle the techniques and concepts of *practical criticism*. (We discuss below some of the explicit and implicit demands of the paper.)

Most teachers we have spoken or written to agree that The Unseen is the most difficult literature paper for which to prepare. Obviously it cannot be 'swotted' in the way that the other papers can be. Under the Cambridge Examining Board the paper is optional, and less than fifteen percent of their candidates are entered for it. What are the reasons for the paper's unpopularity? It is difficult to know precisely the criteria the examiners apply to candidates' work. Who can say exactly what 'critical intelligence' or 'reading sensibility' mean? And, as one teacher remarked, 'How can there not be a high degree of subjectivity in the marking?' We know that there is disagreement among the examiners as to what the paper is trying to achieve. Then there are the practical difficulties of teaching for this paper. Since all poems—and, for that matter, passages of prose—are held to be unique, how can one be certain that one is rehearsing students on the appropriate sort of material? A lot of teachers, it seems, plump for the safe course—using past papers as the basis for discussion and written work. But the Examining Boards reserve the right to change the format of The Unseen without prior notice. Whatever 'critical intelligence' is, it takes rather a long time to nurture. Ideally, each student should receive a good deal of individual attention in his or her pursuit of it, but in very many schools this is not possible. Finally, there is the content of the paper itself. In trying to guarantee that the extracts and poems *are* previously unseen by the candidates, the examiners tend to pick passages and, especially, poems which are obscure. It is often the case that these works are obscure for no other reason than that they deserve to be. Consequently, students are too frequently confronted by writing which is mediocre, conventional and unstimulating. (The Georgian poets seem to crop up more often than seems necessary, although one year the London Board did treat us—if that is the right word— to a poem by Adrian Henri. It seems that A-Level poetry flourished in England between 1890 and 1930.)

What all this adds up to is that, as the Examiners' Reports indicate, poor performance in The Unseen examination is the greatest single reason for failure among A-Level candidates.

It all lends The Unseen a kind of mystique. One senior examiner told us that in his opinion an examination paper was almost an art form, possessing a character, and a unity or integrity of its own. Another advised us not to 'approach this, of all papers, in an examination way.' But how else does one approach an examination? When we said we intended to comment on the nature of the paper, its general character, the criteria it seems to employ, and examiners' comments on the performance of candidates, we were told that 'students will not be and cannot be interested in this aspect of things.' Comments like these reflect an odd protectiveness in the examiners' attitude towards The Unseen. This may possibly be because they are uncertain about its objectives or anxious about the way it is marked. Or, more probably, it may be that The Unseen is considered to involve a degree of specialized discipline not present in other papers, a degree of *mystery* (in the old sense of the word), and some of the skills which identify the literary scholar and distinguish him from other men.

There can be no doubting the validity and usefulness of the general principles and techniques of practical criticism. (In fact, it could only be to the good, if they were considered an essential element of all education. Why is it that we make no methodical attempt to equip *all* pupils and students with the critical skills needed to scrutinize, interpret and evaluate language? Not just literary language, of course, but the language of politics, of advertising, or of broadcasting. Since educationalists constantly bemoan the corruption of language by such agencies, it is surprising that no determined effort has been made to establish elementary critical techniques as an educational prerequisite only slightly less fundamental than basic literacy). Indeed, it can be argued that the Unseen is the only examination which has any validity as a means of assessing a student's abilities as a critical, appreciative and sensitive reader of literature. This only makes more deplorable the frequent predictability and dullness of the paper's content.

II SETTING OUT FOR THE UNSEEN

How may a student best prepare himself for The Unseen? There are two basic requirements: the first is that he should have what the examiners call 'a background of wide-ranging and critical reading'; the second is some familiarity with the procedures of practical criticism. Let us begin with the first of these requirements.

Studying the texts prescribed for the other literature papers is not in itself enough, nor is it sufficient to read a large number of books of only one kind — modern novels, say. A great many students sit The Unseen without having read any English essayists, for example, or any poetry written during periods not covered by the A-Level syllabus. Furthermore, the voracious reader is not always a critical reader, and it is often difficult for such a student to find the opportunity to discuss his extra-curricular reading with someone more informed or experienced than himself. The kind of writing which has often featured in unseen papers is not, it must be admitted, the sort of stuff to which young readers will be attracted instinctively; I cannot recall any student ever approaching me lit up with a new-found enthusiasm for, let us say, Thomas Babington Macaulay or Edward Gibbon.

The acquisition of a 'wide-ranging background' of reading must involve a certain amount of self-discipline and work. One thing you might do is spend an hour or so a week reading from anthologies of prose and verse which include writings from different genres and historical periods. The danger in this is that you may suffer a form of mental indigestion, whereby a great bulk of half-remembered words wallows around uselessly in your mind. The antidote is to *read* rather than merely to consume words. One consequence of our examination-ridden educational system is that students are taught to extract 'ideas', 'points' and 'information' from what they read. The assumption which underlies this sort of activity is that the content, the 'meaning' of a written work can be separated out from its style, form and language, which are mere ornament. This assumption is utterly irreconcilable with the appreciation of literature. When you read you must develop the habit of thinking as much about *how* a writer writes as about *what* he writes. In literature, there is a symbiotic relationship between style and meaning; each exists only by virtue of the other. If this book harps on this point, forgive me—it is of great importance. It also leads us directly to the basic principles of practical criticism.

What is 'practical criticism'? It is a mode of criticism which has been the backbone of literary study for the past fifty years, and is associated with two English critics: I. A. Richards, whose book *The Principles of Practical Criticism* appeared in 1924, and F. R. Leavis. In America, it is commonly called 'The New Criticism', after the title of a book by John Crowe Ransom published in 1941. The essence of practical criticism is contained in the name of the very influential periodical edited by Leavis—*Scrutiny*. At the present time, in some academic quarters, there is a reaction against practical criticism from those more interested in seeing and discussing the relationship between literature and politics, or psychology, or social issues, or some other wider contexts; there is some feeling that it creates narrowness of thought or over-specialization. This debate has not as yet had any effect upon A-Level study, of course, but it is true to say that the examiners do not expect rigorous adherence to Richards' principles, even though their Unseen Exam papers are still, basically, exercises in practical criticism. If, therefore, you can grasp and apply its principles you will be well prepared for your encounter with The Unseen. What are these principles?

First: a work of literature is to be considered a self-defining and unique entity. The critic 'is concerned with the work in front of him as something that should contain within *itself* the reason why it is so and not otherwise. The more experience—experience of life and literature together—he brings to bear on it the better, of course; and it is true that extraneous information may make him more percipient. But the business of critical intelligence will remain what it was: to ensure relevance of response and to determine what is actually *there* in the work of art.'* This warns against the 'background' approach to literature, the attempt to understand a novel or poem by relating it to (a) its historical and cultural context and (b) the author's life-experience. If we read *Paradise Lost*, it helps to know the political background, it helps to know something of Milton's religious and political commitment, it helps to know the literature and mythology to which the poem alludes; but these things cannot themselves reveal the poem's full *meaning* (a word we would have preferred to avoid for now, but . . .) for this depends upon what we might call the 'internal dynamics' of the thing itself. Throughout the following chapters we are at pains to stress the mutuality of form, sound, tone and

*F. R. Leavis: *The Common Pursuit*.

content in poetry and prose. You should consider the purpose of a critical appreciation to be the discovery and discussion of why the writing before you 'is so'—in form and significance—'and not otherwise.' All the evidence and material you will need in writing your appreciation will be contained within the poem or passage itself.

Second: this evidence and material shall arise from close scrutiny and analysis of the language of the text under consideration. This means that you will need to be familiar with some of the techniques of practical criticism. However, we have to add immediately that these are means and not ends. Richards carefully distinguishes between the *technical* and the *critical*. The analysis of metre and rhythm, the discovery of ambiguous significances in words, the examination of the relationship between balanced cadences, and so forth, are technical matters; criticism, on the other hand, is that activity which *uses* this technical knowledge to work towards a 'complete reading'—*not* a paraphrase or 'translation'—an attempt to *experience* the poem. That this last phrase is imprecise and abstract indicates one reason why many students rely too heavily on acquiring a competence in analytical technique and why, consequently, their critical studies are full of dull jargon: the aim of criticism is to express the effect of literature on the reader—i.e. yourself. Thus to write about a poem is, in the final analysis, to reveal yourself. This involves a preparedness to expose your sensitivity, and this takes a certain amount of courage. The over-use of technical jargon is an attempt to conceal sensitivity (or lack of it); and it is also an inhibited refusal to seek imaginative and personal language with which to express your response. But it is the nature, quality and expression of your response to literature which the examiners wish to see; if they do not, then they are doing nothing worthwhile.

Third: the meaning of *meaning* is complex. This is a bugbear of all criticism, and involves us in all manner of convolutions in phraseology. It is a sad fact about the English language that the word 'meaning' refers to the relationship between, say, the word 'pencil' and the definition 'a writing instrument consisting of a thin graphite rod encased in a cylinder of soft wood', and at the same time refers to the significance of *Othello*. When we use the word in a critical context we do not mean to indicate a literal, dictionary definition. A word's meaning is affected by a number of things, such as its context, the tone, its emphasis. (We discuss this at greater length in Chapter 7.) The problem is, of course, far more complicated when language is used figuratively; the total meaning of a metaphor is greater than the sum of the meanings of the component words. For this reason, critics, writers, examiners and the authors of this book are obliged to use the word 'effectiveness' as one means of indicating the 'full meaning' of words, phrases, images or whole written works, and as a means of recognizing that words act upon—affect—the reader's imagination. I. A. Richards suggests four kinds of meaning (*Practical Criticism*, Part III, Chapt. I): *Sense, Feeling, Tone* and *Intention*. He defines these categories as follows:

Sense is the immediate significance of the words—the names of the things, situations, incidents which are offered for the reader's consideration.

Feeling is the writer's attitude towards these things, his 'special direction', 'bias', a 'nuance of interest', which is inseparable from his presentation of the subject matter. Obviously, we may have latent or manifest feelings about these things which differ from the author's. Furthermore, as Richards points out, the speaker may be unaware that he is communicating these feelings and thus revealing his attitude.

Tone is that quality of the writer's 'voice' which reveals or openly expresses his attitude *towards the readers*, his 'recognition of his relation to them.' Again, this may be unconsciously revealed, or even deliberately disguised. (See the discussion of Swift's *A Modest Proposal* in Chapter 7).

Intention is, of course, the writer's aim (conscious or unconscious), 'the effect he is endeavouring to promote.' This purpose modifies his language in any of a number of ways. (Again, irony is a special case; the actual words may be at odds with the intended effect, and a grasp of tone and implied feeling is essential to our grasp of the writer's intention.)

As Richards points out, different types of writing will give prominence to one of these functions. A writer of a scientific treatise will attach greatest importance to *sense* and subordinate his *feelings* for the sake of clarity and objectivity. In poetry, *feeling*—or the manipulation and contemplation of *feeling*—is commonly of greater importance than *sense*; that is to say, the *things* (subject matter) are not to be taken as literal truths, but are means towards the expression of feeling. Likewise, the poet's *intention* may be no more specific than the communication of his feeling or the evocation of a kindred feeling in the reader.

Clearly, then, Richards' categories must be used flexibly and sensitively. (We would, in fact, dispute the need to distinguish always between *feeling* and *tone*; the writer's *tone* would seem to indicate both his attitude towards his subject and the reader.) Yet Richards' four kinds of meaning seem useful lines along which to approach a literary work's effectiveness. Indeed, a recent report by the examiners of the Associated Examining Board recommended Richards' methodology to its candidates.

The complexity of meaning in literature brings us into the more shadowy territory of *interpretation*. Here, the pitfall which claims the most victims is the temptation to go searching for hidden meanings. Commenting on their candidates' essays on a poem by Rudyard Kipling, one Examining Board reported:

> It was rare for candidates to have difficulty with the interpretation of Kipling's poem, but a minority refused to accept the surface meaning and plunged into some mystifying and complex symbolism. Sea-weed became tobacco, deep sexual undertones revealed themselves everywhere; divorce and even Amazonian ladies were seen to be lurking beneath Kipling's innocent diction. This was occasionally amusing, occasionally irritating, but always disturbing. It is unfortunate if candidates are taught to expect every poem to have deep, symbolic meanings.

Indeed it is. Your only safe assumption is that a poem means what it says and says what it means. If it doesn't, then it's not likely to be a good poem. This 'message-hunting' approach is one symptom of a rather commonplace belief: that 'ideas' can and do exist separately from language, and that language functions as a mere vehicle or 'disguise' for these 'ideas'. [To forestall this belief is one concern of this book. For the time being, let us say it is simply wrong, that ideas exist *as* language]. A related illusion is that to be good, a work of literature must convey original, profound or mightily intelligent insights into life. It is not, in fact, the aim of poetry to expand or revolutionize the store of human knowledge in the realms of philosophy, sociology, politics or whatever. At the level of 'message', most poems assert what are simple clichéd truths: 'War is nasty', 'Sex is rather nice', 'It's awful growing old.' But this is irrelevant. Poetry's energies are directed more towards *feeling* truths than towards simple *knowing* them. You may *know*—morally, intellectually—that killing people is wrong, but a poem by Wilfred Owen may make you *experience* that knowledge, and feel its active force. Poetry is more concerned with refreshing vision than with merely adding to it; more concerned with expanding the mind than with expanding knowledge; more concerned with new ways of seeing than with new things to see.

Problems of interpretation relate to the business of *subjectivity*. In haggling over the finer points of a poem's interpretation with students, we are often told 'Well, that's what it means to *me*'—implying that discussion stops there. It doesn't, of course, although there is a problem in that because the relationship between words and meaning is often nebulous, and because a poem's meaning can operate at a number of levels, various interpretations of that work may be possible. As one critic points out, 'One of the things that make paranoia possible is that interpretations can seldom be disproved, even if they are such as no person in his sane sense would accept.' (And it is also possible that a writer's work may have meanings he did not consciously intend). Nevertheless, validity of interpretation can be tested by sensitive reference to a poem's language.

> A single word by itself, let us say 'night', will raise almost as many different thoughts and feelings as there are persons who hear it. The range of variety with a single word is very little restricted. But put it into a sentence and the variation is narrowed; put it into the context of a whole passage, and it is still further fixed; and let it occur in such an intricate whole as a poem and the responses of competent readers may have a similarity which only its occurrence in such a whole can secure.*

Undisciplined subjectivity—which is undesirable—is not at all the same thing as individuality—which is earnestly to be wished for. Your critical writing should have some personality. You are off to a good start if you can regard critical appreciation -as an opportunity for imaginative and creative writing. Do not feel encumbered by the ponderous weight of existing critical opinion. We return to matters of essay style in Chapter 12, but let us try to establish our major point now. You should not separate the interdependent activites of reading and writing. Let what you read—poetry, fiction and criticism—inform your own writing. Inhibition is counter-productive. Imitate, plagiarize, bend, weld and adapt the styles of the authors you encounter until the bits add up to something which suits you. Expand, systematically and continually, your vocabulary. Ideas won't come until the words are already there.

*Richards: *Principles of Literary Criticism*, Ch. 1.

ONE

The Good, the Bad and the Ugly

Having already mentioned, in general terms, the kinds of mistake students tend to make in writing appreciations, we thought it would be only sensible to illustrate some of these mistakes early in the book so that you can avoid them henceforth. As it would be tedious to write a list of 'Do Nots,' our demonstration is in the form of essays by two students who were asked to write a study of W. B. Yeats' *The Wild Swans at Coole*.

The first was written by a student who had only recently begun his A-Level course, while the second is by a student who had already taken the examination. This will be immediately obvious from the greater confidence with which the second writer handles language and her familiarity with, and use of, a number of technical terms. Nevertheless, this comparison should be an efficient and reasonably digestible form in which to make a number of points.

Ideally, you should write your own appreciation of Yeats' poem before reading the two essays and the comments on them.

The Wild Swans at Coole

The trees are in their autumn beauty,
The woodland paths are dry,
Under the October twilight the water
Mirrors a still sky;
5   Upon the brimming water among the stones
Are nine-and-fifty swans.

The nineteenth autumn has come upon me
Since I first made my count;
I saw, before I had well finished,
10   All suddenly mount

And scatter wheeling in great broken rings
Upon their clamorous wings.

I have looked upon those brilliant creatures,
And now my heart is sore.
15   All's changed since I, hearing at twilight,
The first time on this shore,
The bell-beat of their wings above my head,
Trod with a lighter tread.

Unwearied still, lover by lover,
20   They paddle in the cold
Companionable streams or climb the air;
Their hearts have not grown old;
Passion and conquest, wander where they will,
Attend upon them still.

25   But now they drift on the still water,
Mysterious, beautiful;
Among what rushes will they build,
By what lake's edge or pool
Delight men's eyes when I awake some day
30   To find they have flown away?

The study written by 'Ted' (names have been changed to protect the innocent) runs as follows:

This poem describes some wild swans. The writer is very impressed by the sound of their wings and their tireless nature. He describes the swans as 'brilliant' and 'mysterious, beautiful'. He claims that they 'delight men's eyes'. But the
5   writer is not entirely at ease. He says that his 'heart is sore'. He looks back into the past and sees that 'all's changed'. He sees that while these swans will never change their nature the landscape will, as man continues to make it over to his own use. He asks, at the end of the poem, what place the
10   swans will find to make their homes when he 'awakes some day to find they have flown away'.
Although the swans themselves are the main figures in the poem, some attention is given to their surroundings. The swans are not actually introduced until the sixth line of the
15   first verse. This has the effect of setting the scene. We are told that it is autumn and that it is twilight. The water in the lake is calm and undisturbed. Yeats brings this across very

2

effectively in the metaphor 'the water mirrors a still sky'.
Perhaps this tranquil scene mirrors the poet's state of mind
at the beginning of the poem. The water is also described as
'companionable'. By comparing the water to a companion
the writer emphasizes the harmony of the birds and the
landscape. This metaphor makes the change forseen by
Yeats at the end of the poem all the more unwelcome.

When the poet makes his appearance the swans are
frightened and begin to fly about in great circles.

> All suddenly mount
> And scatter wheeling in great broken rings
> Upon their clamorous wings.

The lack of punctuation in these lines suggests a frantic
movement. By describing the swans as 'clamorous' the poet
emphasizes this. He also compares the noise of their wings
to the sound of a bell: he speaks of the 'bell-beat' of their
wings. The sound is loud and monotonous. The metaphor
could imply that the sound of their wings has a summoning
effect.

The swans have a tireless nature. Yeats says that 'their
hearts have not grown old'. They 'climb the air' with the
greatest ease. They are compared to lovers who perhaps
never tire during the early days of their courtship. But the
poet also sees them as passive creatures, as being
'Mysterious' and 'beautiful'. He describes them 'drifting in
the still water'. The long 'i' in 'drift' and 'still' stresses this
passivity.

Numbers seem to figure highly in this poem. Yeats notes
that there are 'nine-and-fifty' swans. This is a rather large
number and must indicate that the pond or lake on which
he sees them must be fairly big. He also tells us that

> The nineteenth autumn has come upon me
> Since I first made my count;

This use of numbers is perhaps a sinister hint that the
number of years that the swans will be able to stay in their
environment at Coole is limited.

The language of the poem is simple and therefore blends in
well with the simplicity of Nature. Alliteration is used a few
times. The repetition of the letter 't' in 'trod with a lighter
tread' has a pleasant-sounding effect. The alliteration of the
letters 'p' and 'c' in

> They paddle in the cold
> Companionable streams or climb the air

3

conveys a feeling of softness. The repetition of 'w' in 'wander where they will' is very positive, giving weight to the idea of the indefatigable swans.

The poem on the whole is regular in form. It has five verses, each with six lines. The rhyme pattern, with a few variations, is a regular A B C B D D.

Generally, the poem is about swans, with some hidden deeper meaning which is a bit confused and obscure. Yeats has perhaps tried to keep himself too disciplined in his rhyme-scheme to make this meaning entirely clear. The poem suggests that the poet sees the swans as a symbol for someone close to him, probably a woman whom he loved and who has left him, possibly for someone else. Perhaps the idea of lost love is˚ reinforced by such words as 'Autumn' and 'October', which herald winter, the symbol of death. Likewise, night is heralded by twilight. In this case, the death is of the woman's love for the poet. The fact that the poet 'awakes' suggests that he was blind to the gradual dying of this love, and he was awakened by her desertion.

The poet seems, finally, to envy or resent the swans because they are still 'lovers'. They are symbolic because the man's heart, since he first visited them, has grown old, whereas the swans seem eternally young. This kind of immortality the poet longs for.

Well, what is good or bad about this essay? What would an examiner make of it?

The basic fault is a *lack of structure*, and from this weakness most of Ted's individual mistakes derive. His study has no logical progression; there is nothing which pulls his ideas together. His first paragraph is really only a paraphrase of parts of the poem. Then at line 11 he begins to go through the poem stanza by stanza (and they are *stanzas*, not 'verses', as he calls them), but almost immediately confuses things by bringing in 'companionable' from stanza four. By the 40th line of his essay he has made a number of comments on the first four stanzas, but doesn't then go on to the fifth. Instead, he makes a few comments on Yeats' use of language. Finally, he devotes two paragraphs to an attempt at interpreting what he calls the poem's 'deeper meaning'.

That the essay lacks organization and coherence is perhaps the result of Ted's failure to detect the structure of the poem itself. He hasn't realized that each stanza marks *a change in the way the poet sees the swans*. He hasn't noticed that the poem begins in a world which is fixed, stable and conventionally beautiful, with the

4

swans numbered and in their places, but ends in uncertainty, with a question which envisages the loss of this stable world, and with the swans no longer familiar but 'mysterious'. He hasn't understood that that the meaning of the poem changes and progresses. As a result, he assumes that the swans have the same significance throughout. Accordingly, his essay betrays a confusion of thought by stringing together quotations from different stanzas. That he does this in his first paragraph is particularly unfortunate; an examiner would be unfavourably impressed from the outset.

Underlying all this is a major error in basic strategy. Instead of trying to get at meaning by means of a close examination of the poem's language, Ted has tried to make the language fit his assumptions about that meaning. He has tried to make his evidence fit the case, rather than build his case upon the evidence. This is the usual mistake made by people who adopt the message-hunting approach to poetry. Matters are made worse by the fact that he hasn't really any idea what the 'message' might be. We can see what goes through Ted's mind as he tackles this poem. He reads the first stanza, noticing the regularity of the rhythm and the generally picturesque effect of the language, and assumes that Yeats is embarking on a 'nature poem' of a 'romantic' variety. But as he reads on, he realizes that there is more to it than that; there is obviously some symbolic significance attached to the swans. It is understandable that he finds this meaning obscure, but his pre-occupation with puzzling it out distracts him. He doesn't go back and re-assess his original assumptions about the poem being a 'romantic' description of a natural scene. Consequently, when he does comment on language and form, he says things which he feels *ought* to be true of the kind of poem he *thinks* it is. Because of this, some of his comments are quite bizarre. He says, for example, that 'the language of the poem is simple and therefore blends in well with the simplicity of Nature.' It is true that the poem's language is simple in that there are few difficult words, but in fact Yeats' use of language is quite complex. And surely 'simple' is the least appropriate word to apply to Nature. He says elsewhere that the alliteration of the letters 'c' and 'p' in

> They paddle in the cold
> Companionable streams or climb the air

conveys a feeling of softness. It is difficult to see how a sequence of *hard* 'c's can convey softness. Or how he can say (lines 39-40) that 'passivity' is expressed by the 'long 'i' ' in 'drift' and 'still', especially since the 'i' is a *short* vowel in each case.

To be fair to Ted, he has not yet acquired the skills of examining language critically, nor is he simply insensitive to sound. He makes

5

these mistakes because his understanding is obstructed by a number of sentimental concepts he associates with Nature and 'nature poetry': Innocence, Simplicity, Softness, Beauty, Harmoniousness, and so forth. (He's also a little obsessed with 'Environmental' matters—Man's intervention in Nature, pollution, and so on. This comes across in lines 6-10 and again in lines 45-49.)

Ted's 'code-cracking' approach is the reason he makes his silliest comment. Unable to find any other secret meaning in the number 59, he concludes that 'it must indicate that the lake is fairly big'.

Because Ted hasn't attempted to get at his 'hidden meaning' by way of questioning Yeats' use of language, such comments as he does make on the poem's linguistic and formal devices are left feebly dangling. They don't lead to any conclusion, and they don't interconnect. He merely says that certain sound-effects are 'pleasant' or that alliterated 'w's are 'positive' (which they aren't). He makes no systematic attempt to relate these phenomena to his interpretative ideas. His feeling is that they are merely decorative or useful for 'emphasis'; he hasn't grasped the notion that verbal effects are *events* in a poem's development. He says that 'on the whole' the poem is 'regular in form', but it turns out that all he means by this is that the stanzas are all of the same length and have the same rhyme-scheme 'with a few variations'. He doesn't seem to think that these variations might be significant, nor does he say where and what they are. But form is not simply a matter of lines in rhyming groups. Form is largely a question of *rhythm* (a word which doesn't appear anywhere in Ted's essay). A stanza is a *rhythmic unit*, and meaning is as much a matter of the order, pace, sound and rhythm of words as it is of the words themselves. Having said that the stanzas were of equal size, Ted should have asked himself whether they all had the same character, the same feeling. They do not, and one important reason why they do not is that Yeats has varied his rhythms from stanza to stanza (and from line to line). The way the 'feel' of the stanzas changes *is* the way the meaning changes.

There are, however, two occasions when Ted does connect his comments on some formal aspect of the poem with his interpretation. He points out (lines 25-29) that the absence of punctuation in lines 4, 5 and 6 of the second stanza 'suggests a frantic movement'. 'Frantic' is perhaps not the best word, but the general idea is correct. Had he realized that punctuation is a *rhythmic device* he might have been led to examine the effect of the poem's rhythms generally.

The second occasion is when he makes the unfortunate remark that the obscurity of the poem's 'deeper meaning' is perhaps a

6

consequence of Yeats' adherence to the discipline of his rhyme-scheme. This raises the complex business of the relationship between form and meaning, which is something we shall have to return to later. For the time being, suffice it to say that Ted's apparent belief that there is some inherent opposition between form and meaning is completely mistaken. In the first place, Yeats *chose* to adopt a rhyming form to express his meaning, so we must assume that the rhymes have some purpose and significance, rather than think that he deliberately created a hindrance for himself.

So much of the poem's meaning depends upon the effect of the sound of the words; the poem is very *musical*, and rhyme is an integral part of this music. Consider, for example, how the approximate rhyme of 'stones'/'swans' has a completely appropriate harmony of sound, yet the sound of 'stones' is not so close to that of 'swans' that we anticipate the end of the stanza's last line; the 'build-up' to swans is not weakened, and the word keeps all the importance and emphasis that Yeats wants it to have. Or consider how not only the sound but also the meanings of 'old' and 'cold' echo each other in stanza four.

We've been rather heavy with the hatchet on poor Ted, so before we look at a more successful appreciation, let us say that his essay is not totally dreadful. He can be forgiven his preoccupation with the poem's 'hidden meaning', since it is, after all, a poem whose central image is symbolic, and no study of it can justifiably avoid seeking the significance of that symbol. Ted's interpretation, although it is rather incoherent, is not completely wide of the mark. He wants an over-precise meaning for the swans, and so believes that they are a symbol for a particular woman. (Ted is a sentimentalist at heart). The fourth stanza in particular provides some grounds for this belief. He has detected the poet's awareness of the unkind passage of time and the mood of imminent death; in the very last lines of his essay he shows he has seen that the swans in some way represent immortality, even if he thinks that the poet 'resents' them for it. (Ted was far less manic in his search for the 'secret message' concealed in The Wild Swans at Coole than were some of his fellow-students. One, who clearly had read something about Yeats' involvement in Irish politics, was convinced that the swans were 59 revolutionaries who had abandoned Yeats and 'flown' to Paris.) He has one or two good insights which, had he followed them up, might have led him somewhere. He suggests, for instance, that the tranquil scene in the first stanza reflects the poet's state of mind, but he doesn't go on to relate subsequent changes in this scene to corresponding fluctuations in the poet's feeling and attitude. He says somewhere else that 'bell-beat' hints at a summons, but fails to see that this gives something of a mystical character to the swans.

Ted's writing style is nervous and less than graceful, but its occasional ugly turns are probably a consequence of his as yet small vocabulary of critical terms.

Let us turn now to an essay printed under the pseudonym 'Joyce':

> The poem is very beautiful, but I don't mean that in any
> sentimental sense. The poem is *about* beauty, I think.
> **(Perhaps that is what the swans represent or symbolize.)**
> Or, more accurately, the poem concerns harmony, the
> 5   harmony between the swans, the swans and their environ-
> ment, and the harmony between the swans and the poet.
> The tone is melancholic because the poet realizes that this
> harmony between the swans and himself is lost, or at least
> transient.
> 10   To a very great extent, the poem depends for its effect
> upon the sound of its language. In terms of meaning, the
> words are quite simple ('Companionable streams' is the only
> phrase I find difficult), but Yeats has been very skilful in
> making sound echo sense. This is true of individual words
> 15   and phrases, such as in line 18 where there is consonance
> between 'trod' and 'tread', but the vowel sound of 'tread' is
> 'lighter'. It is also true of the poem as a whole; shifts in
> mood are conveyed by shifts in rhythm and sound. The
> violent movement in the second stanza is the clearest
> 20   example. Generally speaking, Yeats sets up regular rhythms
> which are then broken at significant points. These varia-
> tions in sound are all the more important because they are
> in a sense the narrative of the poem. There is only one
> actual incident: the sudden uprising of the swans at line 10.
> 25   **The main concern of the poem is the way the meaning of the**
> **swans changes for the poet.**
> The swans are introduced at line 6. The preceding 5 lines
> serve to set the scene, but do more than just that. The
> poem starts off in a conventional, confident way, but the
> 30   third line is difficult to scan. There is a pause after 'twilight'
> where a stress is expected. Also, I half-expected the line to
> end with a rhyme on 'beauty'. After this ruffling of the
> rhythm, the fourth line is very emphatic. The total effect of
> having the first stress on the first syllable, the alliteration of
> 35   'still sky', and the semi-colon, is to stop the reader in his
> tracks for a moment (as the poet stopped, perhaps, on
> seeing the swans). This pause is dramatic in that it antici-

pates the poem's key image. It also seems to 'freeze' that image. The opening stanza as a whole is a picture, like a
40 photograph. The scene is motionless, perfect, seemingly permanent. We come finally to the swans, where the rhythm evens out (Yeats writes 'nine-and-fifty' rather than 'fifty-nine' in order to get this evenness) and it is clear at this point that the swans are to be the poem's subject.

45 But this changes when the second stanza begins. Several things happen. We realize the poet is actually there, and our attention shifts from the natural scene to him. There is a movement in time, to the past. (The time-changes are confusing throughout the poem, and I'm not sure whether
50 'saw', in line 9, refers to the present or to the time nineteen years previously.) We get the first suggestion that the poem is concerned with time and with time's passing. The phrase 'has come upon me' has a sad and perhaps resentful ring. Because of this, the imagery of the first
55 stanza takes on new meaning. Until the poet makes his appearance, the autumn woodland and the twilight are to be taken literally, but now we pick up their associations with ageing and fading. The most noticeable change is in the swans themselves. From being static 'props' in the
60 pastoral scene of the first stanza they are transformed into figures of great and anarchic power. The harmony is shattered by a sequence of words suggesting dischord: 'suddenly . . . scatter . . . broken . . . clamorous.'

This vigorous movement by the swans brings with it a
65 deepening in tone. The poet has studied the swans and now his 'heart is sore.' Because the two statements are connected by 'and', it is not necessarily the case that he is grieving because of the swans, but that suggestion is there. 'All's changed', and although what 'All' is, is not made
70 clear, there is a feeling of loss. The loss, it seems, is the poet's youthfulness; nineteen years on from his first visit to Coole, he walks with a heavier tread. But I feel his unhappiness is not caused by age alone. There has been a change in the way he sees the world. (It was twilight
75 nineteen years ago, but it did not seem so significant then.) The swans, at this point in the poem, begin to take on symbolic qualities. 'Bell-beat' describes the heavy rhythm of the birds' wings, but for me the phrase has connotations of a vaguely religious nature, and bells are a signal or summons.
80 It is as if the swans were leading him then, or even perhaps lifting him in some way.

In the fourth stanza the swans are certainly symbolic. They are 'lovers', and constant lovers too. By contrast with the man they are 'unwearied'. They are at home in both elements, the 'cold/companionable streams' and the air. They are ageless, their 'hearts do not grow old' (nor 'sore'). But it is the last couplet of this stanza which is most important in conveying the symbolic character of the swans.

Passion or conquest, wander where they will,
Attend upon them still.

The word 'attend' tells us that the birds do not have to seek passion and conquest, but that passion and conquest are in some way servants of the swans, following them wherever they care to wander. The swans are noble or regal, perhaps even god-like. A number of words in this stanza ('lover', 'companionable', 'hearts', 'passion', 'conquest') hint that the poet is brooding over a lost lover, but his sorrow seems to have more to do with his inability to be like the swans than with disappointed love. Despite the feeling of sadness, there is a return to calm in this stanza. The word 'still' occurs twice. The rhythm is in a more or less regular iambic metre and soft consonants dominate. There is only one word which has any hardness ('conquest'). Line 22 is smoothed even more by the long alliteration of '. . . conquest, wander where they will.'

This air of stillness continues into the final stanza. There is a return to 'now'. The poem ends with a question, and the word 'awake' comes as a surprise: the swans are a dream or an illusion.

Exactly what the swans symbolize is difficult to say. Perhaps one would have a better idea of their meaning after reading more of Yeats' poems. In this, the symbolism remains rather vague, and this must be deliberate. It is clear that the swans have greater significance at the end of the poem than at the beginning. It is also clear that they are eternal, outside time. ('Still', in both places in stanza four can mean 'always' or 'forever'.) Therefore they remind the poet that he is not. It may be that he will 'awake' only when he dies. The fact that he comes to Coole every year suggests that his counting is some kind of ritual. The recurrence of references to age and the autumn twilight lead me to think that the swans represent his past (perhaps he is 59 years old) or his youth. 'Passion and conquest' indicate youthfulness. This would explain why they will have flown away when he dies. But the thing is that the poet doesn't

125   complete his ritual counting. Before he had 'well finished',
      the swans 'suddenly mount/And scatter'. It's as if they
      refuse to be pinned down and numbered, refuse to be
      controlled or owned by him. So that whereas at the beginning
      of the poem the swans are numbered, static figures in a still
130   landscape, at the end they are drifting, and they are remote,
      'mysterious'. In the end, the poet seems to accept this. The
      last emotion is 'delight'. He overcomes his melancholy by
      realizing that although he may die, or merely lose his youth-
      fulness, the immortal swans will continue to delight other
135   men who are still young and passionate. Finally, the swans
      are beautiful *because* they remain aloof and mysterious.

First of all, we want to say that we do not intend you to take this
essay as a 'model answer'. It is by no means perfect. However,
Joyce does avoid the traps which caught Ted. Most importantly,
she does attempt to reach an understanding of the poem by means
of a sensitive look at its language and Yeats' technique. The
results of her adoption of this method are threefold:
  (i) Her appreciation has a simple but adequate structure—a
      beginning (two paragraphs of introductory remarks which,
      although they are of a general and tentative nature, make
      specific references to the text), a middle (a paragraph, more
      or less, on each stanza) and an end (twenty-odd lines on the
      symbolism).
  (ii) She has a fair amount of material, and her essay is a better
      length than Ted's.
 (iii) Her interpretation of the poem's meaning—whether it is satis-
      factory or not—is based squarely on the text. She doesn't
      formulate a theory and then try to make the poem conform to
      it.
Of course, Joyce's study has its flaws. For one thing, it is rather
uneven. She makes some good analytical comments on the way
Yeats uses rhythmical variations in the first stanza, but doesn't go
into equal detail elsewhere, even when considerations of metre
and rhythm are equally important if not more so. Of the fourth
stanza she says (line 90) only that 'the rhythm is in a more-or-less
regular iambic metre' and leaves it at that. Judging by the amount
of care she takes over the poem's opening lines, she could have
been a good deal more precise. She is good at detecting the
changes that take place between stanzas, but says little about the
continuity of ideas and images *across* the stanza divisions. She
misses the connection between 'bell-beat' and 'clamorous', for
instance. She says nothing about rhyme, even though some
attention paid to the approximate rhyme in lines 5 and 6 would

have helped her to make her point about the 'dramatic' introduction of the swans. But when Joyce does have difficulty over particular phrases or ideas she has the sense to say so; at least an examiner would know that she is aware of the problems, even though she cannot see their solutions.

These things aside, the appreciation is pretty competent. The writing style is fairly free and self-assured; the reader doesn't hear the sound of nail-biting in the background. There is a reasonable balance between technical detail and her more personal conjectures. Best of all, she *reasons* her way towards a general interpretation. Because she begins with the way the language achieves its effects, she has, by the time she has gone through the five stanzas, ample material with which to build her argument about the symbolism of the swans. As it turns out, her interpretation is quite convincing. She does not insist on an over-precise meaning. She doesn't jump at the red-herring possibility that 59 was Yeats' age, even though she was tempted. (In fact, Yeats was 54 when the poem was published.) Her most valuable insight is that it is not the actual *number* that matters, but the act of *counting*. She sees that by counting the swans the poet is trying to 'pin them down', to make then a part of his personal 'ritual', as she calls it. He hopes that by numbering them he can symbolically *own* them. When they become violently animated (stanza two) they assert their independence of the poet, who is only mortal. His initial reaction is a rather self-centred sorrow, but Joyce puts the emphasis in the right place when she says that at the end the poet comes to terms with the swans' freedom (and therefore with his ageing). She is quite right when she says that the final question is not envious, but actually optimistic. In view of all this, it seems reasonable to conclude that the swans are symbols of youth or vitality.

Let's hope that you have found this exercise in comparison useful, even though it is more than a little unfair. The problems it raises will be our concerns throughout this book, and eventually we shall risk formulating some advice on how to present a good essay in appreciation. In the meantime, it will be obvious that we have two mottoes which we hold almost sacred. They are, of course:

Always work from the particular to the general

and

A poem will only deliver up its secrets (if it has any) if you ask it the right questions.

TWO

Questioning a Poem — and
Surviving Panic

You are sitting in the examination hall. You turn a page and
hastily read an unheard-of and anonymous poem. You have an
hour or so in which to convince a faceless examiner that you
appreciate its argument, its images, its subtleties. But you do not
'understand' it. What does it *mean*? Panic begins to fill you like
black water.

Or a pleasantly confident lecturer at your first-choice university
welcomes you to your interview by handing you a sheet of paper
upon which a poem is printed. He says he has somebody else to
talk to, and in the meantime would you read the poem and write
down your reactions to it? You look at the poem, which has a title
something like *Canto XXII*, and suddenly you feel rather like a
burglar caught in the beam of a flashlight.

Or, simply, you are reading, at your ease, a poem which
interests or moves you. But it is irritating that you do not really
understand *how* it interests or moves you; something has evaded
your grasp.

The degree to which you are baffled in situations like these
depends very largely upon how committed you are to the 'message-
hunting' approach to poetry. We discussed some of the problems of
'meaning' in the Introduction and in Chapter 1, but it will be useful
to restate here one or two basic principles. A poem is not a coded
message which, to be understood, has to be translated into
'ordinary' speech or prose. Nor is it a message in a finely-wrought
box which is to be appreciatively admired and then broken open.
Meaning is not the same as *message*. A poem's meaning grows
from the language of which it is built, and our understanding of a
poem therefore depends upon our ability to question and compre-
hend the way the poet has used language.

13

The following exercise suggests one way of approaching poetic meaning through an examination of language. It seems, perhaps, a little mechanical or systematic, but is in fact the kind of thing a sensitive and alert reader will do instinctively—as he reads.

In the face of bafflement, then, cross-examine the poem's language:

A Singular Metamorphosis

We all were watching the quiz on television
Last night, combining leisure with pleasure,
When Uncle Henry's antique escritoire,
Where he used to sit making up his accounts,
5   Began to shudder and rock like a crying woman,
Then burst into flower from every cubbyhole
(For all the world like a seventy-four of the line
Riding the swell and firing off Finisterre).
Extraordinary sight! Its delicate legs
10   Thickened and gnarled, writhing, they started to root
The feet deep in a carpet of briony
Star-pointed with primula. Small animals
Began to mooch around and climb up this
Reversionary desk and dustable heirloom
15   Left in the gloomiest corner of the room
Far from the television.
                I alone,
To my belief, remarked the remarkable
Transaction above remarked. The flowers were blue,
20   The fiery blue of iris, and there was
A smell of warm, wet grass and new horse-dung.
The screen, meanwhile, communicated to us
With some fidelity the image and voice
Of Narcisse, the cultivated policewoman
25   From San Francisco, who had already
Taken the sponsors for ten thousand greens
By knowing her Montalets from Capagues,
Cordilleras from Gonorrheas, in
The Plays of Shapesmoke Swoon of Avalon,
30   A tygers hart in a players painted hide
If ever you saw one.
                When all this was over,
And everyone went home to bed, not one
Mentioned the escritoire, which was by now
35   Bowed over with a weight of fruit and nuts

And birds and squirrels in its upper limbs.
Stars tangled with its mistletoe and ivy.

Howard Nemerov

Without hazarding guesses as to what the poem may be 'about',
and leaving aside the more or less irrelevant matter of how much
you like or dislike it on a first reading, try to answer the following
questions:

1 Why 'We all were . . .' rather than 'We were all . . .'?
2 Is 'combining leisure with pleasure' merely a facile rhyme, or
   does the phrase have any other significance?
3 Why are lines 7 and 8 in parenthesis, and what effect, if any,
   is achieved by the battleship image?
4 What do you notice about the language in line 10?
5 Could you, and would you, punctuate line 10 differently?
6 Is there a purpose in the poet's choice of briony (11) and
   primula (12) rather than other flowers?
7 What is the effect of the full stop in line 12?
8 What is achieved by using the slang word 'mooch' in line 13?
9 What are the relevant meanings of the word 'reversionary'
   at line 14?
10 There is an unexpected rhythm to lines 14 and 15. How is this
   achieved, and why? What is the effect of the enjambment*
   upon line 16?
11 Is there some point to the repetition in 'remarked . . .
   remarkable . . . remarked'?
12 Why is the policewoman named Narcisse? What is the *pun* in
   this line?
13 'Greens' ('greenbacks') is slang for 'dollars'. Why is the slang
   preferred?
14 What are the two plays suggested by lines 27 and 28, and why
   are the names of their characters (and their author) garbled?
15 Line 30 is a quotation (almost) from Robert Greene, a contemporary and rival of Shakespeare. On his death-bed, Greene
   abused Shakespeare as a 'tyger's hart wrapt in a player's
   hide.' This phrase was itself a parody of a line from
   Shakespeare's *Henry VI*: 'O tyger's hart wrapt in a woman's
   hide'. All very interesting, no doubt, but does one need to
   know this to understand the poem better? How does the line fit
   into its context? The poet has inserted the word 'painted' into
   the quotation—for what reason?

*See Glossary, page 201.

CE–B

16 What is the effect of the word 'tangled' in the last line, and why is this line an independent sentence?

From these questions of detail, we may develop questions rather wider in scope:

17 How is the poem structured? How many stanzas are there, and where do they divide?

18 Is there an underlying development throughout the poem—other than the stanza progression? (The vegetation featured in the last lines may offer a clue.)

19 By line 16, does 'television' have a greater significance than it has at line 1? If so, how is this amplified or qualified by the quiz programme sequence (lines 22–31)?

20 By reading the poem aloud, you should be made aware that the poem is very irregular in its rhythms. What effect does this have upon the sense of the poem? Why are some passages more rhythmic than others?

21 What is the poet's tone? What use is made of irony?

22 What is the exact meaning of the word 'escritoire'? What is the significance of this meaning in relation to the emphasis on television in the poem?

Noted down, the answers to these questions should comprise sufficient material for a good written appreciation. More importantly, the close examination of the carefully-created details of the poet's language is a surer basis for an understanding of the poem's meaning than any attempt at a generalized 'translation' could be.

For the purpose of discussion, or as ground-work for a written study, compile a list of questions arising from the following poem.

The Heron

> The cloud-backed heron will not move:
> He stares into the stream.
> He stands unfaltering while the gulls
> And oyster-catchers scream.
> 5   He does not hear, he cannot see
> The great white horses of the sea
> But fixes eyes on stillness
> Below their flying team.
>
> How long will he remain, how long
> 10   Have the grey woods been green?
> The sky and the reflected sky,
> Their glass he has not seen,

But silent as a speck of sand
Interpreting the sea and land,
15   His fall pulls down the fabric
Of all that windy scene.

Sailing with clouds and woods behind,
Pausing in leisured flight,
He stepped, alighting on a stone,
20   Dropped from the stars of night.
He stood there unconcerned with day,
Deaf to the tumult of the bay,
Watching a stone in water,
A fish's hidden light.
25   Sharp rocks drive back the breaking waves,
Confusing sea with air.
Bundles of spray blown mountain-high
Have left the shingle bare.
A shipwrecked anchor wedged by rocks,
30   Loosed by the thundering equinox,
Divides the herded waters,
The stallion and his mare.

Yet no distraction breaks the watch
Of that time-killing bird.
35   He stands unmoving on the stone;
Since dawn he has not stirred.
Calamity about him cries,
But he has fixed his golden eyes
On water's crooked tablet,
40   On light's reflected word.

Vernon Watkins

ASKING THE RIGHT QUESTIONS

As you went through the questions we posed regarding the poem
by Howard Nemerov, it occurred to you, no doubt, that some of
these questions are more important than others. That is to say,
certain questions draw your attention to what we might call the
'surface texture' of the poem (witty use of language, manipulation
of rhythm at particular points, and so on) while others can lead
you beyond this 'surface texture' towards the underlying or
allegorical (in the case of this poem) suggestions which the poem,
in its entirety, attempts to make. Considering that you will have
precious little time in which to conduct your 'cross-examination' of

a poem's language, how can you decide which of the questions that occur to you are the most helpful, the most creative?

Questioning a poem's language in the way we are suggesting should have three main purposes. The first is preventative; it's a way of stopping yourself getting entangled, *prematurely*, in whatever metaphysical or philosophical aspects a poem may have. The second is to provide you with sufficient material out of which to build your argument or discussion of these deeper or more abstract aspects. The third is to test your early assumptions about the poem. Generally, the formulating of actual questions to apply to a poem is a method of disciplining yourself into anchoring your interpretative ideas firmly in that poem's text.

Do not dismiss, without careful consideration, any small detail of a poem's language as incidental or trivial. This is particularly important if you are inclined to be a message-hunter, especially if you are confronted with a poem which has cryptic or symbolic dimensions (and the three poems we have looked at so far are all of this sort). It is from these linguistic details, these individual words, metaphors, rhythms, sounds, that a symbolic image acquires and modifies its meaning. Students who wrote on *The Wild Swans at Coole* rarely paid much attention to the lines 'Passion and conquest. . . ./Attend upon them still.' Most took it to mean something like 'they still have their (sexual) potency'. But as 'Joyce' pointed out, the word 'attend' means 'wait upon' or 'serve', and the word 'still' has the meaning 'always'. These two words, perhaps more than any others in the poem, suggest the god-like or mythic stature of the swans, and their immortality. That line is the clearest indicator of the swans' real significance, and only readers prepared to spend time questioning the *exact* meaning of words will detect its importance.

One of the most common banalities found in students' essays is 'the poet has chosen his words carefully', yet those who write such a comment are very often those who fail to look closely at words' meanings. Similarly, when students discuss *A Singular Metamorphosis*, they frequently make dismissive or contemptuous remarks about the quiz-show sequence (lines 22-31). Having sorted out, to their own satisfaction, the references *to Romeo and Juliet* (Montagues and Capulets), *King Lear* (Cordelia and Goneril), the assorted puns on Shakespeare's name and epithet (Swan of Avon), and on 'greens', 'cultivated', and so forth, students have tended to put down the whole passage as a self-conscious language-game played for Nemerov's own amusement. After all, they say, the poem is meant to be comic, isn't it? Well, yes and no. The passage has a serious point to make. The garbled words and cheap jokes demonstrate, or enact, television's regrettable tendency to

18

turn everything it touches, including Shakespeare, into so much jumbled rubbish. Far from being trivial or self-indulgent, these lines establish the character of television in the poem. While the TV pumps out its mesmerizing garbage, most of us (i.e. most people in the poem) remain oblivious to the truly astonishing events taking place elsewhere. The television is synthetic (it synthesizes words) and fascinating; the 'reversionary' and forgotten desk asserts the power of Nature and is ignored. (This may be taking the poem too seriously for your taste, but although it *is* comic, it is also a parable.)

The important question here is not 'What are these "Capagues and Montalets"?' but 'Why are these names jumbled?'

Finally, a word about *assumptions*. In Chapter 1, 'Ted' formed some early impressions of Yeats' poem, and did not reconsider them in the light of his reading of the whole poem. Be careful not to do likewise. We would say 'Make *no* assumptions about a poem on a first reading', but we are aware that it is natural and inevitable for a reader to have 'first impressions', and everybody knows that they can be influential.

A piece of practical advice, then: if, early on, you make some assumption about a poem (e.g. that it is 'about' such-and-such, or that it is 'really' about something else, or that it is 'sentimental' or 'Romantic' or whatever), then *write that idea down* somewhere. Do not let it remain vague or unspoken; if you do, you will find, perhaps, that it is influencing the way you think and write without you being conscious of it. If your assumption is vaguely silly, then writing it down will make its silliness obvious, and you can abandon it. If, on the other hand, your idea seems reasonable, then having it written out—above the poem on the examination paper, say—will remind and help you to check its validity against your close scrutiny of the text. Both *The Wild Swans at Coole* and *The Heron* tempt the reader to suppose, at first, that they are descriptive verses of a fairly orthodox kind; at what point in Watkins' poem does this supposition become questionable? We think that the significance of the heron changes at around lines 14 and 15. What kind of power is suggested by 'pulls down the fabric'? The word 'interpreting' is rather surprising; what are its possible meanings? As 'Joyce' pointed out, each stanza of Yeats' poem causes us to reconsider the stanza or stanzas preceding it; does *The Heron* have a similar cumulative development? Notice that the last five lines of the poem echo the last five lines of the third stanza. Has the same image taken on a new significance?

The effect of questioning in this way may be to modify your original reading to such an extent that by the end of your essay you are advancing a view of the poem which differs radically from the one you began with. In this there is the danger that your essay may be disjointed or over-tentative. If you are to avoid this danger, you will need to develop a fluid and discursive writing style which allows you to make the transition from one idea to another without a lot of fuss. ('Joyce', you may recall, began by thinking that the swans represent Beauty, but moved to a different interpretation without too much strain.) There is nothing in itself wrong or inept about an essay which shows that its writer has found reason to change his mind.

THREE

A Note on Rhythm and Rhyme

I RHYTHM AND MEANING

> Every work of literary art is, first
> of all, a series of sounds out of
> which arises the meaning.*

Because rhythm is 'the organization of a language's sound-system', it is inseparable from meaning. In English, rhythm is created by varying the position and strength of *emphasis*. 'I'm having that one' differs in meaning from 'I'm having *that* one'. This much is simple and obvious. What it means for the student of literature is that rhythm must be seen as an *intrinsic* part of a poem's total effect; it must not be thought of or written about as if it were a decoration or disguise for the 'real ideas', nor as if it can be distinguished from the particular significance of the words (see Chapter 1, page 6).

For many poets, rhythm has been the first stage of composition. Yeats and Hopkins often formed the 'tune' of a poem before they found the words, and Wordsworth's method of wordless composition alarmed his Lakeland neighbours, who were, on occasion, 'flayt a'most to death . . . to hear t'girt voice a groanin' an' mutterin' an' thunderin' of a still evening.'

This might be an appropriate point at which to pause and consider the way *we* read. When we read prose we tend to read with our eyes only. We read much faster than we can speak. There are even, Heaven help us, correspondence courses which promise to teach you how to gulp up whole paragraphs at a time. Poetry should be read aloud; this is especially so if our concern is to detect rhythms. Unfortunately, there are places and occasions

---

*R. Wellek and A. Warren: *The Theory of Literature* (Peregrine Books), p. 158.

21

where reading aloud is actively discouraged—during examinations, for example. It is necessary, therefore, to develop the technique of reading aloud to yourself *silently*. Slow down your reading speed to speaking speed, pronouncing the words inside your head and listening to them. If you find that a phrase or line is difficult to pronounce do not skip over it, but read it 'aloud' again and take note of the demands made by the verse on the natural pattern of emphasis. 'Reading aloud silently,' will be indispensable when we come to look at *metre*.

Rhythm, in that it is an arrangement of emphases, is one element of language which contributes to meaning; it is also an abstract, musical phenomenon involved in the inception of a poem. But what does rhythm do? The answer will vary from poem to poem, of course, but we may risk two generalizations.

First, it *integrates*. Poetry tends toward a greater degree of organization than does prose, and rhythm is the corner-stone of this organization. It gives shape to the lines we have read and sets up expectations (which may or may not be justified) about what comes next.

Our second generalization is more tentative, because it involves an imaginative process which is, almost by definition, undefinable. The actual sound of the rhythm may have an emotive effect. In this respect poetic rhythm is perhaps akin to certain music, which may create particular emotions in us, or appeal to certain 'ideas', even though the sound of the music has no *literal* meaning. This response to rhythm is *not* dependent upon the rhythm of a poem resembling the rhythm of something else—a funeral march, or waves breaking upon the beach. No, this emotive effect of rhythm has to do with what T. S. Eliot has called our 'auditory imagination', a 'feeling for syllable and rhythm penetrating far below the conscious levels of thought and feeling, invigorating every word.' Just as certain combinations of images or colours may have certain effects upon our visual imagination, combinations of sound and rhythm may evoke a response, inexpressible in words or pictures, which intensifies the significance of the poet's words. This response will be unconscious, but it will be qualified and shaped by the same things that qualify the rhythm itself: the poem's subject and imagery, the sound and meaning of the words.

When it comes to writing about rhythm (and, to a lesser degree, rhyme) students tend to commit two main errors. One is writing short, isolated statements about a poem's rhythms, a practice which implies that rhythm can be separated from its context. The other is offering hazy and subjective imprecisions: 'the poet uses rhythm to reflect his melancholy mood' or 'the poem has a flowing rhythm which creates an impression of peace'. Our concern in this chapter is therefore the problems of writing *meaningfully* about rhyme and rhythm. One prerequisite is a small vocabulary of technical terms and procedures. Let us familiarize ourselves with those first.

II SOME TERMINOLOGY OF RHYME

End-rhyme is that which most people think of as 'rhyme', i.e. rhyming words falling at the ends of lines.

Internal rhyme occurs within the line, e.g.:
Fair <u>Dame</u>, he said, my <u>name</u> is lost.

Slant rhyme (also called *half-rhyme, near-rhyme*) is approximate rhyme, when vowel sounds are similar but not identical: sea/sigh, steel/hill.

Sight rhyme involves words alike in spelling but not in pronunciation: plough/rough, love/move.

The following might also be properly thought of as forms of rhyme:

Assonance, the recurrence (systematic or not) of a vowel sound throughout a passage:

Shark, br<u>ea</u>thing b<u>e</u>n<u>ea</u>th the s<u>ea</u>,
Has no bel<u>ie</u>f, comm<u>i</u>ts no tr<u>ea</u>s<u>o</u>n.

Consonance, the recurrence of consonants throughout a passage:

<u>L</u>i<u>ll</u>ies <u>bl</u>own by the hur<u>l</u>ing wind

Alliteration, the repetition of initial sounds:

With a <u>h</u>eavy and a <u>h</u>ardened <u>h</u>eart

It is almost impossible to make general comments on the *effect* of rhyme, since this will vary not only from poem to poem but from line to line of individual poems. However, we might tentatively suggest that rhyme works in one or both of two ways. First, since rhyme is a matter of sound, it will contribute in some way to the movement and the music of a poem, and thus affect the over-all meaning. One can see this happening clearly in the case of internal rhymes, as in the lines by Ted Hughes at the end of this chapter. Second, rhyme can affect the meaning of the rhyming words. A rhyme casts echoes back and forth; in some way the meaning of one rhyming word can adjust the meaning of another. The effect of rhymes such as Pope/grope, room/tomb, mistress/distress, graced/distaste might be to insinuate an ironic relationship between their component words, or to introduce a third 'idea' not contained in either. 'Easy' or obvious rhymes are not necessarily less effective or intelligent than ingenious rhymes. Indeed, ingenious rhymes tend to attract attention to themselves, perhaps interrupting the 'flow' of the poem, and increasing our awareness of the poet manipulating language. They tend, too, to be comic, like Byron's groan-evoking lines:

> But oh! ye lords of ladies intellectual!
> Inform us truly, have they not henpecked you all?

Strained rhymes like these are, of course, much used by ironists. The above couplet is funny because the rhyme is grotesque; in the following stanza from the same poet's *Don Juan* the rhymes (particularly in the 2nd, 4th and 6th lines) induce an ironic reading although the scene presented is one of passionate romance:

> She loved and was belovéd—she adored
> And she was worshipped; after nature's fashion
> Their intense souls, into each other poured,
> If souls could die, had perished in that passion—
> But by degrees their senses were restored,
> Again to be o'ercome, again to dash on;
> And beating 'gainst his bosom, Haidée's heart
> Felt as if never more to beat apart.

III METRICS

Metre means, literally, 'a measure'. Metrics is the business of measuring the rhythms of poetry. The reader who wanders into the field of metrics will find it populated by such wondrous creatures as the cautious *anapaest*, the daring *dactyl*, the restless *synaphea*, the occasional quizzical *syzygy*. But be not appalled, we are not concerned here with the more far-flung and exotic of metrical phenomena, but only with such processes and terms as you may find useful in writing about rhythm in the context of a poem's total effect.

In all English speech and writing, the basic unit of rhythm is, as we have said, emphasis, or *stress*. Most words of two or more syllables will have one syllable which is given greater stress; in the case of polysyllabic words, stresses may fall on more than one syllable:

ON|ly in|SIS|tant sci|en|TIF|ic SES|qui|ped |AL|ian|ism

(Alter the position of the stresses and you find yourself speaking English as a foreigner might: in sis TANT.) In poetry, it is the pattern of a line's *stressed* and *unstressed* syllables which creates the metre. We can conveniently mark them thus:

only scientific

The opening line of Gray's *Elegy in a Country Churchyard* is stressed:

The cúrfĕw tólls thĕ knéll ŏf pártĭng dáy,

and it should be obvious that it consists of five regular units each of one stressed and one unstressed syllable:

The cúr|fĕw tólls|thĕ knéll|ŏf párt|ĭng dáy,

Each of these units is a *metrical foot*. A foot is (usually) a stress grouped with one or two unstressed syllables. The four most common metrical feet are:

the *Iamb*, an unstressed syllable followed by a stress:

bĕcaúse   cŏrrúpt

the *Trochee*, the reverse of the iambic foot:

péoplĕ   próspĕr

the *Anapaest*, two unstressed syllables followed by a stressed:

ĭntĕrvéne   rĕprŏdúce

the *Dactyl*, the anapestic foot backwards:

póvĕrtў   jóyfŭllў.

The metrical description of a line depends on two things: the *kind* of foot used, and the *number* of feet used. Gray's line, which has five iambic feet, is therefore an instance of *iambic pentameter* (the most common metre in English poetry, incidentally); while this line:

The Ăssў|riăn căme dówn|lĭke thĕ wólf|ŏn thĕ fóld,

having four anapaestic feet, is an example of *anapaestic tetrameter*. And so on. If you find it interesting to work out metres (the process is called *scanning* or *scansion*) you will find more information in the glossary under **metre**, and the bibliography indicates books which go into it in greater detail. If you want to be good at it, practice is the only way; try scanning some of the poems in the practice exercises at the end of this book.

Now, it will have occurred to you, no doubt, that metre, as sketched here, is inadequate to describe the over-all effect of the rhythm of a line of poetry. For one thing, two lines might have the same metre, yet demand reading at different speeds and thus appear to be of different lengths. These lines are an oft-quoted example:

Mid hushed, cool-rooted flowers fragrant-eyed

Keats

25

How soon they find fit instruments of ill

Pope

Both are iambic pentameters, but the first is slower and longer. The assonant phrase 'cool-rooted' fits uncomfortably into an iamb, and the variation in the lengths of the pauses elongates the line. Note the differing effects of the alliterated 'f' in the two lines. Or a line may have, say, five stresses or *beats*, but they need not be of equal weight. Here is another line of Pope:

True ease in writing comes from Art, not chance.

We've marked the position of the stresses, but surely 'Art' has a stronger emphasis than 'comes'; it is important that the line ends with two strong beats on 'Art' and 'chance' because these two antithetical ideas are at the centre of Pope's argument. 'Art' should probably have rather more force than 'chance', since it is Art that Pope is advocating. The unstressed syllables, too, vary in strength. 'True' is more important than 'in' or 'from', and should be stressed only slightly less than 'ease'. 'True' is, in fact, a *secondary* stress, marked thus: Trúe.

A reasonable scansion of the line might then be:

True ease in writ|ing comes|from Art, not chance.

Pope has achieved a good deal of movement and diversity within his metre. This is important to his intentions, because the irregular, assertive stresses of the line contrast with the line that follows it:

As those move easiest who have learned to dance,

which moves with an even rhythm, conveying the sense of both ease and dance. The poet has expressed a good deal of movement and variety within the apparently strict form of a rhyming iambic pentameter couplet. This may seem a lot of trouble to take over two lines of verse (although it's only fair to Pope to do so, since he went to a lot of trouble himself), but it helps us to make two important points. First, metre is not a tight shoe into which the poet has to cram his language. *It is only a simplification of, and a generalization about, what a poem's rhythms tend to do.* But when you are asked to write about a poem in which rhythm plays a significant part (and after all this is the case with most poetry) this simplification or generalization is useful because it can lead you to the poem's underlying structure, its skeleton, so to speak. Moreover, an awareness of the poem's pattern of emphasis is indispensable to an understanding of its meaning. From this develops our second point: it is usually the case that it is not the basic metre itself which is of the greatest interest, but *the movement of the language within it and the deviation of the rhythm from it.* As Richards points out, 'readers who take up a poem as though it were a bicycle, spot its metre, and pedal off on it regardless of where it is going, will naturally, if it is a good poem, get into trouble. For only a due awareness of its sense and feeling will bring its departures from the pattern metre into a coherent and satisfying whole.' We will look again at this matter in a moment but it should be clear that any change in a generally regular metre will attract the reader's attention to the sense and feeling of the words involved. Coleridge summed up the question of metre with this vintage simile:

> For any poetic purpose, metre resembles . . . yeast, worthless or disagreeable in itself, but giving vivacity and spirit to the liquor with which it is proportionally combined.

IV METRE BECOMING RHYTHM

If metre is a simplification and a generalization, then obviously slavish adherence to one metrical pattern will tend to produce poetry which is dull and predictable. (This is true even of poems in fairly complex metres.) We resent being marched soldier-like through a poem. Metre functions better as a 'ghostly voice' (Yeats' phrase) which gives the poem a dimension appreciated almost unconsciously by the reader. What are the ways in which a poet may temper and modulate his metres?

First of all, there is the fact that language is an elastic medium which resists strict discipline. Poetic rhythm is therefore a compromise between artificially patterned stress and the natural rhythms of speech. There is a limit to the extent to which a poet may take liberties with these natural rhythms. For example, we usually resist stressing grammatical words (definite and indefinite articles, conjunctions, auxiliaries, prepositions, etc.) and verb endings. (Although Gerard Manley Hopkins, for one, frequently places stresses on normally unstressed syllables: 'Was deeméd, dreaméd').

Then a poet may make use of *metrical variation*. In extreme cases this may actually explode the verse-form; here is a ludicrous example in which the metrically tight form of the *limerick* falls apart:

There was a poetic young man
Whose verses just wouldn't scan;
When asked about this
He said 'Nothing's amiss,
I just like to get as much into the last line as I possibly can.'

This is an exaggerated instance of what one writer has called 'defeated expectancy', the surprise caused by metrical variation.

Less drastic examples are common in rather more serious verse —the substitution of one kind of metrical foot for another, say, or the use of secondary pauses to 'even out' a line. Two different metres may be used throughout one poem (a procedure sometimes called *syncopation* or *counterpoint*). This technique is used here in this lovely couplet from Marvell's *The Garden*, where the mind 'withdraws into its happiness,'

> Annihilating all that's made
> To a green thought in a green shade.

The long, fluid (yet implicitly violent) word 'annihilating' dominates the first line, which has three rather subdued stresses. The second line, of four stronger beats combined with the repeated long vowel sound of 'green', has a calm, meditative and completed air. The pauses are almost equal in weight to the stresses. The total rhythmic effect—coolness, peace—is precisely appropriate to the subject.

Metre may be qualified and modified by the manipulation of a line's pauses. The main pause in a line of verse is called the *caesura*. The caesura may be emphatic, as when it is indicated by some form of punctuation:

> That thou hast her, ‖ it is not all my grief,

or it may be subdued, existing only as the point at which the line's sense or syntax may be divided, as in:

> And yet it may be said ‖ I loved her dearly,

Other pauses we may generally term *secondary pauses*.

Sound-effects may temper metres; assonance and alliteration, for instance, will affect the way we read a line (as the line by Keats quoted earlier).

But rather than speak in these general terms, let us turn to specific verses and examine in some detail how rhyme and rhythm work.

> The poplars are fell'd, farewell to the shade
> And the whispering sound of the cool colonnade,
> The winds play no longer, and sing in the leaves,
> Nor Ouse on his bosom their image receives.

This is the opening verse of a poem intended to convey human sadness at the passing of time and the transience of pleasure. The poet (William Cowper, 1731-1800) is mourning the destruction of a line of trees which come to symbolize his youth (sturdy but ephemeral) and, by extension, his temporal life. It is a theme to be taken seriously, but any seriousness is almost completely subverted by the jog-trotting banality of rhythm and rhyme. The metre is not exactly regular, in fact. All four lines are tetrameters, but only in the second are all four feet identical; each of the other three lines begins with an iambic foot instead of an anapaest. But this is insufficient variation to break up the inappropriately jaunty pace. Matters are made worse by the placing of a stress on the last syllable of each line, since this attracts our attention to the lack of originality or flexibility in the rhymes. The first line is not end-stopped, but the stress on 'shade' causes us to pause after it anyway, and this has the effect of diminishing the attractiveness of the rather handsome phrase 'cool colonnade' by making it somewhat predictable and flat. In every line, the caesura, the main natural pause, falls exactly half way (i.e. after 'fell'd', 'sound', 'longer' and 'bosom'), and this too appears mechanical. Cowper seems to have tried to modify this in the second line; he has not begun with the iamb, thus delays the first beat, and the line, which is vaguely onomatopoeic, has some sinuousness; But the consonance of 's' in 'whispering sound' and the alliteration of 'cool colonnade' have the effect of separating the two phrases, making them self-contained. Thus the caesura remains noticeable, and the line fails to flow. There are other weaknesses in the verse, such as the clichéd use of anthropomorphization, but it is the absence of harmony between content and rhythm which is the most destructive.

This next extract is far more successful in its use of metrical variation.

> Of these am I, who thy protection claim,
> A watchful sprite, and Ariel is my name.
> Late, as I ranged the crystal wilds of air,
> In the clear mirror of thy ruling star
> I saw, alas! some dread event impend,
> Ere to the main this morning sun descend;

The first two lines are a perfectly symmetrical iambic pentameter couplet. The resulting neatness and briskness are completely appropriate, since Ariel is announcing himself and he is in a hurry to get on to his business, which is the delivering of a warning. We might note one subtlety of metre in the first line: we would not normally emphasize 'thy', but the metre, by requiring a stress, underlines the directness of Ariel's person-to-person address. The introduction over. Ariel becomes more urgent, and the change of tone is marked by a change in stress-pattern. In the third line the first stress falls on 'Late' (meaning 'lately, recently'); in technical terms, Pope (for he it is) has substituted a trochée for the first iambic foot. The punctuated pause after the word is a further break with the quick, even pattern of the first two lines. The same sort of thing happens in the fourth line. Here, the first beat is delayed until the third word, 'clear' (the first iamb replaced this time by an anapaest—'in the clear'). The effect of this, and of the rolling consonance of 'r's, is to quicken the line towards the passage's climax, which is the 'dread event'. The strong pause indicated by the exclamation mark after 'alas' prepares us for this key phrase, which is given suitable weight by its assonance: 'dread event impend'. Pope's use of rhyme is also very skilful. The completeness of the first couplet is enhanced by the full rhyme of 'claim'/'fame'. An equal rhyme in the next couplet might distract us from the flow of the verse towards 'dread event', and so Pope uses the unobtrusive slant rhyme of 'air'/'star'. A full appreciation of the passage would require some discussion of the beautiful images 'crystal wilds of air' and 'clear mirror of thy ruling star'. You may feel that the predominance of imagery involving light and glass is at odds with the verse's subject, the coming of some horrible catastrophe. It is, and deliberately so. The passage is ironic; the 'dread event' occurs when the poem's heroine loses a precious lock of hair at cards.

Our next passage shows a use of rhythm very different from Pope's delicate system of checks and balances.

> Daylong this tomcat lies stretched flat
> As an old rough mat, no mouth and no eyes,
> Continual wars and wives are what
> Have tattered his ears and battered his head.

Here, the poet (Ted Hughes) forsakes any regular metre; the pattern of stresses is conditioned by natural speech rhythms and by sound-effects. Rhyme, in particular, is used with considerable finesse. Of the three rhymes in the first one and a half lines ('cat/flat/mat') only the last is a fully-stressed syllable. This smooths out the rhythm, isolating and thus emphasizing 'no mouth and no eyes'. In subsequent stanzas of the poem the fangs and green 'ringstone' eyes of the cat are in dramatic contrast to this phrase. In the third line the strong alliteration is modified by our natural instinct not to stress 'what'; we pause slightly after 'wives' (picking up the assonant echo with 'eyes'), and run 'are what' on to the beginning of line four. In this last line the internally rhyming words 'tattered' and 'battered' are forceful emphases; the line in fact falls into two balanced parts:

Hăve tát|teréd hĭs eárs‖ănd bát|teréd hĭs héad.

This symmetry comes as something of a surprise, and gives a finalizing roundness to the stanza. The sound and rhythm of line four also convey a sense of the cat's ruggedness.

Clearly, Hughes uses rhythm in a way very different from the way it is used by Cowper and Pope. All our previous quotations were from poems written as *foot-verse*—that is, poems in which metre is a question of *feet* consisting of stressed and unstressed syllables. Hughes' poem is *stress-verse*, in which unstressed syllables do not figure in the metre and may vary in number from line to line. The main metrical concern is with the *number* of beats per line and not their position, which can be freely varied. Hughes' stanza has three stresses in the first and third lines and four in the second and fourth. Although stress-verse is less sensitive to the subtleties of metrical variation than is foot-verse, it has greater flexibility and greater rhythmic scope. It has a long tradition in English poetry; the Anglo-Saxon poets used it, as did Chaucer. In much modern poetry, stress-verse and *free-verse* (see below) have gained predominance over foot-verse. This is in part one consequence of the literary 'revolution' which centred around Ezra Pound and T. S. Eliot during the early decades of this century and which was itself (among other things) a reaction against 'the tyranny of metre'.

Free-verse is, by definition, almost indefinable. The term originates from the French phrase *vers libre*. During the 1880's certain French poets rebelled against laws or orthodoxies of versification which dictated the numbering of syllables, the positioning of the caesura, and so forth. But because there are fundamental differences between French and English—notably that words and syllables are not stressed alike in both languages—*vers libre* and free verse are not the same thing.

In English poetry, free verse came to a signify not only a breaking away from metrical structures but also a more general rejection of conventional forms, rhythm patterns and subjects. At the same time free verse was a hostile reaction to the qualities of late Victorian and Georgian poetry. (See Chapter 10 and **Georgianism** in the Glossary.)

Free verse does not conform to any 'rules' of metrics, nor are stresses organized as they are in stress-verse (although it is common to find, in free verse poems, passages of metrical verse used for particular effects). Free verse is structured according to what are often called *cadences*, i.e. the natural risings and

31

fallings in the sound of speech. (This means, first of all, that to appreciate free verse you must have a 'good ear', a sensitivity to the way sound is modulated in speech.) *Form* in free verse is therefore a matter of the balancing of phrase against phrase, line against line, somewhat in the manner of musical composition. Many of the devices which may be used to manipulate cadence will already be familiar: rhyme, alliteration and assonance, various forms of repetition, variations in the number of syllables in a line, and so forth. Since the free verse poet is not concerned with metre, it follows that he has freedom in the matter of line-length. It is important, therefore, that when you are considering free verse you pay particular attention to *lineation*, because the relative lengths and weights of lines are one of the most significant elements of form in free verse. This should become clear to you when you read William Carlos Williams' *The Red Wheelbarrow* (Chapters 9 and 10) and Theodore Roethke's *The Visitant* (Chapter 11).

It is over this subtle matter of form in free verse that students seem to experience most difficulty (and for this reason we have more to say about free verse in the *Note on Form and Structure*). It is a serious mistake to assume that free verse is devoid of form which can be used to the same *effect* as form in conventional verse. Because form is indispensable in poetry, the abandoning of traditional formal devices (metrics, regular rhyme-schemes et al.) obliges the poet to develop his own poetic forms. Otherwise, his poems will lack unity and meaning. T. S. Eliot, certainly a modern master of free verse, has this to say: 'The division between conservative verse and free verse does not exist, for there is only good verse, bad verse, and chaos.'

Since our overriding concern was with rhythm, commentaries on the extracts in this chapter should not be seen as miniature 'model appreciations'. In the Introduction we discussed some of the criteria of the A-Level examination and it seems appropriate to restate here one or two points.

Metrical analysis and its terminology are *tools*. An essay on a poem's metrical structure is not at all the same thing as an appreciation of that poem, and an essay larded with technical terms and detailed anatomizations will not impress the examiner, who wants to see some evidence of your awareness of the contribution made by rhythm to a poem's total effect. We included a very brief account of metrics in this book for two reasons: (a) to underline the importance of rhythm and the care good poets take over its management and (b) to offer you a few technical terms which you may find useful when you need to make *precise* comments on rhythm. It would be a waste of time and energy writing three paragraphs or so on the use of anapaestic substitutions in a trochaic pentameter poem, or somesuch. On the other hand, it is useful to be able to say something like 'By switching to a regular iambic pentameter in line 10 the poet accelerates the rhythm,' rather than have to settle for a vaguer comment such as 'The rhythm changes in line 10,' or for a muddled sentence which fails to identify exactly the change that has taken place. Nevertheless, a good appreciation, which demonstrates a sensitivity to the interplay between all a poem's elements, will not be thought less of because it employs no technical terminology.

We suggest you finish off this chapter by attempting brief appreciations of the following 3 short passages, paying particular attention to the organization and effects of rhythm and rhyme.

I hear an army charging upon the land,
    And the thunder of horses plunging, foam about their knees:
Arrogant, in black armour, behind them stand,
    Disdaining the reins, with fluttering whips, the charioteers.
James Joyce

Room after room,
I hunt the house through
We inhabit together.
Heart, fear nothing, for, heart, thou shalt find her—
Next time, herself!—not the trouble behind her
Left in the curtain, the couch's perfume!
As she brushed it, the cornice-wreath blossomed anew:
Yon looking-glass gleamed at the wave of her feather.
Robert Browning

And if tonight my soul may find her peace
in sleep, and sink in good oblivion,
and in the morning wake like a new-opened flower
Then I have been dipped again in God, and new-created.

And if, as weeks go round, in the dark of the moon
my spirit darkens and goes out, and soft strange gloom
pervades my movements and my thoughts and words
then I shall know that I am walking still
with God, we are close together now the moon's in shadow.
D. H. Lawrence

FOUR

Two Prose Passages

This far we have concentrated on poetry. It is time to look at some prose. What follows is representative of the kind of thing you may expect to encounter in the Unseen paper at Advanced Level. The two passages are the opening paragraphs of novels. Read them carefully, and then we will discuss the kind of question the examiners ask.

PASSAGE A:

On the 1st. of September, in the memorable year 1832, someone was expected at Transome Court. As early as two o'clock in the afternoon the aged lodge-keeper had opened the heavy gate, green as the tree-trunks were green with
5   nature's powdery paint, deposited year after year. Already in the village of Little Treby, which lay on the side of a steep hill not far off the lodge gates, the elder matrons sat in their best gowns at the few cottage doors bordering the road, that they might be ready to get up and make their curtsy
10   when a travelling-carriage should come in sight; and beyond the village several small boys were stationed on the look-out, intending to run a race to the barn-like old church, where the sexton waited in the belfry ready to set the one bell in joyful agitation just at the right moment.
15   The old lodge-keeper had opened the gate and left it in the charge of his lame wife, because he was wanted at the Court to sweep away the leaves, and perhaps to help in the stables. For though Transome Court was a large mansion, built in the fashion of Queen Anne's time, with a park and
20   grounds as fine as any to be seen in Loamshire, there were very few servants about it. Especially, it seemed, there must be a lack of gardeners; for, except on the terrace surrounded

34

with a stone parapet in front of the house, where there was
a parterre kept with some neatness, grass had spread itself
over the gravel walks, and all over the low mounds once
carefully cut as black beds for the shrubs and larger plants.
Many of the windows had the shutters closed, and under
the grand Scotch fir that stooped towards one corner, the
brown fir-needles of many years lay in a small stone
balcony in front of two such darkened windows. All round,
both near and far, there were grand trees, motionless in the
still sunshine, and, like all large motionless things, seeming
to add to the stillness. Here and there a leaf fluttered down;
petals fell in a silent shower; a heavy moth floated by, and,
when it settled, seemed to fall wearily; the tiny birds
alighted on the walks, and hopped about in perfect tranquillity; even a stray rabbit sat nibbling a leaf that was
to its liking, in the middle of a grassy space, with an air that
seemed quite impudent in so timid a creature. No sound was
to be heard louder than a sleepy hum, and the soft
monotony of running water hurrying on to the river that
divided the park. Standing on the south or east side of the
house, you would never have guessed that an arrival was
expected.

PASSAGE B:

Most people in this world seem to live 'in character'; they
have a beginning, a middle and an end, and are true to the
rules of their type. You can speak of them as being of this
sort of people or that. They are, as theatrical people say,
no more (and no less) than 'character actors'. They have a
class, they have a place, they know what is becoming in
them and what is due to them, and their proper size of
tombstone tells at last how properly they have played their
part. But there is also another kind of life that is not so
much living but a miscellaneous tasting of life. One gets hit
by some unusual transverse force, one is jerked out of one's
stratum and lives crosswise for the rest of the time, and, as
it were, in a succession of samples. That has been my lot,
and that is what has set me at last writing something in the
nature of a novel. I have got an unusual series of impressions
that I want very urgently to tell. I have seen life at very
different levels, and at all these levels I have seen it with a
sort of intimacy and in good faith. I have been a native in
many social countries. I have been the unwelcome guest of
a working baker, my cousin, who has since died in the
Chatham infirmary; I have eaten snacks—the unjustifiable

gifts of footmen—in pantries, and been despised for my
want of style (and subsequently married and divorced) by
the daughter of a gasworks clerk; and—to go to the other
25   extreme—I was once—oh, glittering days!—an item in the
house party of a countess. She was, I admit, a countess with
a financial aspect, but still, you know, a countess. I've seen
these people at various angles. At the dinner table I've met
not simply the titled but the great. On one occasion—it is my
30   brightest memory—I upset my champagne over the trousers
of the greatest statesman in the empire—Heaven forbid I
should be so invidious as to name him!—in the warmth of
our mutual admiration.
       And once (though it is the most incidental thing in my life) I
35   murdered a man. . . .
       Yes, I've seen a curious variety of people and ways of living
altogether. Odd people they all are, great and small, very
much alike at bottom and curiously different on their
surfaces. I wish I had ranged further both up and down,
40   seeing I have ranged so far. Royalty must be worth knowing
and very great fun.

You are now asked to comment on certain phrases from each of
these extracts. You are asked to comment on the *meaning and
effectiveness* of
(from passage A): *hopped about in perfect tranquillity* (36-7)
                               the soft monotony of running water (40-1)
       and
(from passage B): *some unusual transverse force* (11)
                               a countess with a financial aspect (26-7)
                               the most incidental thing in my life (34)

What do the examiners mean by 'meaning and effectiveness'
(sometimes the rubric says 'meaning and aptness')? And why have
these particular phrases been picked out?
       Many candidates make the fundamental mistake of writing about
the 'meaning' of these phrases as if they were being asked to
translate from a foreign language. There is no point at all in
writing that 'hopped about in perfect tranquillity' means 'skipped
about in complete peace of mind'. Many of the phrases you may be
asked to comment on are, on a simple literal level, self-explanatory,
and as long as it is clear from your comments on their 'effectiveness'
that you have understood them, there is no need to write out a
paraphrase. On the other hand, there will be particular words
which do require some explanation; you should be wise to make it
clear to the examiner that you are aware of the meaning or

36

meanings of such words as 'transverse' and 'aspect'. In any case, it is better to write about meaning and effectiveness as if they were (as indeed they are) complementary terms, rather than write one sentence on what an expression 'means' and then a couple of sentences on what it tries to achieve. In other words, your comments should themselves be continuous and unified small passages of prose.

It's pointed out in the second part of our Introduction that the word 'meaning' is, in a literary context, complex; the meaning of a word depends upon its effect, and therefore the examiners are really repeating themselves in asking about 'meaning' *and* 'effectiveness'. So what is meant by 'effectiveness'? This is to ask two questions:

What effect does a phrase have upon its context?
What effect does it have upon me, the reader?

Take the little exclamation by the narrator of passage B: 'oh glittering days!' (25). Within its context it suggests something of the glamour of his experiences in the countess' social circle. That is one of its effects. But the reader may feel that it is a little out of keeping with the narrator's general tone, which is self-consciously worldly and rather cynical; is he then being perhaps a little ironic here? Or is he in fact rather naively in love with the delights of the high life? Another effect of the phrase is to make the reader wonder about the writer's attitude.

A similar effect upon the reader is achieved by the remark 'And once (though it is the most incidental thing in my life) I murdered a man . . .' It's rather a shock, certainly, after such trivialities as spilling wine down a politician's trousers. It arouses the reader's curiosity as to what kind of life can include an 'incidental' murder; it provokes questions about the narrator's morality, perhaps. And what might be the tone of voice for this sentence? Is there a lapse in the predominantly garrulous way of speaking, a drop into a tone perhaps more reflective for a moment? Or is it let slip casually and callously?

A word of warning: when writing about the effect a word, phrase or sentence has upon you, don't overdo it. Do not become over-subjective. Resist the temptation to be merely fanciful, in an attempt to convince the examiner that you have been deeply moved. I remember a student writing that a phrase something like 'through the haze of many summers,' made her think of all manner of nice things from iced cocktails and sunburn to exotic places. Perhaps it did, but it can hardly have been the writer's intention to induce a great burst of free-association in his reader; an examiner might be forgiven for thinking that the girl put it down because she couldn't think of anything more relevant. On the other hand, beware of crude oversimplification: another student wrote that the phrase 'the soft monotony of running water,' has the effect of 'making the reader bored.'

Why were these particular phrases picked out for your comments? It is tempting to reply that these were the only phrases the examiners thought you might just possibly not understand. A more worthy answer has already been implied in the comments on effectiveness. Clearly, they are phrases written for some special effect, some particular function. It is often the case that these words have specific qualities which you are expected to be able to identify. 'A countess with a financial aspect,' for example, contains a deliberate *ambiguity*, and you should make it clear that you appreciate the ways the expression can be taken. 'The soft monotony of running water,' has an *onomatopoeic* ring, and you should say so. Other expressions may make an especially significant contribution to establishing a mood or 'atmosphere', others may be significantly ironic. Be alert, then, to particular techniques and functions of individual phrases.

Now you are asked a wider question. You are asked to compare the two passages *as 'openings' to novels*, giving your opinion as to their success in engaging the reader's interest, their skill in 'whetting the reader's appetite for what is to come,' and to comment on their different styles.

This is a more specific question than many; one is often instructed merely to write a general appreciation of a prose passage. It is surprising that people still fail examinations because they do not pay attention to the specifications of the rubric, so it is worth saying the obvious: select your material and organize your essay around the exact requirements of the question.

We shall discuss matters of style in our next chapter, but for the time being it's suggested that an approach to a question such as this could be organized under three headings:

INFORMATIVENESS

Author A answers the questions a reader instinctively asks when he first opens a novel—Where? and When?—and he does so in the first sentence. Having established time and place, and a certain expectancy (Who's coming?), he establishes a detailed setting of atmosphere (slightly agitated rural placidity), and scene (gently decaying magnificence). B, on the other hand, does not reveal his name, his age or his whereabouts, but plunges us straight into a philosophical speculation about the way people lead their lives. Immediately after this we are told all manner of apparently unrelated biographical details; the passage has some-thing of the quality of a *trailer* for a film. This is a fairly straight-forward appeal to our curiosity.

TONE

Again, this is something that comes up in a later chapter. It should be obvious that the two authors have very different *voices*. They imply two different attitudes towards the reader. A is more leisurely, more relaxed than B, who has impressions he wants 'very urgently' to relate. (B thus implies the reader may expect a fast-paced book. We're not going to be bored, we are assured.) A seems to be at home at Transome Court; B stresses his restless-ness. Accordingly, A is comfortable and restrained; his sentences are longer, more fluid and more circumspect. He spends more time on detail than does B, who is in a hurry to get on to incidents: consequently B's style is more broken. His sentences suffer parenthetical interruptions and ejaculations. His tone is conversa-tional. Tone is closely tied up with:

NARRATIVE POSITION

Where is the author in relation to his subject and the reader? A has a god-like omniscience, able to move, like a free-ranging camera, from place to place, able to see indoors and out, house and village; he can describe every detail of the landscape. When he introduces his characters he will no doubt prove to be intimate with the lives and thoughts of each. What is the effect upon the reader of an author adopting this position?

Whereas A is the 'Invisible Outsider', B is the 'Visible Insider'.*
He is his own major character, and talks to us directly from the world of his fiction. This gives the passage greater immediacy, and perhaps involves the reader more actively because while we can only accept the omniscience of author A, we can actually take issue with the opinions and the view of the world held by B. And, of course, since the novel from which the second extract is taken is related by one of the characters, the narrator cannot pretend to know what takes place in the heads of the other characters or what takes place when he is not there. This naturally gives the reader's imagination more to do. The second passage engages our attention more easily, perhaps, since we are involved immediately with a person, and as readers of novels we are more interested in people than in, say, trees or houses or tranquil rabbits.

As general frames of reference, these three topics seem to us to be useful guidelines for critical appreciations of most extracts from works of prose fiction.

*These are terms used by John Stephens in his book *Seven Approaches to the Novel*, which has a useful chapter on how novels begin.

FIVE

An Approach to Prose

> *Prose:* language spoken or written without metre or rhythm;
> plain matter-of-fact style.
>> *The Penguin English Dictionary*

Like many definitions found in any dictionary, this one is really
only marginally useful. It is unfortunate, for example, that the
word 'prose' sometimes seems to have connotations of tedium and
dullness. It is also obvious, to most people, that there are many
writers of prose whose style could hardly be termed 'matter of
fact'.

Many scholars and critics have tried to reach a precise and
satisfactory definition of this word 'prose', but have rarely
succeeded, primarily because the question 'What is prose?' is such
a large one. What, for instance, have Income Tax forms and the
novels of D. H. Lawrence got in common? Answer: they are both
written in prose. Asking this kind of question is one of these
peculiar exploratory tasks where a satisfactory completion is
probably impossible, but 'getting there' can be interesting.

Because prose is such a highly versatile medium, used as a
means of communication in virtually all human activities, it seems
beyond simple categorization. A medium that can be used by
novelists and writers of Geography textbooks seems as versatile as
'paint', a material which can decorate both the front of a house
and an artist's canvas.

However, there are surely a few comments we can make. We
can say, perhaps, like the dictionary, that prose usually avoids
regular rhythm and rhyme, but if we do, immediately we have
problems before us. It is not hard to find almost regular iambic
pentameters in parts of Dickens' novel *A Christmas Carol*, while
many poems avoid both rhyme and regular rhythm. Much depends
upon the definition we give to the word 'regular'. In other words,

even the most obvious-sounding statement, if looked at closely, is misleading and vague. We must deal in generalities, some of which will, no doubt, be monsters of inaccuracy, but they should help us, if only because we will see that that is precisely what they are.

Many critics would maintain that 'literary' prose seems to contain patterns of thought, imagery and meaning which are more diffuse than those found in poetry. (Which, of course, is not simply to say that novels are, on average, longer than poems!) The novelist especially deals with a more extensive formal system; his effects are likely to be larger in scale, his language less noticeable than the poet's.

It is obviously time to look at some examples of English prose:

i)   The centrifugal water pump and radiator cooling fan are driven together with the dynamo from the crankshaft pulley wheel by a rubber belt. The distributor is mounted towards the rear of the right hand side of the cylinder block and advances and retards the ignition timing by mechanical and vacuum means. The distributor is driven at half crankshaft speed by a short shaft and a skew gear from a skew gear on the camshaft.

ii) Comparison with an earlier oil sketch of the subject shows an uneasiness about the relationship between the flatness of the tapestry covered wall at the back and the adjacent wall opening onto a landscape. In the final version this is not resolved. The space is ambiguous, and it is as easy to read the composition as flat all the way across the back as to imagine that the landscape wall is at right angles to the tapestry, and thus parallel with the right hand side of the table. In his attempt to reorganize pictorial space, Millais found that he was unable to accommodate the daring of his compositional method to the demands of naturalistic perspective.

iii) It was in Burma, a sodden morning of the rains. A sickly light, like yellow tinfoil, was slanting over the high walls into the jail yard. We were waiting outside the condemned cells, a row of sheds fronted with double bars, like small animal cages.

iv) Across the threadbare cuffedge he saw the sea hailed as a great sweet mother by the wellfed voice beside him. The ring of bay and skyline held a dull green mass of liquid. A bowl of white china had stood beside her deathbed holding the green

sluggish bile which she had torn up from her rotting liver by
fits of loud groaning vomiting.

v)   Then I tacked down the snowblind hill, a cat-o'-nine gale
     whipping from the sea, and, white and eiderdowned in the
     smothering flurry, people padded past me up and down like
     prowling featherbeds.

   The first extract differs quite radically from the ones that follow,
primarily of course, because of its context: a car repair manual.
Here the prose *is* 'matter of fact'. The reader of a prose passage
such as this one wants precise and unambiguous information, the
more 'invisible' the prose the better. (Imagine for example a car
manual that began: 'The centrifugal water pump, oakstrong trunk,
yet like a delicate starfish' . . . One would suspect the writer to be
either a poet manqué or a practical joker). The language here is, if
you like, all content and no style. The next extract is also
informative but the information is of a very different kind.
Although it contains technical words (such as 'pictorial space',
'compositional method') it also makes value judgements ('shows an
uneasiness about the relationship') and uses the inherent rhythms
of English prose to emphasize certain ideas—by varying sentence
length for example.
   Extract three is from a contemporary account of an execution by
the writer George Orwell. Although factual (it is about a real
event) the language is, in some ways, drawing attention to itself.
Orwell has used a simile 'like yellow tinfoil' about the light which
is 'sickly'. Accurate reporting does not necessarily preclude the
use of figurative language, especially if, as here, the writer is
attempting not just to inform, but to create atmosphere and elicit a
definite response from the reader.
   Extract four is from the novel *Ulysses* by James Joyce. Here the
language is indeed idiosyncratic, the reader has to work rather
harder to grasp the 'meaning' of all those words. One notable
admirer of Joyce, the novelist Anthony Burgess, has pointed out
that it would be quite possible to re-write this passage as if it were
by a less adventurous, 'ordinary' writer who would, for example,
omit such stylistic mannerisms as compound words, and carefully
explain in his novel that the hero is looking at the bay outside and
day-dreaming of his mother's death, having been reminded of her
bile by the colour of the sea. In short, a more timid novelist would
make the meaning easier for the reader. Joyce is a novelist who
constantly explored the opacity of language, his novels are *about*
language as much as they are about character and incident.
To re-write the novel in this way would, as Burgess points out, be

to misunderstand the sort of linguistic experience to be had from reading the sort of novel that Joyce writes.

Passage five (from *Return Journey* by Dylan Thomas) is, if anything, perhaps even more 'poetic' in the sense that it exploits sound effects ('Smothering flurry'), alliteration ('People padding past') and contains imagery that is at best surreal and disturbing, at worst rather fanciful ('prowling featherbeds'). It is the kind of language that we would expect to find in a poem, but which is unusual in most prose. As readers, we would no doubt willingly accept and enjoy this kind of writing in a short story, but whether we would have the stamina for such dense language were it to last the length of a novel, is another matter. Some readers might well find such self-referring language irritating if they are mainly interested in character and plot and are frequently 'interrupted' by the writer's language. Others might well enjoy the verbal acrobatics for their own sake.

Which brings us to another, again fundamental and complex, distinction between the function of language in prose and the function of language in poetry. Many poets have stressed, perhaps rather confusingly and tautologically, that poetry is primarily a matter of *words*. That is to say, the language of poetry is, in general, 'foregrounded' or 'opaque' whereas the language of prose tends to be 'invisible' or 'transparent'. When we read our car manual we obviously want to look *through* the words to the information presented and the things referred to. We do not want the writer's style to interpose itself between us and the facts and instructions. To a less obvious extent, the same is true of many novelists. Although we may well admire, enjoy or even become excited by a novelist's style, we are also interested in other matters such as plot, character and physical or social environment. If the language of the novelist we are reading is extremely opaque or even obtrusive, like surface noise on a record, we may well become irritated because we have been deprived of our primitive need for story. What Kingsley Amis, the British novelist, calls:

a high idiosyncratic noise-level in the writing with
plenty of rumble and wow from imagery, syntax and diction . . .

can be, at best, demanding, at worst, little more than a surface mannerism. It is because of this almost hidden dual role of language in prose that the criticism of prose is, in some ways, a more demanding activity than the criticism of poetry. The prose of many novelists can often seem apparently effortless and transparent and we, as readers, are often not immediately aware of its qualities as language. It is usually the ideas, or facts that the language contains, that are of immediate interest and the tendency to 'see through' and 'ignore' the prose is dangerously easy. Fortunately perhaps, it is rare to find extracts from car manuals in the 'A' Level Practical Criticism paper. Indeed, because of the very nature of the examination, the extracts used are virtually always from prose that might be loosely called 'literary', that is, novels, biographies, essays, journalism, histories and so on.

Some Boards tend to present the prose passage in the form of a sophisticated comprehension test, with questions that are sometimes helpful and sometimes misleading. Others will simply ask the candidate to comment on the passage, paying particular attention to the writer's style. The candidate has, therefore, in the space of an hour or so, to subject the extract to a barrage of searching questions with the aid of all the analytic tools he has found in this book and elsewhere, remembering that often the functions and origins of prose are not automatically identical with those of poetry.

There is obviously not time, in a book of this nature, to examine the more complex questions such as 'When does a writer use prose, and when does he write a poem?' or 'Why are some writers novelists and some poets?' They are what they are. Herbert Read, in his excellent book *English Prose Style* has some suggestions which may help to illustrate some of the issues involved:

> Poetry is creative expression: prose is constructive expression . . .

> . . .Poetry seems to be generated in the act of condensation; prose in the process of dispersion.

Words like 'constructive' and 'dispersion' do, at first glance, seem to be establishing prose as the poor relation of poetry. However, a novel hardly ever attempts to achieve the kind of intensity and condensation that is often to be found in a poem. For many poets, especially nineteenth and twentieth century poets, the act of writing poetry does seem to be a kind of very intense activity, akin to verbal necromancy; it has often been suggested that words and their sounds are to the poet precursors of thought itself.

To finish this section, we might refer to two writers who excelled in both media: Thomas Hardy and D. H. Lawrence. In one of Hardy's notebooks we find:

> It is certain that the poetic form, by music, as well as brevity, has conveyed you out of yourself and made its whole effect more swiftly; and this may be a sign that poetry is made out of feelings, not necessarily deeper than the feelings in prose, but more intensely concentrated.

Sandra Gilbert in her critical book on D. H. Lawrence, *Acts of Attention*, believes that for poets such as D. H. Lawrence:

> The poet is more passive than the novelist; his whole being is concentrated in pure awareness of the thing itself. The novelist, on the other hand, because of the greater length and complexity of the form in which he works must be . . . active in a way that the poet is not, for the structures of relationships that he raises on the foundation of his primary perception of man in the universe requires him to manipulate his material more extensively.

THE 'CLASSIFICATION' OF PROSE

As we have seen, one can make no prescriptive statements on the meaning of the word 'prose'. However, one useful and traditional method of approaching any subject is to break it down and then to classify it. One very obvious way of 'attacking' prose is to categorize it according to the purpose for which it is being used. It is a good idea to examine the unseen passage of prose one is faced with in an examination and ask oneself whether or not it has distinctive characteristics of one particular category. Again, a classification by function is necessarily arbitrary; prose being such a slippery concept, one may well find that a prose extract belongs to several simultaneously. However, as we have said before, the 'journey' may well be a helpful one. A simple classification might be as follows:

Informative Prose

This is prose which avoids, as a matter of principle, such things as ambiguity and the irrational. At one extreme end of this classification stands the technical report, where the language is as 'transparent' and 'invisible' as possible. The car manual would obviously come into this category, as would textbooks, encyclopedias, some newspaper articles, and so on.

Emotive or Expressive Prose

This is prose in which language is used, not just to give information, but also to change or create attitudes, feelings or emotions in the reader. This is the kind of prose most commonly found in A-Level examination papers and could itself be sub-divided into further categories:

Discursive Prose

This is the prose used by writers such as philosophers, theologians and politicians for example. Its purpose is to present a series of ideas and/or arguments. It is a kind of writing that can appeal to the intellect or the emotions, or, of course, both. A philosophical work may attempt to persuade primarily through an appeal to the intellect, a political pamphlet may well appeal to the emotional prejudices of a specific audience.

Contemplative Prose

Although less prevalent as a kind of writing nowadays, the 'essay' is often chosen by examiners for the A-Level practical criticism paper. An essay is a sometimes speculative and often whimsical piece of writing on virtually any subject. A brief glance at *The Pelican Book of English Essays* reveals titles such as *On Travel, Sunday in the Country* and *The Praise of Chimney Sweepers* by the famous essayists Bacon, Addison and Lamb.

Narrative Prose

Any extract from a novel would be narrative (although incidentally it might well contain prose which is contemplative—perhaps spoken by one of the fictional characters). This category would also include the short story, as well as biographies and auto-biographies. Narrative means not just story or action, but includes the more subtle and detailed aspects of fiction such as the examination of character and motivation and the relationship between the individual and his environment. Narrative prose contains far more than prose which is simply informative; indeed, some novelists resent the necessity of having to provide any simple 'story' information in their work.

Categorizing sometimes becomes a facile substitution for real thought. A prose passage from a novel may well be discursive, and could certainly be informative in part. No doubt one could find an extract which could belong equally to all of these categories or none of them. However, it is often useful to make some kind of decision as to what sort of prose one is reading. It would, for example, be unhelpful to read a section from Swift's *Gulliver's Travels* as if it were a piece of informative prose, thereby fail to recognize it as narrative, and fail to see that it was probably more complex in terms of tone. By examining each passage in terms of its content, vocabulary, syntax, rhythm and sound, one can usually make a tentative and perhaps useful decision as to what kind of prose one is dealing with, and therefore begin to ask what it means.

Another useful method of attack is to examine some of the other varied factors which determine the different ways that writers put their words together.

One obvious factor is the geographical one. A writer who writes about characters who come from a specific place may have a unique style; there are many dialects in the English language. Look for example at these extracts:

I try to tell her where he was but she say she can't hear properly. Fifteen minutes she came in a car, she was looking vex and sleepy and I went up to call him. The door was not lock, I went in and touch his foot and call him very soft, and he jump up and begin to shout.

'Come wench,' said Job, 'don't look so gloppened because thou'st fallen asleep while an oud chap like me was talking on oud times. It were enough to send thee to sleep. Try if thou canst keep thine eyes open while I read thy father a bit on a poem as is written by a weaver like oursel'.

So we turned into Barney Keirnan's and there sure enough was the citizen up in the corner having a great confab with himself and that bloody mangy mongrel, Garryowen, and he waiting for what the sky would drop in the way of drink.

All three extracts contain words which are obscure (vex, gloppen, confab) although one can guess at their meanings from the relevant contexts. The second extract attempts to reproduce dialect typographically, a method commonly used by writers such as Dickens, Thomas Hardy and D. H. Lawrence.

If we were linguists, we might notice certain things about each extract, such as the peculiar and fascinating verb forms in extract one, the archaic second person singular in extract two, as well as the omission of certain consonants such as 'l' and 'v' sounds, and the verb forms again in extract three.

All possess grammatical peculiarities of specific dialects. The first, from a short story by V. S. Naipaul, captures the unique dialect of the West Indies, and one character in particular. The second, from the novel *Mary Barton* by Elizabeth Gaskell, shows us not just the peculiarities of place but also those of class, a point we shall look at later. The last extract, again from Joyce's *Ulysses*, is an example of the Dublin Irish accent, an accent used not surprisingly, by many of the characters in that novel. As Anthony Burgess has pointed out, the novel is as much a 'glorification of the linguistic resources' of Dublin as it is a book which exploits all varieties of different English prose styles continually and almost exhaustively.

Geography may well be an important aspect of a writer's style; dialect is often as rich and varied as any Standard English, as well as being a language which reveals the unique and individual peculiarities of any specific culture.

Just as language has a complex and two-way relationship with environment, so it reflects social and educational differences. This is, of course, a subject best left to linguists and sociologists, but there is no doubt that novelists have been, and no doubt always will be, fascinated by class and the role that language plays in establishing often very subtle divisions between people. Such differences in language have, partly for this reason, sometimes been called *codes*.

Jane Austen, a novelist who wrote primarily about a fairly narrow social range, uses very subtle linguistic distinctions to differentiate between her characters. Mrs. Elton in *Emma* continually reveals the fact that she is *nouveau riche*, not because of any dialect she uses, but through the syntax and vocabulary of her language, whereas Fanny Price in *Mansfield Park* uses language which subtly indicates that she is worthy of a higher position in society than her humble origins would seem to suggest.

Although the writer of prose does have an extremely wide range of linguistic resources, in practice there may well be certain limitations placed on him by factors such as his subject matter, intention, audience, tone and personal idiosyncracies. For example, a sports reporter probably cannot deviate markedly from the language and jargon associated with a particular sport. More subtly perhaps, a writer such as Jane Austen has self-imposed and quite specific limitations of subject matter, and so the language that she uses, however complex, is restricted by the scope of her fictional environments, and the way her characters speak reflects this. This kind of limitation is, of course, obvious when we read informative prose, which has often to employ a specific technical vocabulary. Some writers may try to escape the limitations of language imposed upon them by subject matter, limitations which they may feel are more apparent than real. This may well help to explain why the language of James Joyce is dissimilar to that of other more 'ordinary' novelists.

The *intention* of the writer may be, at first, obscure, but it is nevertheless vital. A private letter to a friend will vary enormously in style and tone from one written to a bank manager. The language of one context will be highly unsuited to the requirements of the other. The language used by a novelist will obviously be different from the language used by the author of a technical report, and perhaps more subtly the language used by an essayist or short story writer. When language normally used in one context is transferred to another, the results are often bizarre and comic, as in this extract from Peacock's ironic novel *Headlong Hall*:

> His ascent being unluckily a little out of the perpendicular, he descended with a proportionate curve from the apex of his projection and alighted, not on the wall of the tower, but in an ivy bush by its side which, giving way beneath him, transferred him to a tuft of hazel at its base, which after upholding him an instant, consigned him to the boughs of an ash that had rooted itself in a fissure about halfway down the rock, which finally transmitted him to the waters below.

Similarly, the reader has an important part to play, especially if it is obvious, for example, that the language of a piece of prose has been tampered with or simplified in some way. A writer of popular and explanatory textbooks may set out to avoid using jargon and end up sounding moronic; a writer of children's books must use language that is simple and yet avoid a tone that is condescending. Whether a writer should write with a particular readership in mind is of course another problem altogether.

Finally, and perhaps most difficult of all, one factor that cannot be quantified (except perhaps by computer) is the extent to which a writer has his own unique language. Writers, human beings like the rest of us, have their own unique personalities and language, although some writers do have a style which is more readily recognizable than others. A writer will have his own distinctive patterns of sound, syntax and vocabulary, according to his physical and social environment, perhaps, his education, his vision of both real and fictional worlds, and his concept of what a writer is and/or should do, as well as the sort of language he should use. Here however, we enter the realms of linguistic philosophy and psychology and fascinating but dubious conjecture; from which we must beat a hasty but dignified retreat.

RHYTHM AND SOUND

> He had already inherited then, without even having seen it, the big old bear with one trap-ruined foot that in an area almost a hundred miles square had earned for himself a name, a definite designation like a living man—the long legend of corn cribs broken down and rifled, of shoats and grown pigs and even calves carried bodily into the woods and devoured and traps and deadfalls overthrown and dogs mangled and slain and shotgun and even rifle shots delivered at point blank range yet with no more effect than so many peas blown through a tube by a child—a corridor of wreckage

and destruction beginning back before the boy was born, through which sped, not fast but rather with the ruthless and irresistible deliberation of a locomotive, the tremendous shaggy shape. It ran in his knowledge before he ever saw it. It loomed and towered in his dreams before he even saw the unaxed woods where it left its crooked print, shaggy, tremendous, red-eyed; not malevolent but just big, too big for the dogs which tried to bay it, for the horses which tried to ride it down, for the men and the bullets they fired into it; too big for the very country which was its constricting scope.

Dixon lit another small cigarette, jabbing with the match at the sandpaper as if it were the driver's eye. He had, of course, no idea of the time, but estimated that they must, by now, have covered five of the eight or so miles to their destination. Just then the bus rounded a corner and slowed abruptly, then stopped. Making a lot of noise, a farm tractor was laboriously pulling, at right angles across the road, something that looked like the springs of a giant's bed, caked in places with earth and decked with ribbon-like grasses. Dixon thought he really would have to run downstairs and knife the drivers of both vehicles; what next? What next? What actually would be next: a masked holdup, a smash, floods, a burst tyre, an electric storm with falling trees and meteorites, a diversion, a low-level attack by Communist aircraft, sheep, the driver stung by a hornet? He'd choose the last of these, if consulted. Hawking its gears, the bus crept on, while every few yards troupes of old men waited to make their quivering way aboard.

You are probably already aware of the fundamental role of rhythm both in the poetic process itself and the consequent relationship it has with a poem's meaning. It seems that most poems have to be read aloud if they are to be fully understood. To a lesser extent, the same is true of prose. Because the reading of novels is nowadays primarily a silent and private activity, then the less obvious rhythms of prose are often neglected more than those of poetry, but they are nevertheless very important. The two passages you have just read are, of course, very different in subject matter and style. The first passage (from William Faulkner's *Go Down Moses*) possesses very distinct rhythms which are ideally suited to the subject of the seemingly invincible old bear, a real animal, and a symbol of the mysterious and vaguely threatening American wilderness.

The rhythms of this passage can obviously not be scanned in the same way that regular metre can be in some poetry. However, it would be either insensitive, or more probably impossible, to read this passage aloud and ignore the very distinct and sonorous rhythms it contains. The three stressed words 'big old bear' are followed by a kind of repetitive and rhythmic incantation: 'of corn-cribs broken down, of shoats and grown pigs, and traps . . . and dogs . . . and even rifle shots'. The rhythm itself is highly suited to these themes of geographical immensity, the passing of time and the majesty of this animal and symbol which moves, as the rhythm of the words themselves suggest, with 'irresistible deliberation'. William Faulkner is, partly because of his highly idiosyncratic syntax, a writer who demands considerable concentration from his readers.

These immensely long sentences are not a sign of casual craftsmanship, but the very opposite; the sound and rhythmic effects of Faulkner's unique language are inseparable from the meaning of the extract.

The second passage (from *Lucky Jim* by Kingsley Amis) is somewhat different. The writer here is using rhythm for comic effect. A man who wishes to reach his destination is delayed by a series of what seem to him malicious, rather than fortuitous, interruptions to his journey. A summary such as this one is of course inadequate partly because it ignores the role of rhythm in the passage. The presence of certain stressed words this time conveys the irritation felt by the character Dixon:

> He had, of *course*, no *idea* of the time, but estimated that they *must*, by *now*, have covered *five* of the eight or so miles to their destination.

Sometimes, of course, writers will indicate where the stresses should fall by italicizing key words. Both Faulkner and Amis leave this kind of decision to the reader himself.

The rhythm then becomes cumulatively staccato, as we enter the head of a frustrated man; Dixon the protagonist becomes virtually hysterical:

> What next? What next? What actually would be next: a masked hold-up, a smash, floods, a burst tyre. . .

Admittedly, much of the humour of this passage lies in the increasing absurdity of the improbable hazards, but the prose rhythms convey very clearly the agitation and sense of exasperation felt by one who feels frustrated and powerless.

Prose which is simply informative will, in general, be less rhythmic than prose which is deliberately or subconsciously emotive or persuasive. There is clearly some very close connection between rhythm and emotion, and we have seen, or rather heard, the way rhythm can convey a sense of awe or irritation. One kind of prose which sets out quite deliberately to produce an emotional response is *oratory*. Politicians and preachers, for example, often hope to move and persuade voters and congregations, partly through the use of very pronounced and often repetitive rhythms.

The Authorised Version of the Bible contains a good deal of prose which, in its rhythms, often approaches the condition of blank verse:

> Vanity of vanities, saith the preacher, vanity of vanities; all is vanity. What profit hath a man of all his labour which he taketh under the sun? One generation passeth away, and another generation cometh: but the earth abideth for ever. The sun also ariseth, and the sun goeth down, and hasteth to his place where he arose. The wind goeth toward the south, and turneth unto the north; it whirleth about continually, and the wind returneth again according to his circuits. All the rivers run into the sea; yet the sea is not full; unto the place from whence the rivers come, thither they return again. All things are full of labour; man cannot utter it; the eye is not satisfied with seeing, nor the ear filled with hearing. The thing that hath been, is that which shall be; and that which is done is that which shall be done; and there is no new thing under the sun.

If you have listened carefully, you will have heard that the rhythm of this passage is very pronounced—primarily because it is based upon specific sentence patterns. One obvious pattern is the balanced opposition of two initial clauses, followed by a more definite and stressed third clause:

> One generation passeth away, and another generation cometh; but the earth abideth for ever.

Quite simply, the passage does not inform us about the ephemerality of earthy existence, it makes us *feel* these things.

Similar kinds of rhythmic structure are to be found in many writers who have based their prose style and hence their rhythms on the Authorised Version. (Writers such as Bunyan and John Donne). This kind of rhythm is found in patterned prose produced by certain sixteenth and seventeenth century writers such as Francis Bacon:

> Men in great places are thrice servants—servants of the sovereign or State, servants of fame, and servants of business; so as they have no freedom, neither in their persons, nor in

their actions, nor in their times. It is a strange desire to seek power and to lose liberty or to seek power over others, and to lose power over a man's self. The rising unto place is laborious, and by pains men come to greater pains; and it is sometimes base and by indignities men come to dignities.

The initial triple statement continues as a three part structure throughout his essay on those *Of Great Place*, and it is probably less immediately effective than the passage from Ecclesiastes, as a piece of persuasive writing. The use of systematic clauses here is in some ways similar to the use of the formal disciplines of metre and rhyme by many poets. This balanced rhythm is partly a result of Bacon's attempts to give his sentences a positive structure, a structure often missing in the sentences of many earlier prose writers of English whose language was often lively and immediate, but whose sentences were frequently loose and amorphous.

Listen now to part of the speech made by Thomas Wentworth, Earl of Strafford, to the House of Lords on the 13th April 1641:

My Lords,—This day I stand before you, charged with high treason. The burden of the charge is heavy yet far the more because it hath borrowed the authority of the House of Commons. If they were not interested,* I might expect a no less easy, than I do a safe, issue. But let neither my weakness plead my innocence, nor their power my guilt. If your Lordships will concede of my defences as they are in themselves, without reference to either party—and I shall endeavour so to present them—I hope to go hence as clearly justified by you, as I now am in the testimony of a good conscience by myself.

My Lords, I have all along, during this charge, watched to see that poisoned arrow of treason, which some men would fain have feathered in my heart; but in truth, it hath not been in my quickness to discover any such evil within my breast, though now, perhaps, by sinister information, sticking to my clothes.

It is, in some ways, stylistically very different from the Bacon essay, primarily because of the felt presence of a speaking voice; the prose is dramatic as well as discursive, but there is the same kind of rhythmic balance:

But let neither my weakness plead my innocence, nor their power my guilt.

*i.e. if they were unbiased.

However, Strafford perhaps recognized that the constant balancing of ideas could impede as well as advance his cause, and consequently varies the rhythm of his speech to 'isolate' some of his very graphic language:

> Though now, perhaps, by sinister information, sticking to my clothes.

Here is a man attempting to persuade the House of Lords of his innocence; unfortunately, his eloquence did not have the desired effect.

Finally, look and listen to the prose rhythms of another famous orator, Edmund Burke:

> But the colonies will go further. Alas! Alas! When will this speculation against fact and reason end? What will quiet these panic fears which we entertain of the hostile effect of a conciliatory conduct? Is it true that no case can exist, in which it is proper for the Sovereign to accede to the desires of his discontented subjects? Is there anything peculiar in this case, to make a rule for itself? Is all authority of course lost, when it is not pushed to the extreme? Is it a certain maxim, that the fewer causes of dissatisfaction are left by government, the more the subject will be inclined to resist and rebel?
>
> All these objections being in fact no more than suspicions, conjectures, divinations; formed in defiance of fact and experience; they did not, Sir, discourage me from entertaining the idea of a conciliatory concession, founded on the principles which I have just stated.

Although perhaps not the best example of Burke's linguistic abilities we can see how the long-practised art of political oratory, works partly through the repetition of certain key words and rhythms. Look, for example, at the cumulative barrage of rhetorical questions which he hopes must inevitably evoke a negative response, as well as the contemptuously stressed 'suspicions, conjectures, divinations'.

We might conclude this section on oratory and the rhythms of prose with an ironic comment from Thomas Paine on another work by Burke:

> He has produced his clauses, but he must produce also his proofs.

In other words, powerful and emotive rhythm is no guarantee of emotional honesty or logical thought. Indeed, the very nature of oratory tends to preclude at least the latter. As with a poem, it is vital to ask oneself whether in fact the rhythm of a prose passage is used to camouflage a lack of any real thought, or stirs the emotions of the reader or listener by means of rhythms which are at best, skilful, at worst, facile.

In the same way that rhythm can, as it were, take over a poem, so it can become a somewhat glib and facile technique in prose oratory, and occasionally in other kinds of writing.

To conclude this section we might look at another kind of sound effect sometimes found in prose. When Kenneth Grahame, in *The Wind in the Willows*, talks of 'the reeds' soft thin whispering' he is exploiting the varied sounds of individual words; the sibilants they contain (s, z and sh sounds) appeal to the ear; the meaning is conveyed through the sounds of the words as well as by their actual and literal significance. You have, no doubt, come across words like this before in poetry; words such as 'bubble', 'rustle', 'hiss' and so on, which are called 'sound' or onomatopoeic words. These words seem to retain in their sounds some echoic effects which associate them with, or make them representative of, the things or sounds they mean. They are at their most obvious when a writer such as Grahame describes or evokes sound, such as that made by swallows:

> They fell a-twittering among themselves once more, and this time their intoxicating babble was of violet seas, tawny sands, and lizard-haunted walls.

One might not notice that the second clause of this extract is virtually metrical but it is clear that Grahame also uses onomatopoeic words such as 'twittering' and 'babble' to imitate the sounds his animal characters make. As with poetry, short vowels can sometimes suggest more rapid movement than long ones, harsh consonants in words like 'clatter' and 'clank' may suggest more harsh sounds than soft consonants ('murmur', 'innumerable').

However, passages such as the following work not just by using aurally suggestive individual words but also by creating a complex pattern of sound, including an often very delicate yet almost mimetic rhythm:

> Water welled up among the pebbles. It stirred them slightly, paused, then sank away while the pebbles clicked and chirruped. It swilled down past his body and pulled gently at his stockinged feet. He watched the pebbles while the water came back and this time the last touch of the sea lopped into his open mouth. Without change of expression he began to shake, a deep shake that included the whole of his body. Inside his head it seemed that the pebbles were shaking

because the movement of his white hand forwards was matched by the movement of his body. Under the side of his face the pebbles nagged.

It is not easy to analyze the sounds and rhythm of a passage such as this one (an extract from William Golding's *Pincher Martin*). Prose is rarely arranged in systematic or precise rhythmic patterns, but is more often an arrangement of stresses and pauses which are an integral part of the ideas or events expressed in the passage as a whole.

Where does one begin? Well, in the same way one approaches a poem: it is best to examine the rhythm and sound effects of a piece of prose with meticulous care and sensitivity. Ask yourself how it adds to (or perhaps detracts from, or is irrelevant to) the essential meaning of the passage.

When describing rhythm in an essay on a prose extract, words like 'flowing' or 'muscular' are of little use much of the time, and are unfortunately all too common in A-Level essays on the rhythms of prose. Another great danger lies in 'finding' (or rather inventing) onomatopoeic words to please the examiner. There are many vowel and consonant sounds in the English language, and combinations of them are not invariably striving for the kinds of effects we have examined. Look, for example, at this passage:

Miss Brooke had that kind of beauty which seems to be thrown into relief by poor dress. Her hand and wrist were so finely formed that she could wear sleeves not less bare of style than those in which the Blessed Virgin appeared to Italian painters. . . .

One student wrote about this passage:

The alliteration of 'Brooke', 'beauty' and 'be' from the very beginning of Eliot's novel *Middlemarch* links these three words violently together. Dorothea's troubles will be those of identity and superficial relationships based purely upon her surface attractiveness later on in the novel. The frailty of her person and situation is echoed by the thin vowel sound of the passage.

Well, the alliteration he mentions is interesting, but probably fortuitous, and certainly not 'violent'. And where are these 'thin' vowel sounds?

This student is searching, somewhat desperately, for something to say, and by so doing has invented a 'major' theme (that of

56

'surface attractiveness') which does not really stand up to intelligent close scrutiny. It is all too easy to attribute mimetic sounds to words which do not really possess them, by a kind of misguided transference from the words' meanings. Dr. Johnson probably summed up this problem in the most coherent manner:

> The fancied resemblances, I fear, arise sometimes merely from the ambiguity of words; there is supposed to be some relation between a soft line and a soft couch, or between a hard syllable and hard luck.

And finally, if short vowel sounds suggest rapidity, and long ones lethargy, how does one explain words like 'leap' and 'drag'? In other words, as you have probably already found out, when one writes about poetry and prose, there are no simple rules.

GRAMMAR

Word: a unit of language expressive of some object, idea, or relation.

Poets are continually searching for new ways to use words, an activity T. S. Eliot called 'the intolerable wrestle with words and meanings'.

Prose writers are perhaps more fortunate in this respect. They are not always required to begin 'a raid on the inarticulate' every time they write, although, of course, many of them do. We have seen how certain prose writers experiment continuously with words and the relationship that they have with meaning. Writers such as James Joyce, Dylan Thomas and many new American novelists enjoy not just exploring existing words, but inventing their own. Henry Williamson in *Tarka the Otter* invents words whose origins are obviously primarily animal sounds. He talks of cubs 'yikkering threats to each other', the drake 'quapping' with its bill, and so on. (Some linguists in fact believe that all early words were onomatopoeic in origin.)

A different kind of word invention (sometimes called *neologism*), is that of compound words:

> The ferreteyed porkbutcher folded the sausages he had snipped off with blotchy fingers, sausagepink. Sound meat there like a stallfed heifer.

Compound words like 'ferreteyed' and 'sausagepink' are omnipresent in *Ulysses*. The interesting thing about them is that, as with most compound words, a new concept has been formed which is not merely the sum of two other concepts. This is at its most obvious with words like blackbird, rainbow and highway: a highway is not necessarily high. A greenhouse can be white. 'Sausagepink' defines a new, unique and somewhat disturbing mixture of the macabre and domestic. In short, Joyce has struggled with language to produce an idea or, here, a disquieting texture, and has produced his own word as a result.

Some writers in the past, and perhaps a few now, feel, in spite of the fact that the English Language is a mixture of many different languages, a 'Saxon' vocabulary is in some way preferable to words derived from elsewhere, the argument being usually that Saxon words are more immediate and direct in some way. However, there are no simple rules about language such as: 'the older or simpler or shorter the word the better it is'. The problem and the arguments are similar to those about the whole concept of 'poetic diction': is there a language suitable for poetry or are no words barred?

Latinate words, because they are often longer and perhaps more cerebral or abstract, can, however, be used to camouflage unpleasantness or disguise a lack of real thought. The real objection that certain writers have to words of Latin or Greek origin is that they are frequently used in pseudo-scientific jargon. People are encouraged to convert 'Twinkle little star' into 'Oscillate diminutive sidereal body' because it gives the illusion of a brain at work. Long words are not inevitably a sign of an intelligent mind.

The English language is, and always has been, extremely flexible; it borrows words from other languages with ease, it changes meaning as rapidly as people require it to. There are no words a writer 'should not use'. We, as readers, have to decide about a writer's vocabulary on evidence that is more subtle. A description of the problems of medicine or psychiatry would be absurd if a writer attempted to substitute Saxon words for the more technical Latinate ones, and it is unlikely that anyone would try to do this. However, we should be suspicious of a writer or fictional character if they continually use long words when there appears to be no reason for doing so. As Dorothea Brooke, the heroine of George Eliot's *Middlemarch*, finds out *after* she has married the wretched Casaubon, anyone who uses 'inflated' vocabulary to propose marriage is someone to avoid:

> It was, I confess, beyond my hope to meet with this rare combination of elements both solid and attractive, adapted to supply aid in graver labours and to cast a charm over vacant hours; and but for the event of my introduction to you (which

let me again say, I trust not to be superficially coincident with foreshadowing needs, but providentially related thereto as stages towards the completion of a life's plan), I should presumably have gone on to the last without any attempt to lighten my solitariness by a matrimonial union.

In short, the Latin versus Saxon war is a red herring. It does not matter where Casaubon's words come from, it is the ones he chooses which tell us so much about him.

> *Because English is, in the main, an analytic language, the sentence is the most important unit of English speech. The sentence is more important even than the word.*
> *Simeon Potter*

The order of the words contained in a poem is, of course, extremely important. The prose writer probably has less freedom in this respect, but does not inevitably stick to the 'accepted' word order.

Coleridge described poetry as 'the best words in the best order'. The same is likely to be true (although in different ways) of the sentence.

The usual sentence pattern is constantly ignored or inverted in poetry, sometimes simply to accommodate rhyme and rhythm. When this order is changed in prose, then the reasons are likely to be different. On the whole, more emphasis is placed by a reader on a word, phrase or clause that is at the beginning of a sentence than one which appears in the middle or at the end. Obviously then, certain writers will ignore the usual word order of the English sentence if they wish to emphasize an idea:

> Dead she was—committed to the deep while still on the southward track, for the boats from Bombay cannot point towards Europe until Arabia has been rounded; she was further in the tropics than ever achieved while on shore, when the sun touched her for the last time and her body was lowered into yet another India—the Indian Ocean.

The end of Mrs. Moore, in *A Passage to India*, who learns that 'Everything exists, nothing has value' is described here by E. M. Forster with consummate and delicate irony. Notice however, that it is the word 'Dead' that receives the emphasis in this sentence; we are surprised by the unusual word order of the first blunt statement.

59

Altering the accepted word order changes both the rhythm, perhaps the tone, and certainly the meaning of this sentence. Sometimes, an experimental writer, such as James Joyce, will change the word order of his sentences to make them almost mimetic of an action:

> Out of shells, periwinkles with a pin, off trees, snails out of the ground, the French eat, out of the sea with bait on a hook.

This kind of unusual syntax becomes a technique in the hands of an orator who wishes to stir his audience with emotive rhythm:

> Little did I dream that I should have lived to see such disaster fallen upon her in a nation of gallant men, in a nation of men of honour and cavaliers.

Of course, quite often this kind of inverted word order serves to join two sentences together and permit a more elegant juxtaposition of ideas:

> Certain readers failed to appreciate or even recognize Swift's irony in this extract. Such readers, the examiners considered, must have been either unprepared or unintelligent.

As well as having the freedom to alter the usual word order of the English sentence, many prose writers may well omit certain parts of speech altogether. This is done for many reasons: to achieve the similar condensation of language found regularly in poetry, to relate ideas more directly, to emphasize certain ideas, to produce a scene or set of ideas with more immediacy and so on. The verb 'to be' is one that the grammar of the language often seems to require although it is not often necessary for meaning alone. Dickens' novel, *Bleak House*, omits this verb in the opening paragraphs:

> Fog everywhere. Fog up the river, where it flows among green aits and meadows; fog down the river, where it rolls defiled among tiers of shipping, and the waterside pollutions of a great (and dirty) city. Fog on the Essex marshes, fog on the Kentish heights. Fog creeping into the cabooses of collier-brigs; fog lying out on the yards, and hovering in the rigging of great ships; fog dropping on the gunwales of barges and small boats.

Dickens assumes, quite rightly, that his readers will provide such words as 'there was'; indeed, if one did pedantically interpolate the predicate throughout this passage, the impact and immediacy would be irrevocably damaged. When combined, as here, with a powerful and unique rhythm, such stylistic mannerisms can produce prose which is extremely effective. In lesser hands though, the omission of certain parts of speech can be an altogether facile method of creating 'poetic atmosphere'.

Sentences themselves can be classified formally (*simple, compound and complex*) and stylistically (*balanced, loose* and *periodic*). A very common kind of *complex* sentence is one which positions modifying or qualifying clauses after the main or independent clause. The first clause makes the initial statement (although not necessarily the most central or important one) which, in itself, would make perfect sense if supplied with a full stop. This kind of sentence is called '*loose*'. A good example is the opening sentence of Defoe's *Robinson Crusoe*:

> I was born in the year 1632, in the city of York, of a good family, though not of that country, my father being a foreigner of Bremen, who settled first at Hull: he got a good estate by merchandise, and leaving off his trade, lived afterward at York, from whence he had married my mother, whose relations were named Robinson, a very good family in that country, and from whom I was called Robinson Krueutznoer; but, by the usual corruption of words in England, we are now called, nay, we call ourselves, and write our name Crusoe, and so my companions always called me.

As Simeon Potter in *Our Language* points out: 'We seem to hear the author talking quietly to us in the first person and telling us the story of his life. . . . All is easy and natural.' When we speak to friends, our sentences tend to be loose; this does not, however, mean that loose sentences are necessarily always as garrulous as this one from *Robinson Crusoe*.

The main point about a sentence such as this one, is that it could finish virtually after any clause, or could go on, it seems, for ever. The first clause has its own independent meaning, the clauses follow on adding and qualifying, until the sentence is complete.

With the *periodic* sentence, the main clause is left until the end. The reader is kept waiting, the writer delays the whole of his meaning until he feels that he has driven his point home. It is, of course, a grammatical form often used by orators:

> Will posterity believe that, in an age in which men whose gallantries were universally known, and had been legally proved, filled some of the highest offices in the state and in the

army, presided at the meetings of religious and benevolent institutions, were the delight of every society, and the favourites of the multitude, a crowd of moralists went to the theatre, in order to pelt a poor actor for disturbing the conjugal felicity of an alderman?

Well, this periodic sentence, from an essay by Macaulay, doesn't really seem to have the kind of effect that he obviously desired it to have. He wished, presumably, to arouse feelings of outrage in the reader but because of the inelegant and not very relevant descent from the general to the particular, he fails to evoke the kind of response one should get from a rhetorical question of this nature, mainly because the reader has forgotten his initial premise by the time he reaches the final and main clause.

Periodic sentences can, however, be very effective indeed when the reader is made to descend down a staircase of subclauses to be met, sometimes with profundity, sometimes by bathos. Here are two examples. One is from Dickens, one from Gibbon:

> From the master, upon whose impaling files reams of dusty warrants Jarndyce and Jarndyce have grimly writhed into many shapes; down to . . . the copying clerk in the six clerks' office, who has copied his tens of thousands of Chancery folio pages under that eternal heading; no man's nature has been made the better by it.

> Had I believed that the majority of English readers were so fondly attached to the name and shadow of Christianity; had I foreseen that the pious, the timid and the prudent, would feel, or affect to feel, with such exquisite sensibility, I might perhaps, have softened the two invidious chapters.

Both writers might have begun with loose sentences. ('No man's nature has been made the better by' . . . 'I might perhaps, have softened the two invidious chapters had I . . .') but this would be to miss the point. The emphasis and distinctive rhythms of both extracts would disappear, Gibbon would lose his almost contemptuous tone, Dickens would lose the impression of tedium and boredom he gives the reader. We, if you like, have to wade through both sentences, in the same way that Gibbon had to deal with nonsensical complaints, and Dickens' clerks and bureaucrats with the law.

As you might suspect, periodic sentences have the air of being planned carefully and to some end, and are therefore usually more suited to discursive or rhetorical oratory than they are to a prose

62

passage which wishes to sound immediate or spontaneous. It is a kind of sentence construction more suited to a writer who wishes to persuade or cajole rather than to one who wishes to minimize the distance between the reader and, say, a fictional narrator.

Of course, sentences are not always either loose or periodic. A complex sentence may, for example, contain a subordinate clause, an independent main clause followed by subsequent further subordinate clauses. Such a sentence is called *mixed*. It is neither periodic nor loose, but has similarities with both. Another sentence from *Bleak House* is an example:

> Seated at the same table, though with his chair which was modestly and uncomfortably drawn a little way from it, sits a bald, mild, shining man, who coughs respectfully behind his hand when the lawyer bids him fill his glass.

Loose and mixed sentences are very common in the English language, periodic ones are fairly rare.

The *balanced* sentence has a long history. It contains ideas or concepts which are balanced or contrasted antithetically, often in pairs of clauses. Francis Bacon's famous essay *On Travel* contains a much quoted example:

> Travel, in the younger sort, is a part of Education; in the elder, a part of experience.

It is, in some ways, a fairly self-conscious construction, but it does serve to make ideas memorable, and has, as we have already seen, a controlling formal effect like that of rhyme and rhythm in poetry. Gibbon uses it frequently:

> But in the militia I was armed with power; in my travels, I was exempt from control. . . .

> I was introduced to . . . the first names and characters of France, who distinguished me by such marks of civility and kindness as gratitude will not suffer me to forget, and modesty will not allow me to ennumerate.

Because this kind of balanced sentence is so controlled and graceful however, it is probably not very suitable for outpourings of the heart or spontaneous feeling. Gibbon says, in his auto- biography, that when he returned to England, his father forbade him to marry:

After a painful struggle I yielded to my fate; I sighed as a lover, I obeyed as a son; my wound was insensibly healed by time, absence, and the habits of a new life.

It is because of the careful balancing of 'lover' and 'son' and the meticulous rhythm of the last three ideas, that the passage does not really convince us that the writer 'means' what he says; the prose is too nicely polished to convey any painful feeling. The dangers of this kind of sentence are obvious. As a basis for prose style it can sound artificial and hollow like poetry whose rhythm is glib and unconvincing. Hazlitt was very critical of this sort of balanced and rhetorical prose, when writing about Burke:

The words are not fitted to the things, but the things to the words. . . . Where there is no room for variety, no discrimination, no nicety can be shown in matching the idea with its proper word.

Coleridge, perhaps unfairly, said the same of Dr. Johnson, who was also fond of the balanced sentence:

The antithesis of Johnson is rarely more than verbal.

In other words, both balanced and periodic sentences, if not used carefully, and perhaps sparingly, can destroy rather than elucidate meaning.

In spite of all this categorization of sentences and syntax it is, in fact, not always easy to trace the relationships between that indefinable thing we call a writer's 'style' and the structure of his sentences. If a writer wished to give the impression of speed or irritation, he may use short sentences and prefer the connective 'and' to others which imply causal relationships. (I ran out the door *and* he was coming after me. I was scared. He was big. He could run faster *and* he was catching me up. . . .) But again, there are no rules. A writer such as William Faulkner can create a sense of panic by using sentences that are unusually lengthy. A writer can be very skilful, like Hemingway, and yet use sentences that are extremely simple in construction. Henry James uses sentences which have a very complex structure indeed, because he is exploring shades of meaning and the minutiae of the emotions of his fictional characters. *The Language of Prose* by Robert Millar and Ian Currie states the problem succinctly:

It is very difficult to define just precisely what contribution the sentence structure of a passage makes to its general signifi-

64

cance, and very little work has been done upon this aspect of style.

To conclude this section, let us examine four sentences:

'You find me my dears,' said Mrs. Jellyby, snuffing the two great office candles in tin candlesticks which made the room taste strongly of hot tallow (the fire had gone out, and there was nothing in the grate, but ashes, a bundle of wood, and a poker) 'you find me, my dears, as usual very busy; but that you will excuse.'

So that it may appear this uncomely company hath had a long continuance, but then nothing given so much to pilfering, picking and spoiling; and, as far as I can learn or understand by the examination of a number of them, their language— which they term pedlar's French or canting—began but within these thirty years, little above; and that the first inventor thereof was hanged, all save the head; for that is the final end of them all or else to die of some filthy or horrible disease.

The notice which you have been pleased to take of my labours, had it been early had been kind; but it has been delayed until I am indifferent, and cannot enjoy it; till I am solitary, and cannot impart it; till I am known, and do not want it.

Ruins and basilicas, palaces and colossi, set in the midst of a sordid present, where all that was living and warm-blooded seemed sunk in the deep degeneracy of a superstition divorced from reverence; the dimmer yet eager Titanic life gazing and struggling on walls and ceilings; the long vistas of white forms whose marble eyes seemed to hold the monotonous light of an alien world: all this vast wreck of ambitious ideals, sensous and spiritual, mixed confusingly with the signs of breathing forgetfulness and degradation, at first jarred her as with an electric shock, and then urged themselves on her with that ache belonging to a glut of confused ideas which check the flow of emotion.

Extract one from *Bleak House* appears remarkably clumsy (the reader has to be reminded of Mrs. Jellyby's speech because of the long parenthesis). And yet the structure of the sentence not only illustrates the woman's character (she seems very absent-minded; we, like her audience, have to wait for her to speak), it conveys the impatience of her listeners, and perhaps implies that 'busy' is a relative word when coming from her.

Extract two from *A Caveat for Common Cursitors* is a wonderfully loose and garrulous sentence with no real structure at all. Thomas Harman, the writer, is full of breathless enthusiasm; he wants to get everything down as rapidly as possible, an impression one gets from much Elizabethan and Jacobean prose, and this writer especially.

Extract three is of course full of antithetically balanced clauses. It is from one of the most restrained and yet most insulting letters ever written: from Samuel Johnson to the Earl of Chesterfield. Here one cannot agree with Coleridge that Johnson's antithesis is 'only verbal'; the balance of ideas is masterful, the contempt absolute. (See 'A Note on Meaning, Irony and Tone', p. 81, for further discussion of Johnson's letter to Chesterfield.)

Extract four, from George Eliot's *Middlemarch,* concerns Dorothea, a girl who has been educated on 'art chiefly of the hand-screen sort', and the impressions she receives of Rome on her first visit there. Clause is piled upon clause, the richness and beauty of the city is catalogued, the sense of confusion in Dorothea's mind when faced with something towards which there can be no simple attitude, is conveyed by the length and near confusion of the sentence itself. George Eliot's sentences do not have the kind of polish and neatness of a writer such as Jane Austen, but it would obviously be out of place here to have a carefully balanced and carefully modulated sentence.

You might now look at these sentences yourself and see whether you agree with what has been said and ask whether you have anything to add to this complex matter of the relationship between syntax and meaning.

SIX

A Brief Exercise in Prose Appreciation

Read the extract below very carefully and then:
1. Explain the meaning of:
   a. *Where necessity ends curiosity begins* (line 4)
   b. *such petty conveniences* (line 10)
   c. *superfluities as neither accommodate the body nor improve the mind* (lines 23–24)
   d. *mercenary officiousness* (lines 41–42)
2. Comment on the irony present in:
   a. *species of distress* (line 19)
   b. *the unhappiest of all mortals* (line 29)
   c. *a public benefactor* (line 37)
3. Comment on the contributions made by rhythm and syntax to the meaning of the following sentences:
   a. *By this . . . necessary things* (second paragraph)
   b. *To set himself free . . . carnations.* (fifth paragraph)
4. In one short paragraph summarize the defence the author puts forward for those who produce only 'superfluities'.
5. Discuss the tone of the passage (What kind of relationship does the writer wish to establish with his readers?)
6. Comment on the style of the passage (Such components as rhythm, vocabulary and syntax seem especially worthy of examination and discussion.)

The desires of man increase with his acquisitions; every step which he advances brings something within his view, which he did not see before, and which, as soon as he sees it, he begins to want. Where necessity ends curiosity begins, and no
5 sooner are we supplied with every thing that nature can demand, than we sit down to contrive artificial appetites.

By this restlessness of mind, every populous and wealthy city is filled with innumerable employments, for which the

greater part of mankind is without a name; with artificers
10   whose labour is exerted in producing such petty conveniences,
that many shops are furnished with instruments, of which the
use can hardly be found without inquiry, but which he that
once knows them, quickly learns to number among necessary
things.
15   Such is the diligence, with which, in countries completely
civilized, one part of mankind labours for another, that wants
are supplied faster than they can be formed, and the idle and
luxurious find life stagnate, for want of some desire to keep it
in motion. This species of distress furnishes a new set of
20   occupations, and multitudes are busied, from day to day, in
finding the rich and the fortunate something to do.

It is very common to reproach those artists as useless, who
produce only such superfluities as neither accommodate the
body nor improve the mind; and of which no other effect can
25   be imagined, than that they are the occasions of spending
money, and consuming time.

But this censure will be mitigated, when it is seriously
considered, that money and time are the heaviest burdens of
life, and that the unhappiest of all mortals are those who have
30   more of either than they know how to use. To set himself free
from these incumbrances, one hurries to Newmarket; another
travels over Europe; one pulls down his house and calls
architects about him; another buys a seat in the country, and
follows his hounds over hedges and through rivers; one makes
35   collections of shells, and another searches the world for tulips
and carnations.

He is surely a public benefactor who finds employment for
those to whom it is thus difficult to find it for themselves. It is
true that this is seldom done merely from generosity or
40   compassion, almost every man seeks his own advantage in
helping others, and therefore it is too common for mercenary
officiousness, to consider rather what is grateful than what is
right.

We all know that it is more profitable to be loved than
45   esteemed, and ministers of pleasure will always be found,
who study to make themselves necessary, and to supplant
those who are practising the same arts.

One of the amusements of idleness is reading without the
fatigue of close attention, and the world therefore swarms
50   with writers whose wish is not to be studied but to be read.

SEVEN

A Note on Meaning, Irony and Tone in Prose

When we examined the word 'prose' we discovered that the relationship between words and their meanings is not at all as clear cut as dictionaries might imply. The concept of 'meaning' is an involved philosophical and linguistic problem. However, if we are to come to grips with a concept such as the one we call 'irony', we ought to examine briefly the intricate relationship between words and what it is they refer to.

Certain words in the English language seem to have very little true 'meaning' at all; words which are functional or connective in some way; 'but', 'and', and 'the' are obvious examples. These 'empty' words are normally prepositions, conjunctions, articles, pronouns or auxiliary verbs whose main function is to describe the relationships between other words which possess stronger meanings. Similarly, there are certain words in the language which seem to have undergone a process of 'semantic generalization'. These are words which once had a meaning that was quite precise but which have now often become vague and simple terms of approval or disapproval; words such as 'nice' and 'bad' would come into this category.

Moreover, many words do not have one simple meaning, but several. For example, the word 'head', according to the *Shorter Oxford English Dictionary*, has at least thirty different meanings and many more when it is used in conjunction with other key words. *Polysemy* (the existence of several meanings for one word) in this case, came about through a linguistic process that some scholars call 'radiation', where different meanings are derived from one central idea. Thus, from the simple initial concept, a whole range of new meanings have diffused and emerged into the language (head of a coin, head of cattle, head of a plant, head on beer, head of a river and so on). The growth of new words and ideas (there is some dispute as to which comes first), as is obvious enough from this example, often seems to arise from the apparently instinctive *figurative* use of language.

Not only can a word have several meanings, but the meanings of individual words can change continuously and often confusingly. For example, the word 'nice' in 1560 seems to have had the meaning of 'foolish', but the sense of the word changed gradually into such meanings as strange, rare, delicate, over-refined, modest, requiring great precision, difficult, trivial, accurate, and finally, into 'vaguely pleasant'. Students who ignore this fact of semantic change often make dreadful mistakes when, for example, paraphrasing or interpreting the word 'presently' in a Shakespeare play, or the word 'enthusiasm' in an extract from Swift, or by misunderstanding the complexities of meaning present in a word like 'nature' as it was understood by Pope or Wordsworth.

Words are also notoriously 'slippery' and ambiguous because of their emotive, and, for the scientist or philosopher, often quite undesirable irrational connotations. Poets are constantly aware of, and continually exploit, this fact; indeed, it seems likely that language itself was originally used for emotive rather than for informative reasons. Many words can take on both informative and emotive functions; words such as 'home', 'little', (when contrasted with 'small') or 'heart' (when opposed to 'head' say,) are obvious examples. There are very distinct differences in the meanings of 'little' when used in the contexts 'little use', or 'little orphan'! Less obviously emotive is a word which seems almost 'technical', like 'purple' which could appear to have a fairly precise informative meaning (a colour somewhere between red and blue) and yet it is constantly used by writers because of the connotations of wealth, luxury and royalty that it possesses. The most obvious point is that it is the context in which a word appears which is all-important. Certain words seem to release their emotive charge only in certain prescribed contexts. Look at the different meanings of the word 'public' when used in the different contexts 'public school', 'public house' and 'the general public'.

As is often the case, a writer may well wish to do more than simply present facts to his readers. By an astute and often intuitive selection of specific words, all containing subtly different and varied emotive potential, the author can indicate faint approval or disapproval, exuberant enthusiasm or extreme distaste.

This is one reason why true synonyms are rare. There is a world of difference between someone 'laughing' and someone 'sniggering', but the gradations of meaning can be almost infinitely subtle. We have already seen that 'matrimonial union' does not 'mean' the same as 'marriage' when it is found in a letter of proposal. A writer will select the words he uses according to the attitudes he has towards his subject, his audience, and the medium in which he is working. Often, of course, this selection will be instinctive and unconscious, and then he may well *betray* his own views through his choice of particular words. Context, then, is vitally important when we examine the meaning of words.

If, for example, we see the words 'confession, fire, fallen, judgement' and 'revelation' in close proximity, we would recognize that the words had acquired specific theological meanings rather than the more generalized ones that they possess when out of such a context. As we saw earlier, a writer such as Peacock can manipulate these verbal contexts in such a way as to treat his characters and their ideas ironically.

It is because of this continually shifting relationship between words and meanings, and the fact that context is vital to understanding, that certain writers are able to manipulate language so that the relationship between what the words appear to say and what they actually mean can be almost contradictory. A writer may use words which superficially seem to possess one sense, but which, in fact, have, for an astute reader, a very different or even opposite meaning. This manipulation of language and meaning, where 'information' appears to exist on two or more levels is often known as *irony*.

The 'meaning' of irony, as one might expect, is notoriously elusive; it is probably more useful to try to avoid an exact definition than to provide one. Dr. Johnson in his famous dictionary defined irony as:

> A mode of speech in which the meaning is contrary to the words.

a definition which seems adequate enough until one comes across the series of pictures by Hogarth known as *The Rake's Progress* which are examples of 'visual irony', or until one tries to apply the formula to the more specific term 'dramatic irony'. In short, irony does not seem to be a simple phenomenon.

As a literary term, it has come to mean different things to different critics. Cleanth Brooks, an American, uses the word irony to describe any change or modification of meaning that one element in a literary work undergoes as a result of the 'pressure of its context'; many critics feel that it is a word with so many plausible and possible definitions that it has almost ceased to be useful as a critical term unless it is endlessly qualified.

The word irony itself has had a long and involved semantic history; the meanings it has possessed range from 'dishonest or fraudulent persuasion' to 'the perception of the essential unpredictability and contingency of life itself.'

One obvious way of approaching the subject might be to examine a list of extracts from various sources, extracts which have all, at one time or another, been called 'ironic'.

1. Is not a Patron, my Lord, one who looks with unconcern on a man struggling for life in the water, and, when he has reached ground, encumbers him with help?

2. It was a disheartening circumstance, but a melancholy fact, that even these readers persisted in wondering. They wondered about human nature, human passions, human hopes and fears, the struggles, triumphs and defeats, the cares and joys and sorrows, the lives and deaths, of common men and women. They sometimes after fifteen hours' work, sat down to read mere fables about men and women, more or less like themselves, and about children, more or less like their own.

3. These reasonings will furnish us with an adequate Definiton of a true Critick; that, He is a Discoverer and Collector of Writers' faults.

Extract one is from that famous and insulting letter from Dr. Johnson to the Earl of Chesterfield. Johnson feels that patrons should offer their services before, rather than after, a writer has become famous. The irony here is 'simple', in that the definition Johnson suggests for the word 'Patron' is the opposite of its usual meaning. He has produced a rhetorical question which blatantly and necessarily elicits the answer 'No' from the reader. The irony here is obvious and the tone sarcastic; as invective, it is extremely effective.

The irony in extract two, from Dickens' *Hard Times*, is again 'simple', but not easy; the questions it raises about meaning are more involved. The narrator is describing the inhabitants of the monotonous industrial city of Coketown, and tells us that they seem to prefer 'fancy' to 'fact' as well as welcoming those things that are apparently 'irrational', including (and here there is a kind of 'double' irony) works of fiction. Obviously, Dickens does not want us to swallow the attitudes presented here. The fact that people who live in Coketown still have enough independence of mind to cling to those things that are symbolic of imagination (the 'novel' itself immediately comes to mind) is the opposite of 'disheartening' and 'melancholy'. Dickens is also suggesting perhaps that 'mere fables' are essential to human life and sanity.

Extract three is from *A Tale of a Tub* by Jonathan Swift. Any simple definition of irony such as 'language which means the opposite of what it says' is here obviously inadequate. A 'Critick' is more than simply a 'Discoverer and Collector of Writers' Faults', but not the opposite. The irony here lies in the writer presenting a partial truth as if it were the whole picture; Swift's ironic implication being that ignorant and partisan modern critics confuse criticism and censure, and are thereby unworthy of the labels they pretend. The word 'Collector' also implies a kind of schoolboy maliciousness; these critics are able to categorize and tabulate but cannot respond to works of art with any sympathy or real understanding of the artistic process. This kind of rhetorical technique is common among artistic ironists. By playing something down in order, paradoxically, to magnify it, one uses the distortion of meaning sometimes known as 'understatement'. 'Overstatement', as one might expect, is the praising of something in order to condemn it; Chaucer uses this kind of irony constantly in *The General Prologue* where his garrulous narrator calls even the most overtly villainous characters 'worthy'.

4. Laws are best explained, interpreted, and applied by those whose Interests and Abilities lie in perverting, compounding and eluding them.

5. When they perceived her to be little struck with the duet they were so good as to play, they could do no more than make her a generous present of their least valued toys. . . .

6. Whether the Nymph shall break *Diana*'s Law
   Or some frail China Jar receive a flaw;
   Or stain her Honour, or her new Brocade;
   Forget her Pray'rs or miss a Masquerade.

These three extracts are similar in terms of satiric technique. They all rely heavily on bathos or anti-climax for ironic effect. Some critics have tried to explain the effects upon the reader of this kind of rhetorical device by using the term 'defeated expectancy'; the reader often tends to 'jump ahead' of the text, and for this reason expects to hear from Swift (extract 4) that 'Laws are best explained . . . by those whose interests and abilities lie in . . . disinterested analysis and legal knowledge' (for example), but, finds, of course, that this is not the case.

Swift, in this extract from *Gulliver's Travels* is implying, through his ironic spokesman, the King of Brobdingnag, not only that there are undoubtedly too many corrupt lawyers in the world, but, more profoundly, that the law itself is perhaps complex not because it deals with involved issues, but is perversely *made* so, so that it can provide income for those who 'interpret' it to ordinary men and women. Swift often delights in this thought-provoking confusion of cause and effect; the irony here also seems to imply that there is an obvious moral conflict in a legal profession which is stirred both by money (interest) and hollow technique (abilities) rather than by the search for truth and justice. The king is also implying, perhaps not necessarily ironically, that frauds, crooks and charlatans are more aware of defects in the law than honest men; lawbreakers would, in fact, make the best lawyers.

The meaning of extract five (from Jane Austen's novel *Mansfield Park*) is equally complex because of the presence of irony. Two characters in the novel, Julia and Maria Bertram, are 'to afford leisure for getting acquainted with' their poor cousin, Fanny Price. They are revealed by the irony as condescending ('were so good as to play') as well as selfish. Austen's irony 'works' very often through the use of what critics sometimes call 'internal contradiction', which, in some ways, is a kind of bathos *and* defeated expectancy. By implying that obviously dissimilar words, by virtue of their context, can have similar or related meanings ('generous . . . least valued') Austen continually calls the surface meaning of her language into question, thereby forcing the reader to re-examine the motives and behaviour of many of her fictional characters. Most of Austen's heroines themselves are faced with this problem: it is vital, if you are looking for a suitable marriage partner, to be able to distinguish between the 'temper' (social and therefore public charm) and 'character' (moral and often private beliefs) of the young men that surround you. The reader of the novels often has to exercise the same kind of perception when examining and evaluating the fictional characters, basing his judgements upon the expertise he receives from the 'irony' present in all the novels.

Extract six, from Pope's *The Rape Of The Lock*, illustrates another kind of bathetic irony. The poem employs an ironic device common to certain satirists, that of *zeugma*. (One predicate referring to two or more words which are incongruous or incompatible. See Glossary.) Here, of course, Swift is implying that the sylph (who protects Belinda from various threats to her person) and her charge, have moral attitudes which are essentially trivial. Belinda is equally worried about her 'Honour' and her 'new Brocade' and the 'economy' of the sentence structure indicates the blandness of her responses to all things that affect her.

Much of this poem is concerned with the essential difference between a concern for reputation and a sincere devotion to 'honour'; Pope illustrates this ambivalence by using the verb 'stain' in both a literal and a metaphorical sense, to refer to the trivial and the ostensibly important, thus implying that the 'spiritual' qualities of the heroine of the poem are more crudely physical in origin than she would care to admit.

This kind of irony, is of course, something one finds constantly in the poetry of Chaucer. Duke Theseus of *The Knight's Tale* comments upon the youthful enthusiasm and foolishness of the two lovers Palamon and Arcite. They love the heroine Emelye to distraction and death and yet, says the Duke:

> She woot namoore of al this hoote fare,
> By God, than woot a cokkow or an hare!

Thereby implying, by the use of this somewhat incongruously domestic simile, not that Emelye is impure in any way, but that the game of love seems at times, a little ridiculous. It is the sort of incongruous juxtaposition that we find in the next extract.

7. My female Friends, whose tender Hearts
   Have better learn'd to act their parts,
   Receive the News in *doleful Dumps*,
   "The Dean is dead (*and What is Trumps?*)
   "Then Lord have Mercy on his Soul.
   "(Ladies I'll venture for the *Vole*)".

This extract (from the poem by Swift, *Verses on the Death of Dr. Swift*) imagines the reactions that society ladies of his acquaintance might have towards the news of his own death. By using apparently 'random' but obviously 'ironic' juxtaposition of snippets of conversation he implies that they would no doubt play cards and discuss the death of friends with little real change of mood or tone. It is the kind of seemingly fortuitous (but, of course, carefully planned) juxtaposition that we find in Pope's poem, when he describes the articles found on Belinda's dressing table:

> Puffs, Powders, Patches, Bibles, Billet-doux.

thereby implying that all are of similar or equal importance in the shallow Society world she inhabits.

As Arthur Pollard, in his excellent book *Satire*, points out, irony is rarely suited to the exploration of self; it is a mode of expression which seems to demand a distancing objectivity and coolness. When Swift imagines his death, it is not for 'personal' reasons:

'We do not get very near the Dean himself; his feelings or his sufferings; these are not subjects for satire. . . . Swift is, in fact, using the solemnity of death to criticize the superficialities of the living.'

8. Women were expected to have *weak opinions*; but the great *safeguard* of *society* and of *domestic life* was, that opinions were not acted on. *Sane people* did what their neighbours did, so that if any *lunatics* were at large, one might *know* and avoid them.

Another more complex kind of 'double' irony is displayed in this extract. (From George Eliot's novel *Middlemarch*). It contains a comic irony which seems to present conflicting viewpoints, neither of which is 'right' or necessarily more valid than the other. Women should be able to voice their opinions openly and freely; the stability and conformity of a provincial town can no doubt be extremely claustrophobic to certain people. However, is it always desirable to 'act on' opinions, under any circumstances? George Eliot is not offering a simple answer here. Conformity and conservatism have effects which are both good and reprehensible, depending perhaps upon one's position in society and one's consequent point of view. There is probably no simple way of reconciling these opposing viewpoints, except perhaps through irony. George Eliot, throughout this and other of her novels, continually prevents the reader from forming easy and simple opinions and conclusions about characters and events by indicating that there is usually more than one vantage point from which one can view these things. You might like to have another closer look at the extract and decide exactly what the writer means by those words that are italicized.

9. We have had a very dull Christmas; Mr. and Mrs. Musgrove have not had one dinner party all the holidays. I do not reckon the Hayters as anybody. The holidays, however, are over at last: I believe no children ever had such long ones. I am sure I I had not. The house was cleared yesterday, except of the little Harvilles; but you will be surprised to hear they have never gone home. Mrs. Harville must be an odd mother to part with them so long. I do not understand it. They are not at all nice children, in my opinion; but Mrs. Musgrove seems to like them quite well, if not better, than her grandchildren.

This extract, from another novel by Jane Austen, *Persuasion*, shows how irony can emerge from the style and linguistic mannerisms used by a fictional character either in conversation or, as here, in written correspondence. The character, Mary Musgrove, is full of egotistical self pity, she is a snob ('I do not reckon the Hayters as anybody'), she condemns others for feelings that she unconsciously reveals herself as having. ('I believe no children ever had such long ones. . . . Mrs. Harville must be an odd mother to part with them so long'). One of Austen's many ironic methods is the art of allowing her fictional characters to betray their true 'character' is this way, rather than always commenting upon them herself as an omniscient narrator. This brand of irony is often called 'unconscious self-revelation'. The fictional character presented in a novel is less astute about his real motives than the reader, who, as with all of Austen's novels, is allowed to feel more astute and intellectually and morally superior. Unlike Emma, the heroine in the novel of that name, Mary Musgrove will never undergo a process of education that will enable her to achieve some degree of self knowledge. In some ways, this kind of restricted and denied 'knowledge' has parallels with irony we call 'dramatic'.

10. Autolycus: . . . having flown over many knavish professions, he settled only in rogue. Some call him Autolycus.

11. Lear: . . . 'tis our fast intent
To shake all cares and business from our age
Conferring them on younger strengths, while we
Unburthened crawl toward death.

Extract 10 is an example of simple dramatic irony from Shakespeare's *The Winter's Tale*. The audience sees and recognizes Autolycus who, as with many similar stage 'conventions', is concealed from other characters by the flimsiest of disguises. Autolycus here describes himself to another more gullible character and the audience enjoys the comedy of a rogue blatantly describing himself as a rogue.

Extract 11, from *King Lear*, is less obviously a dramatic irony in the sense we have just seen. Unless the audience has seen this play before, it is unlikely to know that Lear, in fact, increases his 'cares and business', and hastens rather than 'crawls' to his death, because of the blind and foolish decisions he makes at the beginning of the play. If the simple kind of dramatic irony we have described does exist here, it is present in the audience which probably suspects that things will not turn out as Lear expects them to; if this were not the case, the play, for one thing, would be extremely short.

The irony that is very evident in an extract of this kind is that which is often called 'Sophoclean' or tragic irony. This concept is essential to the ethical world of tragedy; whatever plans, aspirations or hopes that men have (especially if they smack of ambition or pride), the chances are that things will go wrong. Tragedy is concerned with, amongst other things, the 'human condition'. We, as members of the human race, are in a peculiar and paradoxical situation; we seem to need to pretend that life is generally logical, ordered, rational, and guided by Providence, but the evidence presented by tragedy continually suggests the opposite. This is why when we watch a tragedy which shows an old man preparing for a comfortable if somewhat premature retirement, we automatically expect the worst. The connection between this kind of tragic irony, and the irony one can really describe as being 'verbal', is not wholly clear. The irony of tragedy certainly seems to suggest that human beings, like the actors on the stage, are being watched and probably manipulated by an unseen author and audience.

12. Chaucer, thogh he kan but lewedly
    On metres and on rymyng craftily
    Hath seyd hem in swich Englissh as he kan
    Of olde tyme. . . .

13. Where were we? I was going to comment on the significance of the *viz* I used earlier was I? Or explain my 'piano tuning' metaphor? Or my weak heart? Good heavens, how does one write a novel! I mean, how can anybody stick to the story, if he's at all sensitive to the significances of things? As for me, I see already that story telling isn't my cup of tea: every new sentence I set down is full of figures and implications that I'd love nothing better than to chase to their dens with you, but such chasing would involve new figures and new chases so that I'm sure we'd never get the story started, much less ended, if I let my inclinations run unleashed.

Both Chaucer in the fourteenth century and John Barth, the American novelist in the twentieth, seem here to be claiming that, for one reason or another, they are not very good writers. Or rather more accurately both writers make one of their respective fictional characters voice this opinion. (The Man of Law in the Introduction to his tale, talking to the Host, and the hero of John Barth's novel *The Floating Opera*, Todd Andrewes.) Both authors are being ironic about themselves as writers. They are employing a rhetorical device sometimes known as 'self-disparaging' irony. Chaucer allows his character to claim that he, Chaucer, is an unskilled poet, confidently encouraging the pretence that he is less skilled and knowledgeable than his audience knows he actually is. Known by certain mediaeval writers of rhetorical manuals as 'diminutio' this kind of ostensibly self-destructive irony is an obvious method of gaining sympathy and tolerance from an audience. (It would not work ironically, for example, if the writer claimed that he was inexpert and bad if he obviously was!)

As with much of the irony that we have examined so far, the author and his audience have come to a kind of conspiratorial agreement; similar to the kind of contract that one makes with a playwright when one enters the theatre. Chaucer doesn't really 'believe' what his fictional character says, neither does his audience, but they no doubt welcome his ironic humility as a form of elegant flattery. Chaucer often assumes this sort of 'mask'; he pretends to be ignorant and credulous, and his ironic statements may often depend on this distance he creates between himself as an author and his convenient fictional narrators. Because it is a form of irony used by Socrates, who constantly pretended to be a simpleton in philosophical debate (in order to destroy the arguments of his opponents), it is sometimes known also as 'Socratic' irony.

Barth is a novelist who seems fascinated with the problems of perception and the often tortuous relation that a work of fiction has with the 'real' world, of which, of course, any novel is itself a part. In *The Floating Opera*, as we can see from this extract, Andrewes claims to be an amateur novelist, inventing the novel, its characters and incidents as he goes along. He establishes a kind of eccentric friendship with the reader by putting on the (rarely convincing) self-disparaging mask of a garrulous and incompetent raconteur. Of course, when we read Barth's novel, what we find is a very sophisticated and professionally constructed work of fiction, the main subject of which is the narrator and the often strange workings of his mind, rather than the events and characters which he describes in a highly partisan and suspect manner. The irony then is both self-disparaging and unconsciously self-revelatory; the more one explores irony, in fact, the more one finds that simple labels such as these are only partially useful.

John Barth seems to be calling into question all those assumptions we, as readers of works of fiction, tend to make when we pick up a novel. Barth's novel, like many other recent American novels, implies that all literature is 'ironic' in the sense that there will always be a series of paradoxes inherent in any activity which is both apart from and yet a part of the 'real' world. D.C. Mueke, in his book *Irony* calls this kind of self-conscious and inwardly directed questioning: 'Romantic' irony:

79

> (It) is the irony of a writer conscious that literature can no
> longer be simply naive and unreflective but must present itself
> as conscious of its contradictory, ambivalent nature. . . . We
> come closer to Romantic irony when the work is accompanied
> by a critical commentary on events and characters and closer
> still when the commentary directs its ironic attention to a
> literary composition in general or even to the composition of
> the work in hand.

So, John Barth uses his ironic 'mask' to foreground and emphasize
the artifice of his—and by implication *all*—literary work. Todd
Andrewes reminds and teases the reader about the quite artificial
processes at work when a writer writes and a reader reads.
Barth's novel implies that novels, and the written word itself, are
not, and never were, simple unambiguous windows through which
we can view the 'real' world. Although *The Floating Opera* does
have a narrative (and all that that implies) it is also a novel about
'The Novel' itself.

Let us pause for a moment. It should by now be obvious that the
term 'irony' embraces a wide range of techniques and concerns.
Generally speaking, irony comes into play when the relationship
between words and meaning is ambiguous or is in some way called
into question. This relationship need not involve contradiction or
opposition (as Dr. Johnson suggested), but may involve a meaning
which is different, or wider or deeper than the surface significance of the words. We might say that irony depends upon a
writer leaving something unsaid which has then to be detected by
the reader. There is some sort of *discrepancy* between the words
on the page and their meaning as it is perceived by the reader (or
by the audience in a theatre). This is the case when, for example,
a fictional character says or thinks things which reveal an aspect
of his or her character that he or she is unconscious of (as in
extract 9). But it should be obvious also that there is a considerable difference between the irony employed by Jane Austen and
that present in the extract from *The Floating Opera*. This
difference reminds us that irony is as much a matter of *tone* as it
is a matter of meaning. Tone, as has been said elsewhere, is 'that
quality of a writer's use of language which suggests his attitude
towards his subject-matter and characters on one hand and his
attitude to and relationship with the reader, on the other'. Because
irony involves a complex correspondence between words and
meaning, ironic writing demands that the reader engages in
interpretation and assessment; the reader must be *actively considering* his response to the words on the page. In this way, irony
invites the reader to participate in the fictional work, and by this

80

means the ironic author establishes a closer relationship with the reader. In most of the extracts we have looked at, this relationship is basically amicable. Austen's tone, say, or George Eliot's, suggests that the reader is as astute, informed and sophisticated as the author. The irony is a means of *sharing* insight, a means by which the author recognizes the reader's own ability to appreciate the complexity of things. The author-reader relationship is characterized by mutual sympathy and respect, by *solidarity*. In a very delicate way, the author flatters the reader (and thus, of course, persuades the reader to accept the author's version of reality). The introduction of a persona, a fictional author placed between the real author and the reader, obviously complicates the relationship. It is more difficult for the reader to identify with the writer.

Let us look again at the passage by John Barth. Barth wishes to write about the difficulties and the artificialities of the novelist's art. Clearly, he cannot demonstrate them by writing a novel which is itself chaotic and madly digressive, because the result would be simply a bad novel which would merely irritate and antagonize the reader. Barth therefore creates Todd Andrewes to 'write' the novel for him. Thus the reader is amused by the struggles of this 'author', and engaged in them, but is conscious of the skill of the actual author behind the mask. As a strategy, Barth's use of this ironic device is very different from Austen's poised and cultured ironic tone. But this is the important point—the result is much the same: the reader is granted a somewhat elevated and detached viewpoint from which to regard a novelist's characters and incidents, and at the same time is allowed a cordial and mutually respectful relationship with the author (even though Barth is less 'visible' an author than Jane Austen).

However, any discussion of irony—no matter how brief—which implied that the ironist's relationship with his reader is always one of sympathy and solidarity would be deceptive. This is not the nature of the relationship behind Johnson's letter to Lord Chesterfield (extract 1). Johnson assumes that Chesterfield will understand him, will share his view of things; but this mutual understanding is a means by which Johnson *attacks* Chesterfield. Chesterfield, a patron of the arts, declined to finance Johnson in his work; yet, when that work was completed, he offered his patronage in order that he might claim some share in its prestige. When Johnson writes to suggest that a patron is one who 'looks with unconcern on a man struggling for his life in the water' and only 'encumbers him with help' when dry ground is reached, Johnson knows that Chesterfield cannot agree; yet once Chesterfield says 'No', he has to recognize his own maltreatment of Johnson. The mutual understanding which the writer assumes exists between himself and his reader is here not a cause for complacency on the reader's part, it is the means by which he is satirized.

Because tone is so fundamental to a work of literature—it conditions the style, it conditions our response to characters, it directs attention to different levels of meaning—it follows that even minor variations in tone can have far-reaching effects upon the reader. Drastic variations can bewilder, delight, surprise, shock. When tone is established by a persona, shifts in the manner, character or language of this persona can cause similar disturbances. Let us bring all these matters together by means of our penultimate extract. This passage, which is longer than our previous quotations and requires a very careful reading, is from Swift's satire *A Modest Proposal for Preventing the Children of Ireland from Being a Burden to their Parents or Country and for Making them Beneficial to the Public*. Swift writes in the persona of a 'projector', a developer of schemes and policies who thinks he has the answer to the massive problems of over-population and starvation in eighteenth-century Ireland. 'The present distresses of the kingdom' (paragraph four) refers to the poverty of Ireland, brought about by English landowners ('landlords') who bled white their Irish estates and tenants, by punitive economic policies fixed in London, and by repeated crop failures.

14. I think it is agreed by all parties that this prodigious number of children in the arms, or at the backs, or at the heels of their mothers, and frequently of their fathers, is in the present deplorable state of the kingdom a very great additional grievance; and therefore, whoever could find out a fair, cheap and easy method of making these children sound and useful members of the commonwealth would deserve so well of the public as to have his statue set up for a preserver of the nation. . . .

As to my own part, having turned my thoughts, for many years, upon this important subject, and maturely weighed the several schemes of other Projectors, I have always found them grossly mistaken in their computation. It is true, a child just dropped from its dam may be supported by her milk for a solar year with little other nourishment, at most not above the value of two shillings, which the mother may certainly get, or the value in scraps, by her lawful occupation of begging; and it is exactly at one year old that I propose to provide for them in such a manner as, instead of being a charge upon their parents, or the parish, or wanting food and raiment for the rest of their lives, they shall, on the contrary, contribute

82

to the feeding and partly to the clothing of many thousands.

There is likewise another great advantage in my scheme, that it will prevent those voluntary abortions, and that horrid practice of women murdering their poor bastard children, alas! too frequent among us; sacrificing their poor innocent babes, I doubt, more to avoid the expense than the shame; which would move tears and pity in the most savage and inhuman breast.

The number of souls in Ireland being usually reckoned one million and a half, of these I calculate there may be about two hundred thousand couples whose wives are breeders, from which number I subtract thirty thousand couples who are able to maintain their own children, although I apprehend there cannot be so many under the present distresses of the kingdom; but this being granted, there will remain a hundred and seventy thousand breeders. I again subtract fifty thousand, for those women who miscarry, or whose children die by an accident, or disease, within the year. There only remain a hundred and twenty thousand children of poor parents, annually born; the question therefore is, how shall this number be reared and provided for? . . .

I shall now therefore humbly propose my own thoughts, which I hope will not be liable to the least objection. I have been assured by a very knowing American of my acquaintance in London that a young healthy child, well nursed, is, at a year old, a most delicious, nourishing and wholesome food, whether stewed, roasted, baked or boiled; and I make no doubt that it will equally serve in a fricasée or ragôut. . . . A child will make two dishes at an entertainment for friends, and when the family dines alone, the fore or hind quarter will make a reasonable dish; and seasoned with a little pepper or salt, will be very good boiled on the fourth day, especially in winter. . . .

I grant that this food will be somewhat dear, and therefore very proper for landlords, who, as they have already devoured most of the parents, seem to have the best title to the children.

Irony is generally held to appeal to the intellect. We have used words like 'cultured', 'civilized', 'informed' and 'sophisticated' to describe the ironist's relationship with the reader. But in the hands of a satirist like Swift, irony can be emotional, and savage. Our response to a passage like this cannot be intellectual, cannot be cerebral; it has to be emotional, initially a simple gut-reaction. Let's go through it step by step to see how Swift has used tone to manipulate our emotional responses.

To the first paragraph we can only agree. If this man can solve the problem, we will chip in towards his statue.

The first sentence of the second paragraph gives no trouble. The tone is familiar; it is the tone of those reasonable, pompous men who write letters to The Times or The Daily Telegraph explaining how the country can escape from the present crisis, whatever it is, and pointing out the errors in the proposals of all the other reasonable and pompous men who have already written similar letters. But then: 'a child just dropped from its dam'. This application of the language of the livestock breeder to human birth is disturbingly insensitive. This, and the purely objective remarks on begging, give us cause to suspect the writer of too cold an attitude towards humanity. But we are quickly reassured of the author's good intentions. He aims to 'provide for' these unfortunate people. Perhaps his stockbreeder/accountant language is just his blunt way of speaking. The third paragraph gives further reassurance. 'Poor innocent babes' and 'the most savage and inhuman breast' are clichés, certainly, but good-hearted ones, and we can only share his indignation. The man's a Christian after all. Or then again is he? Paragraph four has an unpleasant flavour. Those cold statistics applied to people are so detached, so objective, when the subject is suffering; and twice more that ugly word 'breeders'. Still, he has to get the hard facts across, and since he is discussing population, statistics are inevitable. And then comes the shock. Confident we will not object, he proposes cannibalism. There is no change in the calm, objective tone. We suddenly realize we have been listening to the perfect logic of a man who is utterly mad. All our previous suppositions or doubts about him and his ideas are turned on their heads. Our sense of outrage is then intensified by the writer's assumption that any small qualms we might possibly have can be dispelled by his assurances as to the tastiness and economy of cooked babies. The genteel phrase 'when the family dines alone' becomes vicious and grotesque when the menu is roast infant. It's difficult not to visualize it. (It gets worse later on, when our projector recommends baby as a dish for special occasions, 'particularly weddings and christenings'.) At this point we may be shocked and outraged; we are also bewildered. Our bewilderment stems from the huge discrepancy between the perfectly acceptable rationality of the man's tone and the awful madness of his vision. And while we are thus bewildered, there comes a dramatic change in tone and direction to add to our confusion. Child meat will be rather expensive, and therefore 'very proper for landlords, who, as they have already devoured most of the parents, seem to have the best title to the children'. Just when we have rejected this man as inhuman and insane, he turns round and makes a point which contains an undeniable truth. We get a taste not of insanity, but aggression; we get a sudden glimpse of the satirist behind the mask. All this is not, after all, a lunatic hypothesis, but a comment on the *actual* situation in Ireland.

What has Swift achieved in this passage? First of all, he has tricked us into listening to a man because that man seems, at first, perfectly rational. He *is* rational—*entirely* rational. Given that there are too many people and not enough food, the only logical course of action is to eat people. As objective reasoning, there is nothing wrong with this. (Besides, as he later says, think of all the beneficial side-effects of the plan: inducement to marriage, greater kindness and attention given to new-born babies, income for impoverished parents, fathers desisting from beating their pregnant wives, etc., etc.). When we reply 'No. Eating people is simply *wrong*, is *mad*', Swift has made his first and most important point. *Purely* objective reasoning *is* madness because it has no human dimension. (Look at the savage irony in 'the fore or hind quarter will make a *reasonable* dish.') What distinguishes man from cannibalistic animals is not rationality but *morality*, and morality asserts emotion over logic. This is Swift's most profound personal belief. But he does not let matters rest there. We might paraphrase him as follows: 'So, you are outraged by the idea of eating children. How is it then that you tolerate the situation in Ireland *now*? To say landlords have 'devoured' the Irish is no mere metaphor; what is the essential difference between systematically driving people to poverty, starvation and death, and eating them? Since we already treat these people like cattle—worse, in fact— why not go all the way?'

What is under attack in *A Modest Proposal* is not, primarily, the ultra-rational projector, nor even those responsible for the Irish situation, but the hypocrisy of Swift's readers. Clearly, Swift does not use irony to establish a sympathetic solidarity with the reader; or, as F. R. Leavis puts it, 'the implied solidarity in Swift is itself ironical—a means to betrayal'.

It is because irony can have such a wide range and involve 'meaning' that is almost infinite in its complexity, that the analysis and discussion of ironic writing is one of the most demanding exercises in 'literary appreciation' required by candidates who sit the Advanced Level English Practical Criticism papers.

As should now be obvious, there is no simple way of spotting and identifying irony in a prose extract or poem. One critic, perhaps facetiously, once suggested that authors could indicate where they had been ironic by employing some kind of typographical symbol, like an exclamation mark, thereby revealing instantly the impossibility of any such simple approach to the subject. All one can do is to be continually alert to the often very subtle varieties and shifts of meaning in literature that is ironic. When reading an extract in the Unseen, the examination candidate should be prepared to look beyond the surface or generalized meanings of the words he comes across, and ask certain questions such as these:

1. Can I see or feel that the writer is being ironic?
2. Are there any verbal clues, or rhetorical devices such as bathos, understatement and so on?
3. Is the relationship between the language and the meaning a simple one, or is some or all of the meaning implicit and covert?
4. Is the subject matter one that could seem to be suitable for ironic treatment? (e.g. hypocrisy, prejudice, pride, conflicting viewpoints, etc.)
5. What attitude does the writer seem to have towards his audience? Is he presenting one sort of information for 'fools' and another level of meaning for the 'astute'?
6. Is the writer comic or amusing at all? If so, is this effect upon the reader partially or wholly achieved by irony?
7. Is the narrator 'trustworthy'? Is he or she a 'mask' used by the author for ironic purposes? Is the reader 'flattered' or 'betrayed' by this mask?
8. If the meaning is not what it at first appeared to be, why is this, and what is the meaning conveyed?

To conclude this chapter on a lighter note, let us consider this passage from Mark Twain's *Huckleberry Finn*. Huck is deliberating as to whether or not he should help free Miss Watson's black slave, Jim.

15. It would get all around, that Huck Finn helped a nigger to get his freedom; and if I was ever to see anybody from that town again, I'd be ready to get down and lick his boots for shame. That's just the way: a person does a low-down thing, and then he don't want to take no consequences of it. Thinks as long as he can hide it, it ain't no disgrace. That was my fix exactly. The more I studied about this, the more my conscience went to grinding me, and the more wicked and low down and ornery I got to feeling. And at last, when it hit me all of a sudden that here was the plain hand of Providence slapping me in the face and letting me know my wickedness was being watched all the time from up there in heaven, whilst I was stealing a poor woman's nigger that hadn't ever done me no harm, and now was showing me there's One that's always on the lookout, and ain't

agoing to allow no such miserable doings to go just so fur and no further, I most dropped in my tracks I was so scared. Well, I tried the best I could to kinder soften it up somehow for myself, by saying I was brung up wicked, and so warn't so much to blame; but something inside of me kept saying, 'there was the Sunday school, you could a gone to it; and if you'd a done it they'd a learnt you, there, that people that acts as I'd been acting about that nigger goes to everlasting fire'.

In this extract, one can see the extent to which irony often makes us question the relationship between words and meanings, which is where this chapter began. The extract also demonstrates how categories like 'self disparaging' and 'unconscious revelation' are useful really only as starting points and are often, as here, only barely adequate. Huck Finn is here unconsciously revealing the hypocrisies and insanities, not of himself so much, but of the society to which he belongs and from which he escapes.

Twain's irony demonstrates how the conventional values of the Southern States of nineteenth century America are contrary to those of Huck himself (and, presumably, to those of the reader). Huck has been 'educated' by a society which regards Negroes as property, property as sacrosanct, and religion as a bulwark for both beliefs: a tortuously deformed system of values which the less 'civilized' Huck has to struggle with in his conscience and eventually reject. The reader is necessarily forced to question the meaning of the words Huck uses. Words like 'low down thing', 'disgrace', 'conscience', 'wicked', 'Providence', 'Heaven', 'stealing', 'learnt' and so on, have here meanings which are far from simple or easy. When Huck says 'they'd a learnt you there that people that acts as I'd been acting about that nigger goes to everlasting fire', Twain is questioning the way that a corrupt society, through the agencies of education and religion (the Sunday school) indoctrinates (surely the true meaning of 'learnt') the individuals in that society to believe in a morality which is almost totally evil in its effects.

Irony, as here, continually forces the reader to grapple with implicit, inherent or inescapable ambiguities of interpretation, makes him explore the ambivalences that are often unavoidable in the values or ideas which the writer wishes to investigate or teach. The reader makes a tacit agreement with the ironist: 'meaning' will not be simple and literal, because things are rarely like that.

CE-D*

EIGHT

An Exercise in Poetic Imagery

Our next chapter will be a discussion of imagery. Before reading it, you might find it beneficial to attempt a study of the following poem, paying particular attention to its images.

White Christmas

Punctually at Christmas the soft plush
Of sentiment snows down, embosoms all
The sharp and pointed shapes of venom, shawls
The hills and hides the shocking holes of this
5   Uneven world of want and wealth, cushions
With cosy wish like cotton-wool the cool
Arms-length interstices of caste and class,
And into obese folds subtracts from sight
All truculent acts, bleeding the world white.

10   Punctually that glib pair, Peace and Goodwill,
Emerge royally to take the air,
Collect the bows, assimilate the smiles,
Of waiting men. It is a genial time.
Angels, like stalactites, descend from heaven,
15   Bishops distribute their weight in words,
Congratulate the poor on Christlike lack,
And the Member for the constituency
Feeds the five thousand and has plenty back.

Punctually tonight, in old stone circles
20   Of set reunion, families stiffly sit
And listen; this is the night, and this the happy time
When the tinned milk of human kindness is
Upheld and holed by radio-appeal.

Hushed are hurrying heels on hard roads,
25   And every parlour's a pink pond of light
To the cold and travelling man going by
In the dark, without a bark or bite.

But punctually tomorrow you will see
All this silent and dissembling world
30   Of silted sentiment suddenly melt
Into mush and watery welter of words
Beneath the warm and moving traffic of
Feet and actual fact. Over the stark plain
The stilted mill-chimneys once again spread
35   Their sackcloth and ashes, a flowing mane
Of repentance for the false day that's sped.

W. R. Rodgers

Comment on the effectiveness of the imagery in lines 2-3, 6-7, 14, 19-20, 31-33, 35-36.

Snow is obviously a dominant theme; what use does Rodgers make of other 'whiteness' images? How are other colours used?

Are there passages in which Rodgers has effectively manipulated sound (e.g. by rhyme or alliteration) in order to strengthen his images?

Do you notice instances of puns or other kinds of deliberate ambiguity?

The poem is clearly satirical; what exactly is Rodgers attacking? Does it work?

NINE

A Note on Imagery

Three words which are crucial to this chapter—image, metaphor, symbol—have meanings which seem to overlap. Of these three, 'symbol', is the easiest to distinguish; a symbol is a kind of image, but it has special characteristics. These are discussed later on, so let us concentrate for now on 'image' and 'metaphor'.

The core of the problem is that we cannot strip the word 'image' of its associations with painting and sculpture. For Shakespeare and writers before him the word meant 'a likeness'—a portrait, a statue. It would not have made much sense to apply the term to poetry. But modern criticism abounds in references to a writer's 'images', and now there are books on 'Shakespeare's Imagery'. The dictionary is little help. *The Shorter Oxford* offers numerous definitions of 'image', most of which refer to visual and optical phenomena—pictures, reflections, photographs and the like, but then adds that an image is also a 'figure of speech' or 'a metaphor'. Yet there are difficulties in using 'image' as a synonym for 'metaphor'. A writer does not create *likenesses*. We may speak of a novelist 'painting' a scene or 'portraying' a character, but this is in fact a sloppy use of words borrowed from a different human activity. Words are the *names* of things, not pictures of them. If I write 'Marilyn Monroe' I am not presenting a likeness, but merely naming. If I add to the name a string of adjectives such as 'glamorous, enigmatic, blond, tragic . . .' I am not 'portraying' her but naming qualities that she possessed (or rather, that she seemed, *to me*, to possess). If while you read this you do 'see' an image of Marilyn Monroe the chances are that it has not been created by the words on this page, but that you have recalled it from photographs or films or other books.

One might say that words somehow release things stored in the mind. Not just in the memory, though; I have never seen a blue daffodil, but I can 'picture it in my head'. We are now talking

90

about 'imagination', and it seems to me that 'poetic images' must be something to do with the activity of the poet's imagination as he writes and the reader's imagination as he reads. 'Images' are produced by words, but are not the words themselves.

Why, you are entitled to ask, am I nagging away at this? If 'image' is so shifty a word, why not drop it altogether and use 'metaphor' instead? Well, because there are problems to do with metaphor, too.

A generally acceptable definition of metaphor might be 'language that implies a relationship, of which similarity is a significant feature, between two things and so changes our apprehension of either or both'.* The basis of metaphor is comparison or analogy. Two (or more, perhaps) things are brought together. The qualities of one thing are expressed by referring the reader to similar qualities in a different thing. A man is of a 'watery disposition', or he 'towers over his fellows' or he has a 'sharp tongue'. A few minutes ago you read a paragraph which began 'The core of the problem . . .' That is a metaphor; the two things brought together are i) a problem ii) an apple—or pear, if you prefer. 'Problem' is abstract, amorphous; to convey the idea of the 'centrality' of it I referred you to something well known to have a centre or 'core'. (I could have said 'heart of the problem'.) But in the 'relationship' between 'problem' and 'apple' how is 'similarity a significant feature'? An apple in no way resembles a problem. If you had contemplated that phrase when you first read it, perhaps you would have imagined—called to mind an image of—an apple and its core and found the analogy with 'problem' very feeble and unilluminating. Yet I suppose you understood me well enough; might this be because the phrase is so familiar that you had no need to 'see' the two terms of my metaphor, and consequently your understanding of it was not interrupted by 'image-making'? But that is not the way we should read poetry, in which metaphorical language is very much a central issue.

> A   He cannot buckle his distemper'd cause
>   Within the belt of rule.

> B   nor Heaven
>   Peep through the blanket of the dark.

As you read those words, did you register, at some level of consciousness, the images of A) a large man failing to get his belt around him and B) a woman ('Heaven', or 'stars' or 'moon' or

*Babette Deutsch: Poetry Handbook (Cape 1958), p. 73.

'dawn' having feminine characteristics, traditionally) peering over bedclothes? Or were such images experienced unconsciously? If they were not experienced at all, how can you have understood what was meant? Both extracts are metaphors, but seem to be dependent upon some image-making faculty. Read next these lines by R. S. Thomas which describe a Welsh peasant farmer:

> churning the crude earth
> To a stiff sea of clods that glint in the wind.

Let us trace the metaphorical usage of the words. 'Churning' is an activity involving liquid—I think of milk, especially. This conflicts immediately with 'crude earth', a thing solid, elemental and heavy. 'Crude' is also a term commonly applied to metal. Solidity and liquidity meet in the paradox of 'stiff sea' (a *frozen* ocean, perhaps?). 'Clods' is one of the heaviest, dullest of words, both in sound and meaning; it jars with the alliterative phrase preceding it. 'Glint' is another change in feeling—a sharp brittle word, associated with metal, again, or glass. Finally, the clods do not glint in the sun (a warm influence having no place in this frigid landscape) but in the wind; the 'glinting' is cold and hard. I think these are fine lines, very successful in conveying vividly the hostility of the environment, the work, and the appearance of the land. The language evokes several concepts which fall into two groups: liquidity and movement on one hand, and heaviness, hardness and solidity on the other. These conflicting ideas move against each other with the rhythm of the lines; the result is a paradox, a kind of harmonious friction. The point I wish to make is that there seems to be too much going on in these lines to be expressed as 'metaphor'; the effect upon our imagination is a more complex one than the perceiving of analogy or comparison could have. I feel it might be better to use the word 'imagery' in this case. It might be more appropriate to use this imprecise word when we are referring to language which operates in a complex way, or to language structures which do more than exploit the similarities between different things. One has the same feeling about this line by Walt Whitman, where he says that grass

> seems to me the beautiful uncut hair of graves.

There is a sort of reversal in this line. Had Whitman written that hair was *like* the uncut grass of graves (the line has that meaning, of course) it would have been a forceful enough simile; but by choosing to arrange his sentence the way he does he gives the idea of 'the hair of graves' its own identity. This way he makes us think

92

(with a bit of a shudder) of corpses inside the graves, and of hair continuing to grow after the body dies, of the hair growing *through* the graves. There's more, besides. 'Beautiful uncut hair' has connotations of youthfulness, and this idea is dramatically at odds with the ideas of age, death and decay usually associated with graves. And there is the disturbing underlying equation of grave and head—both contain dead things, Whitman seems to imply. The line is certainly a very economical use of language; it has taken me 150 words just to mention what Whitman puts into 10. And again, I would be happier to apply the word 'image' or 'imagery' to those ten words. It seems to me that what happens in that line fits uncomfortably with the definition of metaphor. You could say, of course, that Whitman is using a metaphor which has numerous terms of reference: grass, hair, death, youth, growth; but it would be ungainly expression. His words act upon each other and upon our imaginations to create a complex of impressions which do not seem to depend upon only analogy or similarity.

What all this amounts to is that at certain points in this chapter you will find me using the words 'metaphor' and 'image' as if they are interchangeable. Therefore you may feel you ought to be a suspicious reader at such times, knowing that I have not worried overmuch about the strict precision of those terms. I rest my case with that strict critic Dr Leavis, who has pointed out that when a critic uses terms like 'imagery' it doesn't really matter if he cannot define them *precisely*. It's the way he uses his words as 'tools', and what he achieves with them, that matters. And the same applies to you if you are a student one day (soon) to be examined in your critical skills. No one, not even an examiner, is likely to be over-upset if you write 'image' instead of 'metaphor' if your use of the term is a means to express a sensitive perception. As Leavis says, 'it is as pointers for use—*in* use—in the direct discussion of pieces of poetry that our terms and definitions have to be judged'. [That remark by Leavis is quoted in a recent book by P. N. Furbank called (punningly) *Reflections on the Word 'Image'* (Secker and Warburg, 1970).]

It is no waste of time to worry about the meanings of words, particularly at a time when language is sorely abused, but since we set out with the intention of being practical and pragmatic we had better put aside anxieties about semantics if we are to say anything helpful. In any case, the matters raised in these opening paragraphs are so central to discussions of poetic language—and literature generally—that we will inevitably touch upon them again.

Images are the activities of the imagination. The imagination is a two-faced creature. In one direction it inclines toward *fantasy*; it trespasses upon the world of dreams; it sentimentalizes or simplifies or decorates reality; it seeks to escape the uglier aspects of actuality. In an opposite direction it is a *critical* faculty which makes connections between disparate things and enables us to grasp their inter-relationships; it applies language to things and thoughts and thus sharpens, rather than obscures, reality; it increases the number of ways in which we see and understand; it is not afraid of ugliness. It is this second, critical, function of the imagination we seek to find evidence of in good poetry.

Let us take up the idea that the imagination makes connections between things; this will lead us to metaphor. Much of our everyday language is metaphorical. We do not think it particularly imaginative to describe a very intelligent person as 'brilliant' (i.e. shining brightly like the sun or a diamond) or 'sharp'; nor are we conscious of speaking figuratively when we refer to the 'leg' of a table or the 'neck' of a bottle. These expressions have become so conventional that they have lost their figurative character—they have become 'dead metaphors'. This much is obvious, but it draws our attention to two rather significant ideas: first, that the human intellect seeks and uses metaphor instinctively and naturally—we *think* metaphorically; second, that consequently the poet, in that he attempts to find metaphors which are fresh and vital, is in the business of 'refreshing language', as Dylan Thomas put it. His ultimate aim, therefore, is to refine and add to our ability to *see* (in both senses of the word—to 'view' and to 'understand').

Aristotle's long-standing judgement still holds: 'a good metaphor implies an intuitive perception of the similarity in dissimilars' and that for a poet 'the greatest thing by far is to have a good command of metaphor . . . it is the mark of genius, for to make good metaphors implies an eye for resemblances'. This matter of similarity is problematical, yet most important because when we come to comment on a writer's use of imagery one of our criteria must be 'appropriateness'. Let us distinguish first of all between metaphors which rely on *physical* similarity and those which rely on our perceiving intellectually a 'metaphysical' or conceptual analogy. Images which are dependent upon physical resemblances appeal directly to our senses—most commonly to our sight. 'Wreaths of smoke' is an effective visual metaphor, although now commonplace enough to approach cliché. It conveys the appearance of smoke in windless air, and is, at first glance, purely visual. Yet, consciously or unconsciously, we register the connotations of 'wreath'—death, grief, commemoration. These associations give added significance to a wreath metaphor used by Shakespeare:

An adder wreathed up in fatal folds

but do not seem particularly relevant to this image of Tennyson's, which pictures a waterfall:

> . . . thousand wreaths of dangling water smoke . . .

Often we discover that images which seem intended to express only the physical or sensual reality of a thing do more than intensify our sensory perception of it; through an association of ideas they also make an emotional and intellectual impact. When D. H. Lawrence describes a bat as

> Like a glove, a black glove thrown up at the light

he not only evokes our traditional fear of bats and blackness; the forcefulness of the image lies in the word 'glove' which, in this context, has a sinisterly human (funereal?) connotation; we imagine a black hand enveloping and extinguishing the light. And, of course, those things associated with or represented by light are also brought into play, and threatened—life, sight, hope, warmth.

The closer we examine the effect of metaphor, the more we suspect that direct physical and sensory analogy is not its most important element. This is true of even the most conventional metaphors. A lady with lips 'like cherries' would have a rather unfortunate appearance; a loved one like a 'red, red rose' cannot be imagined as having petals and stamen; eyes actually 'like almonds' would be disturbing, to say the least. What is involved in metaphors like these is a mutual agreement between poet and reader about certain unspoken characteristics of the things compared (redness and 'sweetness' in the case of lips and cherries, beauty and voluptuousness in the case of the rose and the lover). At the same time, there cannot be too great a dissimilarity between the subject and the image which expresses it, otherwise absurdity destroys the impact. Witness, for example, Crashaw's notorious metaphor by which Mary Magdalene's weeping eyes are depicted as 'two walking baths'. (Incongruity such as this is well-beloved by satirists—Pope is an expert in its use—but unfortunately Crashaw did not intend to be a comic.) Figurative language which employs visual analogy does not necessarily depend upon our having actually seen the thing to which we are referred. In *Rhapsody on a Windy Night*, T. S. Eliot writes:

> Midnight shakes the memory
> As a madman shakes a dead geranium.

I have never seen a madman shaking a geranium (had Eliot?), but I find the image a powerful one—the madness of trying to revive a dead thing, the past as a dead flower, the despair and futility the poet feels. What happens here is that *my* imagination is engaged in the same sort of activity as the poet's was; my interest and receptivity is intensified because I am not being 'given a picture' but being *asked to imagine*; I am being involved in a creative process.

P. N. Furbank has written:

> An image in the sense of a metaphor is not a likeness of anything. True, a metaphor depends on pointing to a likeness between heterogeneous things. But to say that courtiers fawning on a great man resemble spaniels fawning on their master is not saying that spaniels are a *likeness* of fawning courtiers, as Holbein's portrait is a likeness of Henry VIII. . . . You can never stand back and scrutinize a mental image, since you are fully occupied in creating it—it represents your consciousness in action.*

Earlier on, we distinguished between metaphors dependent upon a physical correlation between two (or more) things and metaphors which call upon our perception of a 'metaphysical' or conceptual analogy. Furbank's idea of image-making and image-receiving as 'consciousness in action' leads us to this second type. We must be aware, however, that 'physical correlation' and 'conceptual analogy' do not exclude one another. On the contrary, we could say that the best images are those which appeal simultaneously to our visual and our intellectual imaginations. Here is a couplet from Shakespeare's *Venus and Adonis:*

> Look! how a bright star shooteth from the sky
> So glides he in the night from Venus' eye,

and this is what I. A. Richards has to say about it:

> Here, the more the image is followed up, the more links of relevance between the units are discovered. As Adonis to Venus, so these lines to the reader seem to linger in the eye like the after-images that make the trail of the meteor. Here Shakespeare is realizing, and making the reader realize—not by any intensity of effort, but by the fullness and self-completing growth of the response—Adonis' flight as it was to Venus, and the sense of loss, of increased darkness, that

*P. N. Furbank: *Reflections on the Word 'Image'*, Ch. 1.

invades her. The separable meanings of each word, 'Look!' (our surprise at the meteor, hers at his flight) 'star' (a light-giver, an influence, a remote and uncontrollable thing) 'shoot-eth' (the sudden, irremediable, portentous fall or death of what had been a guide, a destiny) 'the sky' (the source of light and now of ruin), 'glides' (not rapidity only, but fatal ease too) 'in the night' (the darkness of the scene and of Venus' world now)—all these separable meanings are here brought into one. And as they come together, as the reader's mind finds cross-connexion after cross-connexion between them, he seems, in becoming more aware of them, to be discovering not only Shakespeare's meaning, .but something he, the reader is himself making. His understanding of Shakespeare is sanc-tioned by his own activity in it. As Coleridge says: 'You feel him to be a poet, inasmuch as for a time he has made you one—an active creative being'.*

The poet gives a great deal of sensory stimulation, he feeds our vision, but the important thing is that he makes us 'an active creative being'. This brings us to the heart of the question of what imagery is. Good Doctor Johnson was only half correct when he said that a good metaphor should 'both illustrate and ennoble the subject', and it is wrong to suppose that an image is 'the little word-picture used by the poet to illustrate, illuminate and embellish his thought'.† Statements such as these imply that the poet has his 'thought' and then decorates it for the purposes of poetry; they assume that one can strip away the 'embellishment' to reveal the 'thought'. And this is not so. Lawrence did not think 'there are bats flying around this terrace' and then start looking for a decorative way of saying it; he wrote of the bat as 'a black glove thrown up at the light' because *his thought about the bat included all the connotations of that image.* In other words, that image was perhaps the *only* way he could have expressed his idea; the image *is* the poet's thought. It is not an ornamental accessory.

Thus imagery, as employed by the poet, is a means of sharing thought, a means of involving the reader in the activity of the imagination. 'An image', says Ezra Pound, 'is that which presents an intellectual and emotional complex in an instant of time'. By 'complex' I take Pound to mean a cluster of thoughts, reactions and associations with a common centre. That centre is the image.

Let us turn now to the function of imagery within poems. To state the obvious, this will vary from poem to poem, but we can

*I. A. Richards: *Coleridge on Imagination.*
†Caroline Spurgeon: *Shakespeare's Imagery* (Cambridge 1935), p. 9.

97

risk a few general remarks. In very many poems the effect of images is *accumulative*. That is to say, a poem is likely to be a progression of thoughts expressed as images, and one image may be expected to develop from another in some way. The images, in other words, are rather like stages in an 'argument'. This is a risky word to use, and we do not mean that poems obey the rules of logic; we cannot expect the poet to avoid the irrational, since irrationality is commonly the characteristic of emotion. At the same time, there is such a thing as 'the logic of the poem' which, while not at all the same thing as scientific logic, does give the poem unity, gives it 'imaginative coherence', as Cleanth Brooks calls it. The accumulative, progressional use of imagery is best seen in the work of the metaphysical poets (and in Shakespeare's sonnets). John Donne, in a poem concerned with weeping and separation, uses images drawn from minting coins, reflections, map-making and cosmography, the ocean and lunar tides. But the poem has 'imaginative coherence' because all these images are prompted by the shape, translucency and reflectiveness of tears. We do not expect such 'logic' from all poets, of course, nor do we expect all metaphors to be so 'intellectual'.

On the other hand, if there is a serious lack of unity among a poem's images (or if, as in the case of Crashaw, they are strained to the point of grotesqueness), we may well fail to receive the imaginative experience the poet wishes to convey; we may be confused or disturbed instead. (This of course is no bad thing if it is the writer's intention to disturb us, but it takes a good deal of conscious control and organization to genuinely disturb a reader.) For the time being, anyway, let us say that one criterion we might apply to a poet's use of imagery is the desirability of a certain connectedness among the images, their contribution to the poem's overall sense, their conformity (no matter how diverse their sources) to an 'imaginative coherence'. Shakespeare's best plays have this kind of coherence on a larger scale. There, the imagery can be seen to have certain *themes*, which adds another dimension to the plays' meanings. *King Lear*, for example, is 'about' age, ingratitude and political power, but the predominance of animal imagery makes us aware that it is also deeply concerned with loss of humanity and moral decline. *Measure for Measure* is 'about' law, justice and mercy, but the recurrence of images drawn from decay and disease reveal Shakespeare's preoccupation with corruption.

An image then, can be a component of a poem, a stage in its development. It can also be the poem's end-product. The clearest illustration of this is the Japanese haiku, three-line poems which present clear visual images, often as delicate as silk-paintings:

The falling flower
I saw drift back to the branch
Was a butterfly.

The haiku inspired the American poet Ezra Pound, whose own short verses, while not conforming to the strict structure of the haiku, retain much of their essence:

In a Station of the Metro

The apparition of these faces in the crowd;
Petals on a wet, black bough.

Alba

As cool as the pale wet leaves
                of the lily-of-the-valley
She lay beside me in the dawn.

Pound was a powerful force in a group of English and American poets calling themselves 'Imagists', active in London between (roughly) 1908 and 1917. Their aims were a purity of style and a unity of sense and the avoidance of 'sloppy abstraction'. Their work has strongly influenced both the practice of modern poetry and criticism of it; much of the current debate about 'imagery' stems from Imagist ideas. Here are two poems by writers involved in this group. The first is by Amy Lowell (1874–1925):

Wind and Silver

Greatly shining,
The Autumn moon floats in the thin sky;
And the fish-ponds shake their backs and
                flash their dragon scales
As she passes over them.

The second is by William Carlos Williams (1883–1963):

The Red Wheelbarrow

So much depends
upon

a red wheel
barrow

             glazed with rain
             water

             beside the white
             chickens

The images these poems offer seem self-contained, complete;
they also, paradoxically, seem to have a much wider, echoing
significance—almost mystical. They seek to capture an instant of
time, fix it (do they not seem almost photographic?) and present
that moment as an image of *all* time. Pound says of his *In a Station
of the Metro* that 'In a poem of this sort, one is trying to record the
precise instant when a thing outward and objective transforms
itself, or darts into a thing inward and subjective'.

Williams' *Red Wheelbarrow* has no 'meaning', in the usual
sense, but it is an image of the way our senses perceive things, the
way our sight *composes*, the way we sense the relationships
between things. And 'so much depends upon' our ability to see—
understand—these relationships, these connections, just as the
redness of the wheelbarrow depends upon (is defined by) the
whiteness of the chickens.

Before approaching the matter of criticising a poem's imagery,
we ought to consider one more form of image: the symbol. A
symbol differs from a metaphor in two respects. Firstly, it need
have no visual or otherwise sensory similarity to the thing or idea
it signifies. This is obvious when one considers that symbols are
commonly used to denote abstractions such as faith, knowledge, a
mathematical concept, a national character. Secondly, a symbol is
an image which *persistently recurs*—either throughout history, or
throughout the course of a civilization, or throughout a poet's
work. *Public symbolism* includes symbols drawn from established
religions or religious texts (e.g. the Lamb of God, the Tree of
Knowledge), symbols drawn from mythologies, and symbols which
have become traditional in literature. *Private symbolism* consists
of symbolism developed by a writer in the course of his work, and
a reader would need to have some familiarity with such an
author's writings if he is to receive the full significance of these
images. One often finds that a poet recruits 'public' symbols and
puts them to his own 'private' use.

Thus W. B. Yeats, as well as developing his own symbolism
around such images as the tree, the swan, the tower and the
mask, also employs images from Irish mythology and Cabbalistic
magic. William Blake has a private symbolism in his prophetic books,
but elsewhere in his work Christian and Biblical symbols play a
major part. In *The Waste Land*, T. S. Eliot combines symbols from
Buddhist texts, the Grail legend, the Tarot and the Old Testament.

Each of these writers uses traditional symbolic systems in such a way as to give them new energy. The symbols are felt to be powerful because of their context; they are relevant; we are involved in the imaginative process of applying their conventional meanings to the poems (and *vice versa*).

We must be prepared to discriminate between this use of symbolism—which refreshes symbols—and the cheap, easy use of symbolism by which a writer hopes to add significance to an otherwise banal work. Here, as an instance of this, is the last stanza of a poem which celebrates the joys of cycling down a hill:

> Alas, that the longest hill
> Must end in a vale; but still,
> Who climbs with toil, whereso'er,
> Shall find wings waiting there.*

The comparison is unfairly extreme, but look now at this little poem by Blake in which we can see the potential of the symbolic metaphor realized:

> O Rose, thou art sick!
> The invisible worm
> That flies in the night
> In the howling storm
>
> Has found out thy bed
> Of crimson joy:
> And his dark secret love
> Does thy life destroy.

The rose is perhaps the most frequently occurring flower image in English poetry. It is used to symbolize beauty generally and innocent sensuality in particular. It is feminine. It has, also, religious and mystical connotations; Dante, for one, speaks of 'the Rose of Heaven', and in mediaeval poetry it is often used as the image of the ideal merging of divine and physical love. At the same time, it is ambiguous. The rose is the most fleshly of flowers, the most sensual, the richest in colour, the most heavily perfumed. In Blake's poem, the phrase 'thy bed/Of crimson joy' certainly suggests voluptuousness and sexuality. The poem's other terms are symbolic also. The 'worm' suggests not only infection and disease of a physical sort but also has associations with 'serpent' and thus with devilry, temptation and loss of innocence; it is almost

---

*The guilty party is Henry Charles Beeching (1859–1919).

certainly phallic. 'Flies in the night' continues this Satanic image; night itself signifies furtiveness, the realm of evil, dark forces. The storm is a traditional symbol of chaos and wild passion (one thinks of *The Tempest* and *King Lear*). The way these symbols inter-connect insinuates an underlying sexual image. One critic sees in the poem an 'evil devouring sexuality that destroys instead of creating, bringing mortal sickness to the crimson joy'. Another believes the poem's meaning is less precise: 'Blake's worm-eaten rose symbolizes such matters as the destruction wrought by furtiveness, deceit and hypocrisy in what should be a frank and joyous relation of physical love'. One can believe that the poem expresses an idea as vague as 'the corruption of pure innocence by evil' or something as specific as venereal disease. And, of course, it is also 'about' an actual mildewed rose. Now, the point is that one does not choose one of these interpretations as 'correct'. The poem is capable of carrying all these meanings simultaneously; it is a brilliant demonstration of the powerful ambiguity of symbolic metaphor, and of its *mystery*. The poem *focuses* all the ideas attached to the symbolism it employs. It is 'a radiant node or cluster . . . a *vortex*, from which, and into which, ideas are continuously rushing'. Beeching's little allegorical verse about cycling is, in this light, banal because it supports only one (moralistic) interpretation, and makes sense only if one 'translates' it.

We should apply to an author's use of symbolism the same critical criteria we apply to his use of metaphor and of imagery generally. What are these criteria?

We have already implied certain standards of judgement in our discusson of the nature and function of imagery. An image, we have said, had best appeal simultaneously to our senses and our intellect. But like all generalized statements about poetry, this one is open to doubt. Certain images are forceful because they deliberately confound either our senses or our intellect, and consequently they startle the reader. The German poet Rilke uses the image 'black milk', which is paradoxical and sinister; it shocks the senses, but does it 'mean' anything? Or take T. S. Eliot's famous lines:

> When the evening is spread out against the sky
> Like a patient etherized upon a table.

After we have read the first of these lines we expect . . . what? A sunset, perhaps? Instead, we have an image from the operating theatre. We can make intellectual conjectures about it—the world is sick; who is the surgeon? God? The poet? Will the patient survive? What is the disease?—but the visual imagination is nonplussed. (All this is very subjective, of course. You may have no difficulty in visualizing Eliot's simile.)

We may ask that a metaphor be 'appropriate', and yet a certain kind of inappropriateness may sometimes be desirable. Take these two flower images:

> behold
> A silver shield with boss of gold
> That spreads itself, some faery bold
> In fight to cover!
>
> *Wordsworth*

> the sight is compelled
> By small, coarse, sharp petals,
> Like metal shreds.
>
> *Jon Silkin*

Wordsworth has transmuted colours—white petals to silver, yellow centre to gold—to metals; this gives him a 'shield', but a shield small enough for only a belligerent faery. All this is 'appropriate' in that one concept seems to lead to another, and they are based on the flower's appearance. But it is very feeble stuff all the same. It's feeble because Wordsworth has fallen prey to conventional and sentimental images; the daisy has been *used*, not *seen*, and used as a starting-point for a train of fancy, not observation or thought.

The second extract is from Jon Silkin's poem *Dandelion*. Like Wordsworth, Silkin is put in mind of metal; unlike Wordsworth, he doesn't dabble in conventionally 'appropriate' metaphors, but declares, in the more direct form of simile, that the flower petals look like shreds of metal. It is the clash between what we consider appropriate associations of 'petal' and the appropriate associations of 'metal' which creates that slight shock to the reader, which in turn urges him to *reconsider*, to see anew.

We offered 'the logic of the poem' or 'imaginative coherence' as a criterion for judging a poet's use of imagery. Let us try to apply this to a famous passage from Shakespeare. At this point in the play, Macbeth's sufferings are intensifying. He is haunted by his victim's ghost, he experiences vicious spasms of guilt, his enemies are marching against him, his wife has taken refuge in insanity. And then he is told of her death. We might expect of him some wild and whirling words, and at first glance this is what they seem.

> Tomorrow, and tomorrow, and tomorrow,
> Creeps in this petty pace from day to day,
> To the last syllable of recorded time;

103

And all our yesterdays have lighted fools
The way to dusty death. Out, out, brief candle!
Life's but a walking shadow; a poor player,
That struts and frets his hour upon the stage,
And then is heard no more: it is a tale
Told by an idiot, full of sound and fury,
Signifying nothing.

The movement of the language takes in images of time, light and a 'brief candle', acting and theatre, shadow, and a 'tale told by an idiot'. Yet these disparate images have a connectedness—not of a logical kind, but of an imaginative, associative, kind. Macbeth is a man for whom the universe has ceased to have meaning. The first 4½ lines dwell on the futility not only of human existence but of time itself. Given our misery, he says, time's slow progress is absurd, a taunt. The lines themselves 'creep'; their tone is that of a man dulled by affliction. In the first 3 lines 'day' is a measurement of time. In line 4 it shifts to include the meaning 'a period of light'; but the light serves only to illuminate the way to death. Therefore the light might as well be extinguished—the candle may as well be snuffed. The candle here carries a number of meanings: it is like the light of day and thus (in this context) a symbol of time (candles as clocks); it is a short-lived gesture against darkness; it is a symbol of brief human life and consequently Macbeth's epitaph for his wife—her candle is already out; it is a cry for his own wished-for death. And from here there is a change of tone; Macbeth moves from a poisoned moroseness to contemptuousness; the rhythm is more broken, the words more harsh. As 'tomorrow' in line 1 suggests its opposite, 'yesterdays', in line 4, so light and candle suggest 'shadow'. Man's life is a 'walking shadow' because it is insubstantial and ephemeral and because in the light of day (or of a candle) he casts a darkness (in the metaphorical sense of 'despair'). These two images—the candle and the shadow—seem to have a common Biblical source. In the Book of (long suffering) Job we find:

> The light shall be dark in his dwelling, and his candle shall be put out with him (xviii, 6)

and

> For we are but of yesterday, and are ignorant: for our days upon earth are but a shadow (viii, 9)

'Shadow' leads to the 'poor player' by a double association: shadow-play, and the idea of an actor being a shadow because his rôle is but an imitation of reality. With the introduction of the actor-image, life shrinks to 'an hour' of 'strutting' (a pathetically vain activity) and 'fretting' (useless anxiety). The actor's speech is then an idiot's tale (this reflects back upon 'syllable' in the 3rd line) composed not of words but mere 'sound', not of calm or learning but 'fury'. And it all resolves into that final, deadening 'nothing'. Even without considering Shakespeare's deployment of his poetic techniques (I mean such things as alliteration and assonance, his rhythm changes) it becomes apparent that the passage has 'imaginative coherence'. For obvious dramatic reasons, Shakespeare had to put into Macbeth's mouth the speech of a man close to breaking, a man so full of bitterness and fear that his outburst must reach the edge of incoherence; yet the imagery of the verse has structure and individual images give each other significance.

Some years after Shakespeare's death, Sir William Davenant took it upon himself to improve this speech, removing what he saw as inadequacies in 'reasonableness' and 'correctness'. This is what he came up with:

> Tomorrow and tomorrow and tomorrow
> Creeps in a stealing pace from day to day,
> To the last minute of recorded time,
> And all our yesterdays have lighted fools
> To their eternal homes; out, out, that candle!
> Life's but a walking shadow, a poor player
> That struts and frets his hour upon the stage,
> And then is heard no more. It is a tale
> Told by an idiot, full of sound and fury,
> Signifying nothing.

Is it an improvement? A rhetorical question—obviously it's a minor outrage. Why? Consider: Davenant has changed only 9 words and made 7 alterations to punctuation; what damage, exactly, has he done to the coherence of the imagery? What has happened to the rhythm? And what do you think Davenant found 'unreasonable' or 'incorrect' about those of Shakespeare's words he saw fit to change?

When we are thinking about 'coherence' or 'progression' or whatever, we are of course thinking about the relationship between a number of images. But what further criteria might we apply to the individual image—in so far as it can be singled out? In his book *Literature and Criticism*, H. Coombes says that:

> In a good writer's hands, the image, fresh and vivid, is at its fullest used to *intensify*, to *clarify*, to *enrich*; a successful image helps to make us feel the writer's grasp of the object or

situation he is dealing with; gives his grasp of it with *precision, vividness, force, economy*; and to make such an impact on us, its content, the stuff of which it is made, can't be unduly fantastic and remote from our experience, but must be such that it can be felt by us as belonging in one way or another to the fabric of our own lives. (my italics)

Precision, vividness, force, economy. Although two of these terms are bound up with subjectivity—what is vivid and forceful to me might be feeble and banal to you—they are reasonable demands to make of a poet's language. I am interested in the second part of Mr. Coombes' sentence; the 'stuff' of an image must in some way be part of our experience—emotional and intellectual experience as well as our personal histories, I assume. There is no doubt truth in this; it may have something to do with why of these two images I prefer the second:

> But at my back I always hear
> Time's winged chariot hurrying near;
> And yonder all before us lie
> Deserts of vast eternity.
>
> *Andrew Marvell*

> I have seen the moment of my greatness flicker
> And I have seen the eternal Footman hold my coat,
>   and snicker,
> And in short, I was afraid.
>
> *T. S. Eliot*

Both convey the proximity of death. Both poets personify death. For Marvell, death rides in 'Time's winged chariot'; he is a figure of power, he is supernatural; worst of all, he is 'at my back', urging his victim towards the 'Deserts of vast eternity'. (Note the effect of that everyday word 'all'.) Fear is expressed as loneliness in space. The image as a whole is truly beautiful. But its emotional impact on me is weakened because *magnificence* becomes an attribute of death; the image conveys *awe* more than *fear*. (And I do think that Marvell's intention was to induce fear, since in the poem he is trying to frighten his mistress out of her coy chastity.) Eliot's lines make a deeper impression on me because they make the commonplace extremely sinister. Death is not a great power bearing down, but a servant who helps you into your oblivion; the simple action of putting on your coat takes on a new significance. Then that nasty word 'snicker' suggests that one's death is absurd, ignoble, possibly sordid. And this, in short, makes me afraid. That

106

I *admire* Marvell's image most but *respond* more to Eliot's, has to do with the fact that death is woven regularly into 'the fabric of my life' by newsreel images from Dachau, from Vietnam, from Northern Ireland; I find it difficult to attach awe or grandeur to dying when death is so casually and massively administered. As a modern reader, then, I am more closely attuned to Eliot's nervous irony; he reminds me that what is ordinary is often also terrible, and that the terrible is often ordinary.

What all this amounts to is that one's response to any image will be, at some level, subjective; that the effectiveness of any poem will be conditioned by the reader's personality, his moment in history, his reading, his own experience. But subjectivity is not at odds with cool analysis. Criticism is an investigation into *how* a poem succeeds (or fails) in moving you, and is therefore an investigation into yourself. Fully aware of this, examiners encourage a subjective response ('say what you like or dislike about this poem'). The required skill consists in separating subjectivity from self-indulgence. Self-indulgence is uncritical dipping into your feelings, whereas your writing should demonstrate that you have tried to trace the relationship between what you feel about a poem and the language the poet has used to elicit those feelings. (We have discussed some of the practicalities of this in Chapter 1.) But given the essential subjectiveness of reading poetry, is there any point in developing critical criteria for general application to imagery? The answer is a qualified 'yes'; the use of terms like 'economy', 'appropriateness', 'imaginative coherence' and so on, is a basis from which to communicate your ideas to whoever reads your work, and it imposes some discipline, thus guarding against generalized and self-indulgent gush. What matters is that you use these terms with flexibility and sensitivity. As Cleanth Brooks and Robert Penn Warren point out:

What is to be stressed is the flexibility of imagery and the almost infinite variety of its uses. The degree of explicitness, the amount of ingenuity, in the comparison, the unpoetic and even shocking nature of the terms compared, the subtlety (or lack of it) in the metaphor, the elaboration of the figure or its swift telescoping—all of these will vary from poem to poem and from 'good' poem to 'good' poem. Perhaps all we can fairly ask of any poem is that its imagery shall not be idle and meaningless, dead or inert, or distracting and self-serving, like some foolish ornament that merely calls attention to itself. Every bit of image ought to 'make sense' and to aid the poem in *its* making sense—but, one must concede, there are many ways in which imagery may make its sense and we can only judge its efficiency in terms of the unique context of which it is a part.*

The elements of any poem are interdependent, and the effectiveness of an image will be conditioned by such things as the rhythm of its language, its juxtaposition with other images, and the poet's tone; thus our discussions of these matters continuously involve some of the issues raised in this chapter.

The following short extracts might be the bases of discussions or written appreciations. One final word of advice: if there is one point in this chapter which deserves the greatest emphasis it is that *imagery is a mode of thought*; a metaphor does not decorate an idea, it *expresses* that idea. Therefore it is when you are discussing imagery that you must be especially careful not to think in terms of 'translation', not to use those dread phrases 'what the poet really means is . . .' and 'the poet is trying to say that . . .'. Such an approach is *reductive*, and a successful poem is itself already a distillation, a concentration, of experience.

> My heart is like a singing bird
>   Whose nest is in a watered shoot:
> My heart is like an apple-tree
>   Whose boughs are bent with thickset fruit;
> My heart is like a rainbow shell
>   That paddles in a halcyon sea;
> My heart is gladder than all these
>   Because my love is come to me.
>
> *Christina Rossetti*

> The low downs lean to the sea, the stream,
>   One loose thin pulseless tremulous vein,
> Rapid and vivid and dumb as a dream,
>   Works downward, sick of the sun and the rain,
> No wind is rough with the rank rare flowers;
>   The sweet sea, mother of loves and hours,
> Shudders and shines as the grey winds gleam,
>   Turning her smile to a fugitive pain.
>
> *Swinburne*

*Cleanth Brooks and Robert Penn Warren: *Understanding Poetry* (3rd edition, New York 1964), p. 272.

All through the night we knelt and prayed,
  Mad mourners of a corse!
The troubled plumes of midnight were
  The plumes upon a hearse:
And bitter wine upon a sponge
  Was the savour of Remorse.

Oscar Wilde

I thought of some who worked dark pits
  Of War, and died
Digging the rock where Death reputes
  Peace lies indeed.

Comforted years will sit soft-chaired
  In rooms of amber;
The years will stretch their hands, well-cheered
  By our lives' ember.

Wilfred Owen

Webster was much possessed by death
And saw the skull beneath the skin;
And breastless creatures under ground
Leaned backward with a lipless grin.

Daffodil bulbs instead of balls
Stared from the sockets of the eyes!
He knew that thought clings round dead limbs
Tightening its lust and luxuries.

T. S. Eliot

TEN

A Note on Form and Structure

A moment's thought will persuade you that the structure of language is essential to its meaning. Take any sentence on this page, change its organization, and its meaning will be slightly altered, radically altered, or totally lost. In Chapter 3 we said a similar thing about rhythm—that rhythm (i.e. the arrangement of stresses or emphasis) was indispensable to meaning. Obviously, then, there is some close relationship between 'rhythm' and 'form' or 'structure'. We might express that relationship in this way: rhythm is to a line of a poem what form is to the whole poem. Or put another way, a poem's form is the overall organization of its rhythms. The closer poetry is to its origins in music, the clearer we can see (or hear, rather) form operating as rhythm. We are thinking here of the ballad, which originates in folk song, or the lyric which is composed for musical accompaniment. Here are the first two verses of the anonymous American ballad *Frankie and Johnny.*

> Frankie and Johnny were lovers, O how that couple could love.
> Swore to be true to each other, true as the stars above.
> He was her man, but he done her wrong.

Frankie she was his woman, everybody knows.
She spent a hundred dollars for a suit of Johnny's clothes.
He was her man, but he done her wrong.

The poem's form is a sequence of three-line verses (tercets) with the last line of each a refrain or chorus. The rhythmic element is thus fairly straightforward repetition. There are, of course, practical reasons for this repetitiveness: it makes it easier for the singer to memorize the ballad, and allows for improvisation—a new verse will 'fit' if it retains that last line. But there are other, more subtle, effects of this formal repetition which we should take note of and remember because they are to be found, in varying degrees, in much more sophisticated poetic forms. Firstly, the repeated last line of the tercet contrasts with, and thus draws attention to, the story as it is developed in the other two lines. Secondly, it interrupts that story and consequently increases the audience's desire to know what happens next. Thirdly, any variation in the refrain will be something of a surprise and thus gain impact (as when it changes to 'She shot her man, 'cause he done her wrong').

Of course, not all poems 'tell a story', and not all use repetition so openly, so these comments on the effect of form cannot be generally applicable in a direct way. But most poems have some kind of 'development' or 'movement' which may be said to correspond to the story-line in *Frankie and Johnny*; and repetition (if not of words then of sounds or 'beats') is an element of all rhythm.

Form and rhythm, then, have similar effects. Both give shape and memorability, both integrate. Variations in both have a similar significance. If you are reading lines made of regular iambic pentameters and you encounter a sudden metrical change (as in the third line of the extract from *The Rape Of The Lock* on page 29) you become more alert to the meaning of the words at that point; likewise, if in a poem made of regular 6-line stanzas you encounter an isolated couplet you naturally suspect that those two lines have a particular importance.

Because it is so important—and the source of so many mistakes made by students—let us dwell a little longer on this matter of form and meaning. (One problem is that although they are inseparable, the very act of writing down the two words—'form' and then 'meaning'—makes us think of them separately). Consider this word construction (is it a poem?) by Michael Gibbs. It's called *Avenue*:

```
treestreetree
treestreetree
treestreetree
treestreetree
treestreetree
treestreetree
treestreetree
treestreetree
treestreetree
treestreetree
treestreetree
treestreetree
treestreetree
treestreetree
treestreetree
treestreetree
treestreetree
treestreetree
treestreetree
treestreetree
treestreetree
treestreetree
treestreetree
treestreetree
treestreetree
treestreetree
treestreetree
treestreetree
treestreetree
treestreetree
treestreetree
treestreetree
treestreetree
```

Here, form is precisely the same as meaning: change the arrangement of the words and the 'street' disappears. You may think that using this illustration is rather a cheat, since Gibbs is using words as a *visual* correspondence to the thing 'described'. If so, let us return to a poem already quoted in our chapter on imagery: Carlos Williams' *Red Wheelbarrow*. In that chapter, the poem was cited to illustrate how a poem can 'present' an image and at the same time 'say something about it' (page 100). We did not pause to analyze how it 'works'.

The Red Wheelbarrow

so much depends
upon

a red wheel
barrow

glazed with rain
water

beside the white
chickens.

We said that this poem is 'about' the way we see. Let us now be more specific. We tend to look at objects in a generalized, utilitarian way. We look at a cup, say, or a wheelbarrow; we know what it is called, what it is for, and that's that. We *recognize* and *name* things but rarely, in the ordinary course of events, *look at* or *see* them. One function of art is to make things *particular* rather than general, and thus to emphasize the peculiar, intrinsic qualities of things. The best-known instance of art achieving this, I suppose, is Van Gogh's painting of a chair. The chair is a perfectly ordinary chair—or would be, if we came across it in real life. But Van Gogh's painting makes us see this chair more intensely; we become aware of it as an arrangement of shapes and angles and spaces, an assemblage of differently-textured materials, a design. We see, if you like, the 'chairness' of the chair, its uniqueness. Williams' poem is trying to achieve a similar effect. He doesn't *say* that art individualizes things—he tries to do it, to enact it. He does this through form, by arranging his lines in this unorthodox way. This slows things down (it is essential we pause at line-endings and between each stanza) and stresses the separateness of the objects—barrow, water, chickens—each of which has a 'line' to itself. Even compound words are split into their components: 'wheel/barrow', 'rain/water'. The spatial relationships between things are similarly emphasized; 'upon' stands by itself and is followed by a stanza division, and each of the phenomena observed stands isolated on the page. We are meant, perhaps, to regard the poem as we would a painting—we move from thing to thing, and then step back to reconsider the way they interrelate. The point is, of course, that Williams' success in conveying his meaning depends entirely upon line-arrangement—the form—of the poem. All is lost if we insist on obeying the normal requirements of 'making sense' and run the lines together as continuous prose.

We have said nothing about *rhythm* in Williams' poem. You will notice that each stanza has one line of three words and one line of one word, and that each one-word line has two syllables; are there elements of rhythm here? Or does the eccentric lineation break up any rhythm?

Pursuing this matter of lineation modifying sense and rhythm—what is the difference between:

> I cannot see you leaving me,

and

> I cannot see
> You
> Leaving me,

and does any shift in meaning (however slight) or tone take place? And again, why did Wallace Stevens prefer to write:

> Upon the bank she stood
> In the cool
> Of spent emotions.
> She felt, among the leaves,
> The dew
> Of old devotions.

rather than:

> Upon the bank she stood
> In the cool of spent emotions.
> She felt, among the leaves,
> The dew of old devotions.

Clearly, there are many ways in which line-arrangement can modify sense (i.e. 'feeling' *and* 'meaning'). This in itself demonstrates that metre is not neccessarily 'tyrannical' (as we pointed out in Chapter 3).

The Stevens passage shows that there can be an interesting tension set up in a poem when the verse has a strong, underlying, regular rhythm-pattern (iambic trimeter in this case) which is pulled apart, so to speak, by the linear form. Of course, the *effect* of such a 'tension' will vary from poem to poem, and may be quite complicated. In the Stevens extract we can take note of certain special effects of the lineation. When we arrive at the word 'cool' we have time to take it quite literally; 'she' is by a river in the cool of the evening. But then as we move on to the third line, we realize that 'cool' is also a metaphor; it expresses the calmness which comes when emotion is spent. A similar thing happens as we read lines 5 and 6. 'Dew' is, at first, *actual* dew 'among the leaves', but its meaning shifts when we get to the next line and find that it is also a metaphor for a spiritual feeling. Thus the line arrangement helps 'cool' and 'dew' to achieve the 'double vision' effect of metaphor. In the 4-line version, these two words lose half their impact because they are so tightly connected to 'spent emotions' and 'old devotions'.

As well as giving individual words flexibility, the form of Stevens' poem has a more general purpose: it slows down the reading and brings out the many long vowels and the various assonant sounds, and all this conveys the appropriate feeling of tranquillity and harmony. (The poem from which the passage is taken is *Peter Quince at the Clavier*, and if you wish to see how the inherent music of language can be used, it is a beautiful demonstration).

Having said all this, a problem remains. When we write out the passage in 4 lines, the de-DOM-de-DOM-de-DOM rhythm of the iambic trimeter becomes very obvious. Such a rhythm is brisk and bouncy; regular iambic trimeter is often the metre of comic and bawdy verse and is very much at odds with the feeling Stevens apparently wants to convey. When we read the proper version, this irreverent rhythm doesn't completely disappear but lurks in the background threatening to destroy the serenity of the scene. If we do not pause after 'cool' and 'dew' this rather vulgar metre will assert itself and tranquillity will be lost. Why, you should ask, would Stevens run this risk? Why not simply avoid that metre altogether? The answer to this question brings out the nicest subtlety of the poem. We haven't the space to quote the poem in full, but its second section (from which our extract is taken) and the third are a version of the story, from the Apocrypha, of Susanna and the Elders. Susanna, who is very beautiful, goes to the river to bathe and there, in her nakedness, is spied upon by the elders of her tribe:

> The red-eyed elders, watching, felt
> The basses of their being throb
> In witching chords. . . .

When they have had their fill of voyeuristic thrills, the elders leap out and chastise Susanna for her shamelessness and immorality.

115

What happens in the poem is that the precariousness of Susanna's serenity is expressed by the precariousness of the verse's moods; just as her calmness is menaced by the lascivious old men lurking in the background, so the cool harmony of the words is menaced by the half-hidden presence of an intruding bawdy rhythm. Stevens, like William Carlos Williams, has used the form of his poem to *enact* the situation he is writing about; change the form and the inter-relationships of sound, lineation and rhythm are upset, and consequently meaning is lost. This poem is an instance of a poet using the techniques of poetry in an extremely conscious and ingenious way. Yet it doesn't strike us as being *over*-ingenious or artificial. This is in part because Stevens' skill is such that it is almost invisible—we do not have to analyze what he does in order to experience it—and in part because the poem is as much *about* music as it is about desire, and so it seems completely appropriate that Stevens should 'play' his sounds and rhythms in the way that his Peter Quince plays the clavier.

CONVENTIONAL FORMS

So far we have dwelt upon poets who use form freely; their structures were chosen to perform particular functions. But what of *conventional* forms, which have certain prescribed structural 'rules' governing the poet's language? Can we expect these forms to operate in the same meaningful way even though the poet has, apparently, less freedom to manipulate them? Let us approach these questions by way of the sonnet. The sonnet consists of 14 iambic pentameter lines arranged in certain rhyme-schemes (see Glossary); generally there is a division—clearly defined or not— between the first eight lines (the octave) and the remaining 6 (the sestet). In the sonnet form used by Shakespeare the break between octave and sestet is usually present (often indicated by a strong punctuation mark—full stop, question mark or semi-colon—at the end of line 8), but the Shakespearian sonnet is actually made up of three four-line groups (quatrains), each with a different pair of rhymes, followed by a concluding rhyming couplet. Thus the rhyme-scheme is ABAB CDCD EFEF GG. Here is one of Shakespeare's sonnets:

Sonnet 130

My mistress' eyes are nothing like the sun;
Coral is far more red than her lips' red;
If snow be white, why then her breasts be dun;
If hairs be wires, black wires grow on her head.

I have seen roses damasked, red and white,
But no such roses see I in her cheeks,
And in some perfumes is there more delight
Than in the breath that from my mistress reeks.
I love to hear her speak, yet well I know
That music hath a far more pleasing sound.
I grant I never saw a goddess go;
My mistress when she walks treads on the ground.
And yet, by heaven, I think my love as rare
As any she belied with false compare.

(Some words may require explication. 'Damasked': mingled; 'reeks': emanates, issues; 'go': walk; 'she'—in line 14—woman; 'compare': comparison.)

We tend to think of a disciplined form imposing limitations upon the poet, and in a sense this is so. But in this sonnet Shakespeare is doing something which could not be done effectively in any other form but the sonnet. To grasp this it is necessary to know that a sophisticated Elizabethan gentleman was expected to be able to turn out a competent sonnet—it was one of the social graces. Furthermore, the most fitting subject for the sonnet was thought to be sexual love. The upshot of all this was that by the end of the sixteenth century, Englishmen had produced thousands of amorous sonnets, some superb, some dreadful, some charming, some obscene, most of them mediocre.

Human inventiveness having its limits, certain excessive images and comparisons became established clichés. The poet's lover was all too frequently 'as radiant as the sun' or graced with 'breasts white as snow'; her hair was of 'golden wires', she breathed 'perfume', her lips were 'red as coral', and so on. In his sonnet, Shakespeare finds his lady failing to qualify for these standard comparisons. He goes through the usual list and finds her lacking. It is as if he were saying 'I really would like to write a sonnet just like everyone else's but I just can't make it fit the subject. . .' We might enumerate some of the effects of this strategy. One: by asserting the actuality, the naturalness, of his mistress, Shakespeare satirizes the inflated claims of other sonneteers. Two: he creates surprise by seeming to embark upon an 'anti-sonnet', one that doesn't flatter and even seems to denigrate. Three: this surprise is then swung round by the 'punch-line' couplet, which says, in effect, that he is more entitled to the high-flown language of the sonnet because his lover is 'just as rare'—an irony which implies that she is *more* rare because she is not 'falsified'. Four: he achieves originality within a rather exhausted and cliché-ridden

117

traditional form, and this is ultimately a fine compliment to his mistress in that she is the inspiration for this originality; he flatters by not seeming to.

Clearly, Shakespeare's aims in this poem could be realized only by using the sonnet form. What we see operating here is something different to the formal devices used by Wallace Stevens—an orthodox poetic form is being used to *comment on* that form. But this is obviously a specialized use of form; it has elements of *parody*, and our appreciation of it is to some extent dependent upon our knowing something about the tradition to which it belongs and refers. There still remains the more general question of the function and purpose of conventional poetic forms.

Why, it may be asked, should a poet choose to fit his thought into a form taken 'off the peg' rather than tailor a form to suit his own particular needs? We could evade this question by pointing out that it is irrelevant to the requirements of the Examiners, who ask that you discuss form only so far as it is relevant to the poem or poems under consideration. On the other hand, it is a problem which has bothered many students, who see some kind of conflict between 'expression of feeling' and 'formal discipline'. It is the failure to resolve this problem which leads people to write about the formal aspect of a poem as if it were separable from the poem's meaning, and which was operating in the mind of the student who thought that the 'deeper meaning' of The Wild Swans at Coole remained 'confused and obscure' because Yeats had 'tried to keep himself too disciplined in his rhyme-scheme'. (Chapter 1, p. 4). So perhaps we should say something about this question, even though it raises huge problems, debated since Aristotle, which have more to do with philosophy than with practical criticism.

Sometimes, in class discussions of these matters, this alleged conflict between expression and formal discipline has been spoken of as a clash between 'naturalness' and 'artificiality'. These terms are whale-sized red herrings. Every work of art is by definition an artifice and therefore artificial; to say that a poetic form is 'unnatural' is thus to say nothing at all. It is true that some artistic forms are more 'naturalistic' than others: a nineteenth-century novel is likely to be 'truer to life' than, say, a Greek epic, but all that this means is that the intentions and cultures of their writers were very different; the observation is no valid basis for evaluative judgement. It is true also that certain paintings approach the realistic qualities of photographs, but if we admire such paintings our admiration is surely for the *artistry*, the skill, of the painter. Oscar Wilde dismisses the whole question with his usual elegant arrogance: 'I hate vulgar realism in literature. The man who

118

would call a spade a spade should be compelled to use one. It is all he is fit for'. Beyond all this, of course, there is the fact that the meanings of words change, and the words 'nature' and 'natural' are especially shifty. Pope asserted that poets should 'follow Nature', but his highly-polished verse seems quite 'unnatural' to the modern reader. For Pope, 'Nature' was bound up with ideas of harmony and order; for us the word has connotations of wildness and indiscipline. Let us then drop the words 'natural' and 'artificial'.

Far more relevant to our present concern is a certain sentimental idea of how poems come about. According to this theory, the poet wanders (or just sits) about until such a moment when Inspiration, like Biblical tongues of flame, smites him and he is moved to write in a fever of words. If this is so, then it seems certainly perverse and even destructive that he should then hammer his white-hot insights into, say, fourteen iambic pentameters with a rhyme-scheme laid down by some long-dead Italian. We had thought that this concept of the genesis of a poem had been laid to rest long ago (poets being prepared to make admissions like 'This phrase popped into my head while I was cleaning the car and I fiddled about with it for a couple of months until I had the whole poem'), but student work demonstrates sometimes that it lingers on, albeit in a less absurdly imagined form. Evidence suggests, in fact, that poems are 'worked up'—and this is true of even the most 'inspirational' of poets, such as Shelley, say, or Gerard Manley Hopkins. (This does not mean, of course, that an idea may not suddenly strike the poet, or that several strands of thought may not suddenly pull together in his mind. If you wish to call this process 'inspiration', then so be it.) To say that poems are 'worked up' is to say that in the poet's mind certain ideas, images, verbal sounds and so forth are *given shape*. Without shape, without form, these thoughts cannot be expressed meaningfully. In other words, meaning and form develop simultaneously and are interdependent. Consequently, it is wrong to suppose that there is any basic conflict between expression and form. (As we pointed out in Chapter 1, the student who thought that the 'deeper meaning' of *The Wild Swans at Coole* was obscured by Yeats' determination to adhere to his rhyme-scheme failed to see that this deeper meaning is, in large part, conveyed by the movement and music of the verse, and the rhymes are an essential part of this music.)

It follows from this that the form of a poem is just as much an expression of the poet's personality as is his subject-matter or his thought and feeling about his subject. Poetic form is a *personal* thing. There is an interesting observation by William Hazlitt, a

119

critic and a friend of Coleridge, which seems relevant here. He is talking about the sound of Coleridge's verse as compared with Wordsworth's when the poets read their work aloud.

> Coleridge's manner is more animated, more full, and varied; Wordsworth's more equable, sustained and internal. The one might be termed the more *dramatic*, the other the more *lyrical*. Coleridge has told me that he himself liked to compose in walking over uneven ground, or breaking through the straggling branches of a copse-wood; whereas Wordsworth always wrote (if he could) walking up and down a straight gravel walk, or in some spot where the continuity of his verse met with no collateral interruption.

For these two poets, the forms of their poems (as conveyed by the way they read) arose from their different personal responses to nature; form and feeling developed simultaneously from the same emotional source.

Now, the point unto which we have been leading is this: there is no essential contradiction in a particular poetic form being *personal* and at the same time being *conventional*. The unique and original qualities of a poet's imagination may well find their perfect expression in a form already long-established. Since Shakespeare wrote at least 154 sonnets (and, it seems, for private reasons rather than for publication), we can only assume that the sonnet form in some way corresponded to and expressed a pattern of his thought and imagination. (To try to be more precise would involve making conjectures based on a reading of all Shakespeare's work. In the glossary we discuss in general terms some of the characteristics of the sonnet form; do you see these formal elements operating, on a larger scale of course, in Shakespeare's plays?)

We have tried, this far, to stress the interdependence and simultaneity of meaning, feeling and form. In general, we have agreed with Karl Kraus, who was of the opinion that 'There are two kinds of writers, those who are and those who aren't. With the first, content and form belong together like soul and body; with the second they match each other like body and clothes.'* Yet in the use of traditional poetic forms there may be other motives involved. I asked a student why John Donne chose to express a certain feeling in the form of a sonnet. She said 'To show off'. This was not a very delicate reply, but it contained a grain of truth. Since it is unusual for a poet to receive from the Muse the gift of a

*Quoted by W. H. Auden in *A Certain World*, p. 418.

completely-formed and perfect poem, it follows that a great part of his art is craftmanship, verbal dexterity, 'wordsmithing'. Attempting to master conventional verse forms is a way of developing and testing these skills. It is, after all, difficult to write a good sonnet (try it) and extremely difficult to write one great enough to rise above the others already in existence. True, there is a certain amount of *game* involved in such an exercise, but some games are more serious than others, and it is always satisfying to win. But for a poet to show that he can produce a fine and individual poem while conforming to the accepted rules of its particular form is not merely 'showing off'. Not all poetry is intended to move us to great heights or depths of passion or thought; much of it is content to give pleasure, and a demonstration of expertise gives pleasure. Of course, such pleasure will not be lasting if the poem is *only* craftmanship, devoid of feeling, commitment and insight.

Another attraction of conventional forms is that the effort to master their technicalities may lead to, deepen into, something more important. The poet says to himself 'I think I'll have a go at writing Spenserian stanzas', and while he struggles with the pentameters and alexandrines, certain combinations of words and rhythms, certain balances between phrases, emerge because they 'fit'. But as well as 'fitting', they illuminate some recess of his imagination and connect an idea to another idea . . . and the game becomes more serious; the poet finds that he has something to say. The French poet Paul Valery describes this process:

> My own poem Le Cimetière Marin came to me in the form of a certain rhythm which is that of the ten-syllable French line arranged in the proportion of four to six. I had not, at first, the slightest idea of what content was to fill that form. Gradually, a number of floating words began to solidify. Little by little they determined my subject, and the labour (a very long labour) of composition was forced upon me.

We can imagine something like the reverse of this procedure. The poet is moved by anger, say, or joy, or an obsessive interest, but his thought and feeling will not distil into coherent form or imagery. He chooses, pragmatically, a conventional form as a means to impose discipline upon his ideas, to order them. He takes his imagination to arbitration. Once the rules of this poetic form have shaped his thought into language, he may abandon them and evolve a poem in free verse. But the rules will have served their purpose.

In certain circumstances, the fact that certain forms are highly disciplined may itself be meaningful. Imagine a sonnet about

121

madness, or a sonnet in which the poet describes his own mental turbulence. The strictly-organized, quasi-logical structure of the sonnet would be a dramatic contrast to its subject. This tension between form and content could have the effect of intensifying the reader's impression of imminent madness; the precarious balance may speak for itself. In such a case, form would have an *ironic* relationship to content.

It is at this point that we have to do a little owning up. The fact is that we have used the terms 'conventional forms' and 'traditional forms' for argument's sake, by and large. We have referred to the sonnet almost exclusively, and the simple reason for this is that the sonnet is one of the very few poetic forms we can safely say is 'conventional'. That is to say, the sonnet is one of a very small number of poetic structures still being used in something like its original form.* (This in itself is interesting. Why should the sonnet retain its fascination? Even e. e. cummings, a poet famous for his idiosyncratic use of form, has written beautifully-balanced Petrarchan sonnets (see Glossary). Other named forms, ode, elegy, pastoral and so forth, have deviated, in the hands of poets over the centuries, so far from their original conceptions that their names have ceased to have any consistent meaning. (This is all to the good, since classification is the implacable enemy of imagination.) If we were forced to offer some definition of 'conventional form' we could only come up with something rather feeble: 'the organization of verse into familiar or recognizable metrical and stanzaic structures', or somesuch. When we come to consider twentieth century poetry the whole question of form— whether 'conventional' or not—becomes even more complicated.

Towards the end of our chapter on rhythm and rhyme we mentioned the revolt against 'the tyranny of metre' which took place early this century. It was, of course, a reaction against much more than mere metre. We do not have here the space to digress into literary history in order to trace the complex of historical and social factors which lie behind the dramatic shift in English poetry which we associate with, notably, Ezra Pound and T. S. Eliot. (We suggest you read the brief account of these matters in parts One and Two of Volume VII of *The Pelican Guide to English Literature: The Modern Age*, edited by Boris Ford.) Put simply and crudely, these and other poets were acutely aware that they lived in an age when religious and moral faith, and faith in political and social structures, was in a state of decay and enervation. In the individual, like Eliot's J. Alfred Prufrock, the result was doubt and aimlessness; universally, this spiritual decadence manifested itself

*Although verse-structures closest to music and song have also retained their basic formal qualities.

in the kind of blind barbarity which was exemplified by the stupid savagery of the First World War. In order to express their world-view, these poets found it necessary to reject the kind of middle-class values which tried to hide the hollowness of modern life under a cloak of cosy respectability. There were urgent things to be said, and they insisted that respectability should not impose restrictions upon the content or the form of their poetry. They turned their backs upon 'public' and popular verse; their work appeared difficult, inaccessible and ugly to readers brought up on Tennyson, say, or the Brownings. They renounced the conventional craftsmanship and somewhat woozy pastoralism of contemporary Georgian poetry, seeing the true spirit of the age in the squalid and chaotic life of the city. Despite the contemporaneity of the two poets, there is a world and an age of difference between these lines by the Georgian poet A. E. Housman.

> Tell me not here, it needs not saying,
>   What tune the enchantress plays
> In aftermaths of soft September
>   Or under blanching Mays,
> For she and I were long acquainted
>   And I knew all her ways.
>
> On russet floors, by waters idle,
>   The pine lets fall its cone;
> The cuckoo shouts all day at nothing
>   In the leafy dells alone;
> And traveller's joy beguiles in autumn
>   Hearts that have lost their own.

and these by T. S. Eliot:

> The morning comes to consciousness
> Of faint stale smells of beer
> From the sawdust-trampled street
> With all its muddy feet that press
> To early coffee-stands.
> With the other masquerades
> That time resumes,
> One thinks of all the hands
> That are raising dingy shades
> In a thousand furnished rooms.

Because we are concerned in this chapter with form, what is important for us to note is that in depicting the social and moral disintegration of their times, these iconoclastic poets found it necessary to disown those poetic forms which had become reassuringly familiar to readers of verse. We can generalize two reasons for this. Firstly, if order was collapsing and the world becoming more and more formless, it was plainly absurd to write about that world in cosily conventional literary forms. Secondly, in an alogical and disorderly world, it was mere dishonesty to write poems which suggest coherence by offering clear, logical, easy-to-follow trains of thought; it was necessary, then, to abandon those poetic techniques which create the illusion of logic and unity— regular metres and stanzas, for example. What was needed, Eliot's work suggests, was a violent and troubling juxtaposition of images. All this does not imply, of course, that Pound, Eliot and others wrote 'formless' poetry—the phrase is a contradiction in terms—but that they insisted on freely evolving or adapting poetic forms in accordance with their particular needs and objectives. As Eliot himself points out,

> only a bad poet could welcome free verse as a liberation from form. It was a revolt against dead form, and a preparation for new form or for the renewal of the old; it was an insistence upon the inner unity which is unique to every poem, against the outer unity which is typical.

Our little historical excursion, inadequate as it is, enables us to make the following points. First: the reaction of Pound and T. S. Eliot to their times demonstrates that *form*, just as much as tone or subject-matter, is an expression of the poet's view of the world. Second: the way Pound and Eliot (early in their careers, at least) saw their position as poets in society remains, generally, the way poets see themselves. The poet is at a distance: *in* society, but not *of* it, and maintaining a critical attitude towards his society's myths and values. Many important modern poets have been or are 'alienated' in some way, either because of sexual or political nonconformity, like Auden, or because of a self-imposed, self-effacing withdrawal from crass modernity, like Larkin, or because of a bleak and unpopular view of Man, like Hughes. Poetry remains largely 'private' rather than 'public'. (It seems to be more and more difficult to find a poet of any stature whose manners and forms are 'normal' enough to qualify him for the Poet Laureate-ship.) As nonconformity has been the pervading tone of modern poetry, it is not surprising that there is no consensus of opinion, even in the most general terms, as to what may be the governing criteria in writing verse, nor even any agreement over what poetry actually is. Poets are prepared, sometimes, to say *what* poetry

124

should do, but not *how* it should do it. Brian Patten thinks that poetry should 'lead all those who are safe into the middle of busy roads and leave them there', but he doesn't say how the 'safe' can be persuaded to follow.

What all this adds up to is that because modern poets have to a great extent freed themselves from the demands of formal rules and conventions, because free verse has become a norm of their writing, you must be *especially* careful not to generalize about their use of form. In no way is it merely 'natural' or 'normal' for a modern poet to use rhymes and metres, for example, and therefore when you do encounter them you must take particular care to see how they relate to the poem's other elements. How you do this is, of course, your most pressing problem. How can we write meaningfully about the relationship between form and meaning and feeling? What criteria may we fairly apply?

Well, having gone to some lengths to point out that a poem's form should be considered only in the context of that poem and only as *intrinsic*, we can hardly propose general guidelines. It should by now be obvious that it is worthless to write something like 'this poem is in three six-line stanzas each rhyming ABABCC', and leave it at that. Beyond this negative advice, we think the best we can offer is a series of questions you should ask yourself when thinking about the form of a poem. It will be apparent that to answer many of these questions you will need to read the poem 'aloud' and with care.

(i) Does the poem have perceptible regular form (e.g. rhythmic regularity, rhyme scheme, equal division into stanzas etc.)? If yes, then:

*Is it sufficiently regular in sound and rhythm to achieve certain effects of repetition? Is it like an incantation, for example, or does it have a lulling effect?

*Is it regular enough to set up expectations about what will follow? As you read, do you consciously predict the subsequent pattern? And are these expectations or predictions fullfilled as you read on, or are they overturned?

*Are there deviations from the formal regularity (e.g. metrical variations, stanzas abbreviated or elongated)? Do these indicate changes in pace, feeling, tone, subject?

*There may be a regular rhyme-scheme, but do individual rhymes draw attention to themselves? Are some rhymes stronger or weaker than others? If so, to what effect?

*There may be a regular metrical or stress rhythm, but are some lines longer or slower in sound than others? What devices has the poet used to achieve this effect, and which words or images does it draw to our attention?

*Where do the pauses fall, and which are 'heavier'? Do they have the effect of grouping words in patterns different to the line-length (e.g. by enjambment) and stanza divisions?

*Is there an underlying structure—such as progression of thought or sequence of imagery—and do the stanzas correspond to the stages of this 'argument' or sequence? In this way, does the form of the poem help to clarify the poem's meaning?

If *no*, then:

*Are there repetitions—of phrases, of the positions of pauses, of groups of words similarly stressed? Such repetitions will contribute to the music and the movement of the poem, obviously; are they, in fact, the basis of the poem's form? And what is the effect upon the meaning of a phrase or line if it is repeated? Does it mean the same thing(s) each time?

*Does the lineation follow syntactical sense, i.e. do the words of each line comprise a complete element of a sentence or a whole sentence, and can each line be understood separately? Or is the line division apparently arbitrary, breaking up sentences and phrases (as in *The Red Wheelbarrow*)? Is the effect of arbitrary lineation to make the reader more aware of each word's meaning, or less aware of meaning and more aware of sound?

*Is the poem divided in some way into stanzas or sections? If so, does each have its own unity—in terms of cadences, images, etc.? Does each represent a distinct stage in the poem's development?

*Are there passages which *are* regular in metrical structure or rhyme, or passages which approximate regularity? What is the effect of this?

*If there is no single rhythm (even as a 'ghostly voice') running through the poem, and no striking use of repetition, what, if anything, gives the whole poem coherence? What is it that makes the poem seem a complete and self-contained entity? Is it a sequence of related images, perhaps, or some kind of narrative?

(ii) Does the form of the poem itself have character?

*If the form is regular, highly-organized and polished (as in Pope's work, for example) does this suggest a certain controlled detachment on the part of the poet? Does its *poise* give you confidence in the poet's thought and insight?

*Does a very irregular form necessarily convey turbulent feelings?

*Is it possible that certain metrical forms are best suited to only one kind of verse? Is it true, for instance, that 'triple metres (anapaestic, dactylic) tend to have something vaguely light, comic or superficial about them'? Consider these lines from two poems by Dryden:

> Sylvia the fair, in the bloom of fifteen
> Felt an innocent warmth as she lay on the green;

> After the pangs of a desperate lover,
> When day and night I have sighed all in vain;

(iii) Does there seem to be a lack of harmony between the poem's tone or content and its form?
If yes, then:
*Is this apparent conflict a deliberate device serving a particular purpose (as in the Wallace Stevens poem)? If there were, say, a violent emotion expressed in a closely-knit and tightly-controlled form, could the resultant tension between form and feeling be an expression of a similar conflict within the poet?
*Or is it a weakness, a destructive discrepancy (as in Cowper's *The Poplar Field*)?

Let us see how some of these questions might be applied. W. H. Auden's *In Memory of W. B. Yeats* is an elegy in three sections. We quote the second section, which is a single stanza, and the opening stanza of the third section. The first thing that will strike you is the dramatic change in verse form.

II

> You were silly like us: your gift survived it all;
> The parish of rich women, physical decay,
> Yourself; mad Ireland hurt you into poetry.
> Now Ireland has her madness and her weather still,
> For poetry makes nothing happen: it survives
> In the valley of its own saying where executives
> Would never want to tamper; it flows south
> From ranches of isolation and the busy griefs,
> Raw towns that we believe and die in; it survives,
> A way of happening, a mouth.

Earth, receive an honoured guest;
William Yeats is laid to rest:
Let the Irish vessel lie
Emptied of its poetry.

Does the first of these stanzas have any regular form? Well, there is a pattern of approximate rhymes, but for the most part this is very subdued. There is only one *full rhyme* (south/mouth), and as this falls on the last line it rounds off the stanza, completes it. There is one *identical rhyme* (i.e. the repetition of the same word) in 'it survives'. Identical rhyme is often considered a weakness, unless there is an especial reason for its use; is there such a reason in this case? There is a similar number of stresses in most lines (four or five) but they do not seem to be positioned according to a regular pattern as in stress-verse; rather, they are the stresses of natural prose speech. Let us regard the stanza, then, as free verse and look for the way phrases and lines are balanced against each other. From this point of view, it should be obvious that the most important formal element is the use of *pauses*, particularly the main pause in each line, the *caesura*. Take the first line: the caesura is marked by a colon, and divides the line into two equal halves (each with two stresses). The way these two half-lines balance is the way the line's two sentiments balance. The surprisingly irreverent first statement, that Yeats was 'silly' (and this is supposed to be an elegy!) is counteracted by the second, that his gift was great enough to survive. The line would suffer if the caesura was weakened; it would be much less effective and surprising if it read

You were silly like us but your gift survived it all.

Or take the third line: the main pause is suddenly shifted back, isolating the word 'Yourself'. Again, the effect is to increase surprise—the surprising and unconventional idea that poetry survives not *because of* the poet's personality but *in spite of* it, that somehow poetry exists independent of people. Poets are the instruments of poetry, rather than vice versa. (This idea is continued in the 'vessel' image of the next stanza.)

Go through the stanza yourself and consider in detail the effects of the caesurae and the secondary pauses.

The questions which now arise are: what is the over-all effect of the structure of this stanza? How does its form relate to its feeling and tone?

Auden seems to be writing an 'anti-elegy' in that he doesn't flatter Yeats and at moments is almost insulting, it seems. He praises only by implication, if at all. His theme is the survival of poetry. 'Survive' occurs three times, and twice it is emphasized by its position at the end of a line, preceded by a caesura. Auden's argument might be paraphrased thus: poetry survives because it has an independent existence of its own; consequently it endures despite the death of poets (and despite their mundane lives); it survives the 'real world' of business and money ('executives') because it is of no use or interest to that world; like a river, it continues, in spite of grief and ugliness, to flow; it is simply 'a way of happening'. The thematic images of 'the poet' and 'the river' are brought together in the final word of the stanza. Now, all this is no conventional 'celebration' of either poetry or the poet. In fact, the tone is bleak, almost pessimistic. The images are of unlovely things, and although poetry is compared to a river, Auden suppresses any notions of pastoral beauty we might be inclined to associate with this metaphor. With all this in mind, it seems appropriate that the verse should be formed in a way that avoids the pleasantly musical elements of poetry—smooth rhymes, patterned harmonies of sound and so forth. Heavy punctuation and end-stopped lines obstruct any fluidity. Auden is addressing another poet directly, almost conversationally, but he is "off duty", so to speak, and talking bluntly. The stanza is, in other words, *informal*.

After this, the next stanza comes as something of a shock. There is a switch to regular form, and a rather strictly-organized one at that. Does this form have any inherent characteristics? Yes, it does. If we scan the first lines there is clearly a monotonous trochaic metre:

> Earth, re | ceive an | hon oured | guest;
> William | Yeats is | laid to | rest.

This is a metre both heavy and brisk, one often used in elegies and epitaphs. Compare it, for example, with the opening of William Browne's *On the Dowager Countess of Pembroke* (page 144):

> Underneath this sable hearse
> Lies the subject of all verse:

It's the kind of metrical verse we might expect to find engraved on a tombstone, and the simple full rhyme of the first couplet also seems appropriate for such a use. Auden has adopted a stanza form which is, we could say, the 'official' one for such an occasion. What this suggests is that the poet has consciously 'pulled himself together'. It's as if, aware of the bitterness and personal involvement he has revealed in the previous stanza, he has said to himself 'Come on, this is an *elegy*. Now, what's the proper tone?' He represses his feelings and retreats behind conventional form. He also takes up a more recognizably 'poetic' attitude: he addresses, somewhat grandly, Earth, not a fellow man; there is the euphemism of 'laid to rest', and the rather inflated image of Yeats as the 'vessel' of Irish poetry. Of course, it is all a bit forced, and finally he can't keep up the pretence. The metre and rhyme break down in the fourth line. We cannot stress the last syllable of 'poetry', nor can we pronounce it to rhyme with 'lie'; at least, not unless we make a very strained and artificial reading. So there is a falling-off at the stanza's end; the 'official' voice breaks, and the strength of the poet's feelings destroys his pose.

It is a fine example of a deliberate conflict between form and feelings; the discipline of the form only succeeds in drawing attention to the emotions it is supposed to control. Auden's bitterness, and the anger that later emerges, has causes in addition to Yeats' death. Yeats died in 1939, and his death takes on symbolic qualities. A man whose cause was beauty dies; a period of ugliness and killing waits to be born. Although Auden retains the four-line rhyming stanza through to the end of his poem, the ceremonious trochaic metre is not consistent. After the first stanza in this third section the measured pomp vanishes. Subsequent stanzas are still tightly-organized, but the effect is to make them sharper, more aggressive, even satirical:

> In the nightmare of the dark
> All the dogs of Europe bark,
> And the living nations wait,
> Each sequestered in its hate;

There is much in these extracts from Auden's poem that we haven't considered. We haven't dwelt on particular details of language; why 'ranches', for example? Why 'her madness and her weather'? But we hope that we have shown that a sensitive examination and questioning of a poem's structure, together with an equally sensitive examination of its language, is a viable way, perhaps the best way, of approaching that poem's complete meaning.

ELEVEN

An Exercise in Formal Comparison

Read carefully the following two poems in order to write an appreciation comparing them from the point of view of their different forms and structures.

To Night

Swiftly walk o'er the western wave,
  Spirit of Night!
Out of the misty eastern cave
Where, all the long and lone daylight,
Thou wovest dreams of joy and fear,
Which make thee terrible and dear,—
  Swift be thy flight.

Wrap thy form in a mantle gray,
  Star-inwrought!
Blind with thine hair the eyes of Day;
Kiss her until she be wearied out,
Then wander o'er city, and sea, and land,
Touching all with thine opiate wand—
  Come, long-sought!

When I arose and saw the dawn,
  I sighed for thee;
When light rode high, and the dew was gone,
And noon lay heavy on flower and tree,
And the weary Day turned to his rest,
Lingering like an unloved guest,
  I sighed for thee.

Thy brother Death came, and cried,
               Wouldst thou me?
Thy sweet child Sleep, the filmy-eyed,
Murmured like a noon-tide bee,
Shall I nestle near thy side?
Wouldst thou me?—And I replied,
               No, not thee!

Death will come when thou are dead,
               Soon, too soon—
Sleep will come when thou art fled;
Of neither would I ask the boon
I ask of thee, belovèd Night—
Swift be thine approaching flight,
               Come soon, soon!

The Visitant

1

A cloud moved close. The bulk of the wind shifted.
A tree swayed overwater.
A voice said:
Stay. Stay by the slip-ooze. Stay.

Dearest tree, I said, may I rest here?
A ripple made a soft reply.
I waited, alert as a dog.
The leech clinging to a stone waited;
And the crab, the quiet breather.

2

Slow, slow as a fish she came,
Slow as a fish coming forward,
Swaying in a long wave;
Her skirts not touching a leaf,
Her white arms reaching towards me.

She came without a sound,
Without brushing the wet stones,
In the soft dark of early evening,
She came,
The wind in her hair,
The moon beginning.

132

3

I woke in the first of morning.
Staring at a tree, I felt the pulse of a stone.
Where's she now, I kept saying.
Where's she now, the mountain's downy girl?

But the bright day had no answer.
A wind stirred in a web of appleworms;
The tree, the close willow, swayed.

TWELVE

Hints on Essay - Knitting

It is at this point that you should perhaps re-read the introduction to this book and first chapter, because I am about to embark upon the rather reckless business of advising you on how to conceive, arrange and present an essay in appreciation, and this will involve a certain amount of recapitulation. It will involve, also, a good deal of cold-blooded pragmatism. Let me say something about this pragmatism before we go any further. If you are an Advanced Level candidate your abilities as a critical reader, thinker and writer are going to be tested in extremely artificial conditions. You will have to demonstrate your perceptiveness and expertise in only a couple of hours, in circumstances calculated to create tension, and what you write in those two hours will be marked, in a matter of minutes, by someone who has never set eyes on you. Whether or not this procedure is just or, for that matter, even rational, is not our present concern. Certainly it is not ideal, and this being so we may as well be coldly practical. Because you will have to work against the clock, you will have to be *efficient*. The second part of this chapter is intended to bring together a number of practical suggestions which, we hope, will help you to be efficient, but before we get down to matters of technique, let us dwell a moment on essay *style*.

As the Examiners' Reports regularly and wearily point out, the Unseen Practical Criticism Paper is an *English* examination. This means, simply, that you will be assessed not only on your ability to examine language but also on your ability to *use* language. It is therefore quite reasonable that you should be penalized for writing stumbling, ugly and dull prose, even if you manage somehow to convey a good number of valuable insights. Your style, the way you write, is, for the examiner, the only evidence of the quality of your thought. Moreover, style, remember, has a *rhetorical* function; that is, it seeks to persuade. When you write a critical apprecia-

134

tion, you are trying to persuade an anonymous somebody that you are a perceptive, sensitive, articulate and imaginative person. Spare a thought for this somebody. The examiner is, let us say, a schoolteacher who supplements his or her income by marking Advanced Level exam papers. It is not often a task which brings joy. He has a large number of essays to get through, all of them written about the same pieces of prose and poetry. He is unlikely to be either saintly or superhuman, and is therefore likely to experience moments—long moments, probably—of boredom. He is undoubtedly an inherently generous and fair-minded soul, and struggles to maintain a consistent objectivity, but after being submitted over and over again to similar mistakes and weaknesses, he may be forgiven for yielding to irritation. Why *should* he struggle to puzzle out what it is that the writer of any one essay is trying to say? But let him pick up an appreciation which is lucid, unstrained, fluidly-written, and his eye will moisten with gratitude; unable to convey his gratitude to the candidate in a more personal way, he expresses it by writing on the essay a letter which comes very early in the alphabet. . .

It would be foolish, of course, to try to say what makes a good essay style. Style is a personal matter. There are, though, a few general criteria which you could bear in mind. A good critical essay will have *variety*—variety in the length and structure of sentences, variety of language, a variety of ideas (not a plugging away at one point of view) and, if the poem or passage merits it, a variety of interpretation. By 'variety of language' we mean to suggest that you should be bold enough to write imaginatively and figuratively; at the same time you should be able to balance and enforce your more impressionistic comments with the kind of close examination of the text which often necessitates the use of technical critical terminology. While a command of a quite extensive technical vocabulary is undoubtedly helpful, it must not become a substitute for thought. An essay which relies too heavily on the competent use of technical phraseology is likely to be impersonal and dull. On the other hand, some familiarity with, and use of, critical terminology is essential if you are to discuss a writer's techniques with precision and without awkwardness. *Economy* is a desirable quality in a critical essay. Avoid repetition, and do not suppose you can fool the examiner by making the same point twice under the disguise of different phrasing. Besides, there is not enough time to waste in this way. Finally, an Advanced Level essay should have what we can only term *fluidity*. Fluidity is that quality in writing style which hides the joints; it is the ease with which you move from one point or topic to another. If, when you write a study of a poem, you adopt the method of discussing

135

each stanza in turn, you run some risk of producing an essay which plods along rather predictably. You should, therefore, try to vary your approach to each stanza, and try to make the transitions from one paragraph to another smooth and flexible so that you can, if necessary, interrupt the stanza-by-stanza progress of your essay in order to reconsider early stanzas in the light of later ones. (See the way Joyce tries to do this in the fifth paragraph of her appreciation—see page 9). If you use a different structure, such as considering the poem or prose passage under various headings, such as 'Feeling' or 'Tone', then your writing should be sufficiently fluid to allow you to connect these categories in a natural way. Remember that you should regard a poem, in particular, as a unified entity and that in consequence your study should have a similar unity; you should avoid writing about 'Tone' or 'Sense' or whatever as if they are clearly separable elements.

Developing a good style is simply a matter of hard work. Let us recall a dictum of Pope's which we have already quoted elsewhere:

> True ease in writing comes from art, not chance.

There is no such thing as a truly natural style. A writer whose style seems natural and fluid has achieved that effect by a painstaking process of constant refinement and adjustment. Although it is very difficult, you must always try to read what you have written with the kind of critical objectivity you apply to other writers.

As was said in the introduction, students often make a strange and artificial division between the twin activities of reading and writing. This is perhaps understandable if we consider that the philosophy of education under which we presently labour involves the teaching of literature as an examinable *subject*; a student may then be forgiven for missing the qualitative difference between literature and, say, biology or sociology. Be this as it may, your success as an examinee will depend to some considerable degree on your willingness to study literature in a *creative* way. Study not only in order to learn 'about' literature, but also in order to learn *how to write*. Surely all writers begin by imitating or reacting against what has already been written. Imitation is a blameless activity if one's models are good, and if it can be developed into a style which becomes your own. During your course of study you will no doubt read critics in order to help you understand your set texts. You have probably had some training in abstracting 'points' from critical commentaries, which is all very well, but you should pay just as much attention to *how* a good critic gets these points across, and try to emulate his success, or avoid his failings. It goes without saying, we hope, that you should be willing to learn how to handle language from the authors whose works are your prescribed study. Be something of a magpie, then; pick up words, techniques and phrasing that attract you from wherever you find them. There are, of course, small risks involved in being stylistically adventurous. You risk the embarrassment of being told (kindly, we trust) by your teacher that your writing is somewhat inflated or pretentious, or that you have misused certain words or concepts. But don't let such experiences drive you back to the nervous, neutral jargon that characterizes so much student writing. You have time to adjust, refine, improve.

One last point about style: the line between sophisticated style and sheer blarney is a fine one, but discernable to the experienced eye. Purple prose will not conceal an absence of perception or close textural analysis. To be perfectly honest, students do, occasionally, get away with it. What do you think of this comment on *The Wild Swans at Coole*?

> These 'brilliant creatures' are timeless and unchanging, not growing old and decaying with man, but flitting like shafts of bright sunlight around the universe, impossible to trap. Unlike the poet, they are not drained of their quintessential life force by life itself. It is not for them to have their spirits settle like sediment in once fast-rushing water which is now becoming stagnant.

Somewhere in there a point is being made, and it's a point well worth making; but it's more than a little over-dressed. It isn't the most purple prose we've read, but it has a heavy violet tinge to it. The interesting thing is that it is a rather restrained example of the style usually adopted by a certain student who, shortly after he wrote those lines, went on to obtain a grade A in the examination. One can only assume that somewhere there was an examiner more than usually desperate to read something out of the ordinary. We think that, on the whole, it is rare for a candidate to achieve a good pass on the strength of his or her gift of the gab. You would be very foolish to gamble on impressing the examiner with mere grandiloquence. The essential quality of a truly good critical style is its ability to convey genuine insights with clarity and ease but without strain and fuss.

Now for the practicalities. The most important matter is essay structure, essay form. As we tried to explain in Chapter 10, form and meaning are inseparable. Without structure, words lose their meaning. A recent Examiner's Report contains (like so many others) the following comment: 'Too often, essays were formless . . . at the end, it was difficult to see what point had been made'. It was difficult to see the point *because* the essays were formless. Your observations, comments and ideas must interconnect, and must be seen to progress towards a conclusion. Unless you are confident that you have exceptional intellectual gifts, you would be unwise to begin improvising an essay structure only after you've entered the examination room and read the unseen passages. It is far more sensible to take in with you a preconceived *but flexible* plan for an essay. There are a number of ways of organizing a critical appreciation, and by the time you sit the exam, you should have experimented with more than one and decided which you find easiest to handle. Ideally, of course, you should be adept at organizing your material in more than one way.

Structuring an essay means, simply, mustering your various comments and observations into coherent groups, and then arranging these groups into a logical sequence. Let us suppose that you are about to embark upon your appreciation of a poem, and let us suppose you:

> *first:* read the thing straight through, probably more to satisfy your curiosity than anything else. As a result of this reading you feel either relieved, depressed, baffled or elated.

> *second:* read again, but this time more slowly and, very importantly, you read it 'aloud' silently. Thus you come to grips with the poem at its primary level, that of patterned sound. On this second reading you should become aware of the poem's overall rhythmic scheme and of certain techniques used by the poet to manipulate sound—metrical variations, or alliterations, or assonances or whatever—and where these occur you underline or otherwise mark the text in some way.

> *third:* read the poem yet again, perhaps noting technicalities you missed on your second reading. By now you should have some grasp of the poem's general characteristics, and you should write down a number of words which you think adequately describe the mood—the feeling and tone—of the poem. You should also, by now, be able to note down your general ideas or assumptions of what the poem is 'about'. 'e.g. Is it

'about' the images or the subject or actually 'about' the poet's attitude to them? Is it 'objective' or 'introspective'? Are there allegorical or symbolic levels to be considered? Does the poem present a problem and does it implicitly or explicitly resolve this problem? Does the poem assert a belief or does it express a question or a mystery?)

It is at this point that the hard work begins. You have a number of comments or questions of a general applicability to the poem, and you have noticed a number of linguistic phenomena. Now you should undertake a more methodical questioning of the poem's language (see Chapter 2) and its form (see Chapter 10). As we pointed out in those chapters, there are two main advantages to this close questioning: it enables you to test and adjust your already half-formulated general ideas, assumptions and opinions; and it enables you to justify your interpretative comments by means of detailed reference to the text.

All that we have described so far are preliminary stages of investigation to be undertaken before you begin to write or think about the structure of your essay. Written out in this step-by-step fashion they seem laborious and time-consuming. With practice, however, these preliminaries can be quite quickly completed; and of course, our division of them into distinct steps is artificial and made only for convenience. A well-prepared candidate should not have to proceed strictly in this 'by numbers' fashion. But we must stress that too many students produce poor critical appreciations because they spend insufficient time in reading the text carefully, and in gathering and arranging their material before they begin writing. Unless you are a painfully slow writer, you can safely spend one third of the allowed time preparing your essay.

Now, let us assume you have a good deal of material, consisting of generally applicable ideas, on the one hand, and detailed textual observations on the other. How can these be brought together into coherent groups? A recent Examiner's Report recommended that its candidates consider as 'workable guideline for analysis' the terms suggested by I. A. Richards: Feeling, Intention, Tone and Sense. This seems reasonable enough. Group your material under these headings. Let us suppose that at some point in the poem under consideration there is a noticeable deviation from the prevailing rhythm. Does this fluctuation indicate a change in the poet's *tone* (i.e. his attitude towards his subject-matter or towards the reader)? Or would it be more accurate to say that this rhythmic device has some effect upon the *sense* of the words at that point? If there is a sudden abruptness in the poet's diction (indicated, perhaps, by punctuation or by crisp alliteration), does it reveal something about his *feeling* or is its purpose to emphasize, and thus clarify his *intention*? Obviously, if you adopt Richards's categories, you must use them flexibly; they are *guidelines*, not strict divisions. If the basis of your essay-structure is to be the close examination of the poem stanza by stanza, you could apply these terms to each stanza in turn. In this case, your problem will be how to vary the emphasis on each, and how to connect your comments on, say, tone *across* the stanzas without being tiresomely repetitious. If, on the other hand, you decide to gather together points from different parts of the poem under these general headings, you will have to take care to show your awareness of the way Feeling, Intention, Tone and Sense *change* and *modulate* from stanza to stanza.

Another handy formula is 'the three Ts': Theme, Tone and Texture. *Theme* is not only the poem's subject-matter, but also the sequence of its images and thought; *tone* indicates the author's attitude towards his theme; and by *texture* we mean the way the writer uses language to achieve his effects. As we have said elsewhere, comments on texture—rhyme, sound-effects, rhythm, etc.—are meaningless unless you perceive their significance; you must try to say how they illuminate the poem's other elements. *How* you do this, and, for that matter, how you make the connections between ideas grasped under convenient headings, is almost entirely a matter of style and your personal vocabulary. You may find it easier to write one or two paragraphs at the end of your essay which pull together the threads of your essay, and thereby make an overall interpretation or evaluation; or you may find that your style lends itself to interspersing textual analysis and interpretative comment consistently throughout your essay. The important thing is to *be conscious of the direction your essay is taking*; the obvious practical advantage of planning your essay in advance is that you know what is to come next, and you can *write towards it*. Fluidity of style and clarity of presentation is, in the final analysis, dependent upon coherent structure. So if you do make an essay plan, keep to it.

Students have often said to us 'I'm all right once I've got started', or 'I didn't really know how to end it. . . .' Introductions and conclusions to essays are admittedly tricky. As far as writing introductions is concerned, perhaps the best advice would be simply 'don't'. It seems to us that lots of candidates write 'introductions' just to make sure their pens are working properly. A 'general introduction' is almost certain to irritate examiners, who like specifics; and until you've written some close textual analysis, your marker has no way of knowing if you are 'waffling' or not. The best thing is to get straight down to it. An appreciation which begins: 'This poem is very moving. Its imagery is drawn largely from Nature and is effective; the rhythm is regular and musical . . .' is likely to get a hostile reception. One that begins something like: 'Until I read the fifth line I thought the poem was going to concern itself with . . .' will do better. Remember, once more, our poor examiner who has already marked many papers; he needs to be stimulated by your essay from the very first. I once read an essay on *King Lear* which began: 'King Lear is a stupid old man. . . .' The essay then commenced to qualify the statement, but this opening was outrageous enough to provoke interest. We are not suggesting that you should practise dramatic opening lines, but your first sentence, and your first paragraph, could be at least business-like and energetic.

'Conclusions' to essays are equally full of pitfalls. Too frequently, a concluding paragraph has been a lame repetition or rephrasing of what has already been said. If a conclusion has nothing new to add, then it isn't worth writing. Should you find yourself trying to round off your essay with a paragraph that begins: 'Thus it can be seen that . . .' or 'On the whole, then, this poem . . .' it is time to stop and ask yourself if you really have anything else to say. There is, in this respect, an advantage in writing the kind of essay which follows the poem stanza by stanza or section by section and develops your interpretation as you progress; you can frame your commentary on the poem's ending so that it brings your study to a natural conclusion.

It has been assumed, in this book, that you have been asked to write an appreciation of all the aspects of a single poem, but the comments are applicable (with commonsense modifications) to questions which ask you to compare two poems, or which specify certain facets of a poem or poems upon which to concentrate. In the latter case, where the examination rubric may instruct you to 'Compare the relationship of the speaker of each poem with the natural world' or to 'discuss the way in which the poet conveys his feelings about war', you must obviously direct your questioning of the poems' language and form towards these ends. Examiners' Reports are often at pains to point out that candidates have blithely ignored the specifications of a paper's rubric and written general appreciations. It is frequently said that essays in comparison are easier to write than 'straightforward' appreciations of single poems. This is true only in that you have more 'raw material'; the problems involved in organizing your essay are more complex. When you are comparing two poems (or two pieces of prose) you should not be constantly switching (or twitching, rather) from one to the other, endlessly contrasting

141

points of detail. As one Examiners' Report put it: 'too many answers chopped and changed from one [poem] to the other without ever allowing themselves sufficient breathing space to develop an argument satisfactorily'. You would do better to compare, say, the *tone* of each, then move on to discuss the *sense* of each, and thus bring together points from both poems into coherent topics. Since in comparing two pieces of writing some kind of evaluation is almost inevitable, it is no bad idea to begin by stating which you prefer, and to develop your essay as a carefully contextualized justification of this preference.

Most of the suggestions that have been made in this chapter may be applied (again with qualifications) to prose also. Although in a passage of fiction you will have to consider such matters as narrative technique, dialogue, and so forth, you can apply the same kind of linguistic scrutiny to prose as to poetry. You might find too that it is useful to consider a prose extract by means of the concepts suggested as guidelines for poetry appreciation—theme, tone, texture; feeling, intention, tone and sense.

Practice Exercises

The 'Papers' that follow do not attempt to imitate the format or the rubric of those of any one particular Examination Board. Rather, we have tried to select for question poems and prose passages fairly representative of the material used by all Boards and relevant to the needs of all candidates. Some of these exercises involve the comparison of two pieces and some do not. The questions we have posed are perhaps more precisely directed than many asked by examiners; they are meant to be helpful suggestions as well as interrogations. (This is because we have often found that the unqualified command 'comment on the style of the following passage' produces paralysis of the mind.)

I

The following two short poems commemorate dead ladies.

A.   **On the Dowager Countess of Pembroke**

     Underneath this sable hearse
     Lies the subject of all verse,
     Sidney's sister, Pembroke's mother;
     Death, ere thou hast slain another
5   Fair and learn'd and good as she,
     Time shall throw a dart at thee.

B.   **Epitaph on the Lady Mary Villiers**

     The Lady Mary Villiers lies
     Under this stone; with weeping eyes
     The parents that first gave her breath,
     And their sad friends, laid her in earth.
5   If any of them, reader, were
     Known unto thee, shed a tear.
     Or if thyself possess a gem
     As dear to thee as this to them,
     Though a stranger to this place
10   Bewail in theirs thine own hard case,
     For thou perhaps at thy return
     May'st find thy darling in an urn.

Both are composed to be engraved on a tomb. Compare and evaluate the effectiveness of each, bearing in mind these questions:
To whom is each addressed?
What is the *tone* of each?
How does each achieve a certain surprise effect? (Consider use of metrical and rhythmic variations, rhyme and imagery.)
Does one or both somehow manage to transcend the merely commemorative function of the epitaph?

Read the following passage carefully and then:
1.   Comment on the meaning and aptness of:
     a. allowed herself to collapse (4)
     b. meditative tone (13)
     c. languid stroll (18)
     d. the sentimental foolish Snort (35–36)
2.   Comment on the contributions made by the rhythm and syntax
    to the meaning of the sentence:
    The two children . . . lumps of earth (27–30).

144

3. Comment on the meaning and significance of this encounter between a father and his two children.

Jenny had got up and wandered away among the trees; her legs too were bare and dirty, and her dress had a large green stain at the side. She had been in the pond. And now Kate allowed herself to collapse slowly out of the swing and lay on
5   her back with her hair tousled in the dirt, her arms thrown apart, her small dirty hands with black nails turned palm upwards to the sky. Her cocker bitch, Snort, came loping and sniffing, uttered one short bark and rooted at her mistress' legs. Kate raised one foot and tickled her stomach, then rolled
10 over and buried her face in her arms. When Snort tried to push her nose under Kate's thigh as if to turn her over, she made a half kick and murmured, 'Go away, Snort.'
'Stop it, Snort,' Jenny echoed in the same meditative tone. The sisters adored each other and one always came to the
15 other's help. But Snort only stopped a moment to gaze at Jenny, then tugged at Kate's dress. Kate made another more energetic kick and said, 'Oh, do go away, Snort.'
Jenny stopped in her languid stroll, snatched a bamboo from the border, and hurled it at Snort like a spear.
20 The bitch, startled, uttered a loud uncertain bark and approached, wagging her behind so vigorously that she curled her body sideways at each wag. She was not sure if this was a new game, or if she had committed some grave crime. Jenny gave a yell and rushed to her. She fled yelping. At once Kate
25 jumped up, seized another bamboo and threw it, shouting 'Tiger, tiger!'
The two children dashed after the bitch, laughing, bumping together, falling over each other and snatching up anything they could find to throw at the fugitive: pebbles, dead daffo-
30 dils, bits of flower-pots, lumps of earth. Snort, horrified, overwhelmed, dodged to and fro, barked hysterically, crazily, wagged her tail in desperate submission; finally put it between her legs and crept whining between a broken shed and the wall.
35 Robert was shocked. He was fond of the sentimental foolish Snort, and he saw her acute misery. He called to the children urgently, 'Hi, Jenny—don't do that. Don't do that, Kate. She's frightened—you might put her eye out. Hi, stop—stop.'
This last cry expressed real indignation. Jenny had got hold
40 of a rake and was trying to hook Snort by the collar. Robert began to struggle out of his chair. But suddenly Kate turned round, aimed a pea-stick at him and shouted at the top of her

voice, 'Yield, Paleface.' Jenny at once turned and cried, 'Yes, yes—Paleface, yield.' She burst into a shout of laughter
45 and could not speak, but rushed at the man with the rake carried like a lance.

The two girls, staggering with laughter, threw themselves upon their father. 'Paleface—Paleface Robbie. Kill him—scalp him. Torture him.'
50 They tore at the man and suddenly he was frightened. It seemed to him that both the children, usually so gentle, so affectionate, had gone completely mad, vindictive. They were hurting him, and he did not know how to defend himself without hurting them, without breaking their skinny bones,
55 which seemed as fragile as a bird's legs. He dared not even push too hard against the thin ribs which seemed to bend under his hand. Snort, suddenly recovering confidence, rushed barking from cover and seized this new victim by the sleeve, grunting and tugging.
60 'Hi,' he shouted, trying to catch at the bitch. 'Call her off, Kate. Don't, don't, children.' But they battered at him, Kate was jumping on his stomach, Jenny had seized him by the collar as if to strangle him. Her face, close to his own, was that of a homicidal maniac; her eyes were wide and glaring,
65 her lips were curled back to show all her teeth. And he was really strangling. He made a violent effort to throw the child off, but her hands were firmly twined in his collar. He felt his ears sing. Then suddenly the chair gave way—all three fell with a crash. Snort, startled, and perhaps pinched, gave a
70 yelp, and snapped at the man's face.

An Elementary School Classroom in a Slum

Far from gusty waves, these children's faces.
Like rootless weeds the torn hair round their paleness.
The tall girl with her weighed-down head. The paper—
Seeming boy with rat's eyes. The stunted unlucky heir
5 Of twisted bones, reciting a father's gnarled disease,
His lesson from his desk. At back of the dim class,
One unnoted, sweet and young: his eyes live in a dream
Of squirrel's game, in tree room, other than this.

On sour cream walls, donations. Shakespeare's head
10 Cloudless at dawn, civilized dome riding all cities.
Belled, flowery, Tyrolese valley. Open-handed map
Awarding the world its world. And yet, for these
Children, these windows, not this world, are world,
Where all their future's painted with a fog,
15 A narrow street sealed in with a lead sky,
Far far from rivers, capes, and stars of words.

Surely Shakespeare is wicked, the map a bad example
With ships and sun and love tempting them to steal—
For lives that slyly turn in their cramped holes
20 From fog to endless night? On their slag heap, these children
Wear skins peeped through by bones and spectacles of steel
With mended glass, like bottle bits on stones.
All of their time and space are foggy slum
So blot their maps with slums as big as doom.

25 Unless, governor, teacher, inspector, visitor,
This map becomes their window and these windows
That open on their lives like crouching tombs
Break, O break open, till they break the town
And show the children to the fields and all their world
30 Azure on their sands, to let their tongues
Run naked into books, the white and green leaves open
The history theirs whose language is the sun.

Comment on the significance and effectiveness of:
  (i)   *The stunted unlucky heir*
      Of twisted bones, reciting a father's gnarled disease,
    His lesson from his desk. (stanza 1)

(ii) The shifts in meaning of the word *world* in the second stanza.
(iii) *For lives that slyly turn in their cramped holes*
      From fog to endless night   (stanza 3)
(iv) The imagery of the final four lines of the poem.

Write an appreciation of the poem, considering such matters as imagery and rhythm, and trying to convey the way in which the poet expresses his attitude towards the situation of the children and the way they are educated.

Read the following passage carefully and then:
(i)   comment on the meaning and aptness of
      a. *magistrates and the like* (line 5)
      b. *toiling away in solemn foolery* (line 45)
      c. *one world less* (line 53)
(ii) *A dreadful thing happened.* . . . Explain the significance of the episode involving the dog.
(iii) What attitude does the writer have towards
      a. his colleagues,
      b. the prisoner?
(iv) How would you classify this writing as a piece of prose? Give your reasons.

We set out for the gallows. Two warders marched on either side of the prisoner, with their rifles at the slope; two others marched close against him, gripping him by arm and shoulder, as though at once pushing and supporting him. The rest of us,
5   magistrates and the like, followed behind. Suddenly, when we had gone ten yards, the procession stopped short without any warning. A dreadful thing had happened—a dog, come goodness knows whence, had appeared in the yard. It came bounding among us with a loud volley of barks and leapt
10 round us wagging its whole body, wild with glee at finding so many human beings together. It was a large woolly dog, half Airedale, half pariah. For a moment it pranced round us, and then, before anyone could stop it, it had made a dash for the prisoner, and jumping up tried to lick his face. Everybody
15 stood aghast, too taken aback even to grab the dog.
    'Who let that bloody brute in here?' said the superintendent angrily. 'Catch it, someone!'
    A warder, detached from the escort, charged clumsily after the dog, but it danced and gambolled just out of his reach,
20 taking everything as part of the game. A young Eurasian jailer picked up a handful of gravel and tried to stone the dog away, but it dodged the stones and came after us again. Its yaps

148

echoed from the jail walls. The prisoner, in the grasp of the
two warders, looked on incuriously, as though this was
25 another formality of the hanging. It was several minutes
before someone managed to catch the dog. Then we put my
handkerchief through its collar and moved off once more, with
the dog still straining and whimpering.

It was about forty yards to the gallows. I watched the bare
30 brown back of the prisoner marching in front of me. He
walked clumsily with his bound arms, but quite steadily, with
that bobbling gait of the Indian who never straightens his
knees. At each step his muscles slid neatly into place, the lock
of hair on his scalp danced up and down, his feet printed
35 themselves on the wet gravel. And once, in spite of the men
who gripped him by each shoulder, he stepped slightly aside
to avoid a puddle on the path.

It is curious, but till that moment I had never realized what
it means to destroy a healthy, conscious man. When I saw the
40 prisoner step aside to avoid the puddle I saw the mystery, the
unspeakable wrongness, of cutting a life short when it is in
full tide. This man was not dying, he was alive just as we are
alive. All the organs of his body were working—bowels
digesting food, skin renewing itself, nails growing, tissues
45 forming—all toiling away in solemn foolery. His nails would
still be growing when he stood on the drop, when he was
falling through the air with a tenth of a second to live. His
eyes saw the yellow gravel and the grey walls, and his brain
still remembered, foresaw, reasoned—even about puddles. He
50 and we were a party of men walking together, seeing,
hearing, feeling, understanding the same world; and in two
minutes, with a sudden snap, one of us would be gone—one
mind less, one world less.

III

Both of the following extracts are concerned with the effects of
industrialization on the English landscape. Extract A is from an
essay, extract B from a novel. Read them both carefully and then:

Extract A
1. Comment on the meaning and aptness of:
   a. palmy Victorian days (line 4)
   b. a blind reaching out (line 11)
   c. competition of mere acquisition (line 35)
2. Examine and discuss the stylistic methods used by the writer to
   put over his point of view.

Extract B
1. Comment on the meaning and aptness of:
   a. the painted face of a savage (line 4)
   b. interminable serpents of smoke (line 5)
   c. the head of an elephant in a state of melancholy madness
      (lines 11-12)
   d. pious warehouse (line 29)
   e. fact (lines 39–40)
2. Comment on the rhythm and syntax of the following sentences:
   a. It contained . . . and the next. (first paragraph)
   b. The M'Choakumchild school . . . Amen. (final paragraph)

From both Extracts
1. In what ways are the approaches by these different writers
   towards this subject a. Similar?
                        b. Different?
2. Which do you personally feel is the more effective? Give your
   reasons.

A   Now though perhaps nobody knew it, it was ugliness which
really betrayed the spirit of man, in the nineteenth century.
The great crime which the moneyed classes and promoters of
industry committed in the palmy Victorian days was the con-
5   demning of the workers to ugliness, ugliness, ugliness: meanness
and formless and ugly surroundings, ugly ideals, ugly religion,
ugly hope, ugly love, ugly clothes, ugly furniture, ugly houses,
ugly relationship between workers and employers. The human
soul needs actual beauty even more than bread. The middle
10 classes jeer at the colliers for buying pianos—but what is the
piano, often as not, but a blind reaching out for beauty? To the
woman it is a possession and a piece of furniture and something to feel superior about. But see the elderly colliers trying

150

to learn to play, see them listening with queer alert faces to
15 their daughter's execution of 'The Maiden's Prayer', and you
will see a blind, unsatisfied craving for beauty. It is far more
deep in the men than the women. The women want show. The
men want beauty, and still want it.

If the company, instead of building those sordid and hideous
20 Squares, then, when they had that lovely site to play with,
there on the hill top: if they had put a tall column in the middle
of the small market-place, and run three parts of a circle of
arcade round the pleasant space, where people could stroll or
sit, and with handsome houses behind! If they had made big,
25 substantial houses, in apartments of five or six rooms, and
with handsome entrances. If above all, they had encouraged
song and dancing—for the miners still sang and danced—
and provided handsome space for these. If only they had
encouraged some form of beauty in dress, some form of beauty
30 in interior life—furniture, decoration. If they had given prizes
for the handsomest chair or table, the loveliest scarf, the most
charming room that the men or women could make! If only
they had done this, there would never have been an industrial
problem. The industrial problem arises from the base forcing
35 of all human energy into a competition of mere acquisition.

B   It was a town of red brick, or of brick that would have been
red if the smoke and ashes had allowed it; but, as matters
stood it was a town of unnatural red and black like the
painted face of a savage. It was a town of machinery and tall
5 chimneys, out of which interminable serpents of smoke trailed
themselves for ever and ever, and never got uncoiled. It had
a black canal in it, and a river that ran purple with ill-
smelling dye, and vast piles of building full of windows where
there was a rattling and a trembling all day long, and where
10 the piston of the steam-engine worked monotonously up and
down, like the head of an elephant in a state of melancholy
madness. It contained several large streets all very like one
another, and many small streets still more like one another,
inhabited by people equally like one another, who all went in
15 and out at the same hours, with the same sound upon the
same pavements, to do the same work, and to whom every day
was the same as yesterday and tomorrow, and every year the
counterpart of the last and the next.

These attributes of Coketown were in the main inseparable
20 from the work by which it was sustained; against them were
to be set off, comforts of life which found their way all over

151

the world, and elegancies of life which made, we will not ask
how much of the fine lady, who could scarcely bear to hear
25 the place mentioned. The rest of its features were voluntary,
and they were these.

You saw nothing in Coketown but what was severely
workful. If the members of a religious persuasion built a
chapel there—as the members of eighteen religious persuasions
had done—they made it a pious warehouse of red brick, with
30 sometimes (but this only in highly ornamented examples) a
bell in a bird-cage on the top of it. The solitary exception was
the New Church; a stuccoed edifice with a square steeple over
the door, terminating in four short pinnacles like florid wooden
legs. All the public inscriptions in the town were painted
35 alike, in severe characters of black and white. The jail
might have been the infirmary, the infirmary might have been
the jail, the town-hall might have been either, or both, or
anything else, for anything that appeared to the contrary in
the graces of their construction. Fact, fact, fact, everywhere
40 in the material aspect of the town; fact, fact, fact, everywhere in the immaterial. The M'Choakumchild school was all
fact, and the school of design was all fact, and the relations
between master and man were all fact, and everything was
fact between the lying-in hospital and the cemetery, and what
45 you couldn't state in figures, or show to be purchaseable in
the cheapest market and saleable in the dearest, was not, and
never should be, world without end, Amen.

Write a study of the following poem, paying attention to such
matters as imagery, the modulation of sound and rhythm, and the
poet's tone. Say, too, what you like or dislike about it.

The Survivor

Yesterday I found one left:
Eighty-five, too old for mischief.
What strange grace lends him brief
Time for repenting of his theft
Of health and comeliness of her
Who lay caught in his strong arms
Night by night and heard the farm's
Noises, the beasts moan and stir?

The land's thug: seventeen stone,
Settling down in a warm corner
By a wood fire's lazy purr;

A slumped bundle of fat and bone,
Bragging endlessly of his feats
Of strength and skill with the long scythe,
Of gallantry among the blithe
Serving women, all on heat

For him, of course. My mind went back
Sombrely to that rough parish,
Lovely as the eye could wish
In its green clothes, but beaten black
And blue by the deeds of dour men
Too like him, warped inside
And given to watching, sullen-eyed,
Love still-born, as it was then.

Wake him up. It is too late
Now for the blood's foolish dreaming.
The veins clog and the body's spring
Is long past; pride and hate
Are the strong's fodder and the young.
Old and weak, he must chew now
The cud of prayer and be taught how
From hard hearts huge tears are wrung.

Read this extract carefully, and then answer the questions below. (Norman Mailer, the American writer, has been arrested for his part in a political demonstration outside the Pentagon, Washington. He contemplates the Marshals on duty at the prisoners' 'reception centre.')

(i) Explain the meaning and comment on the effectiveness of the following phrases:
    a. *those subtle anomalies of the body* (line 17)
    b. *odd cleaving wrinkles* (line 22)
    c. *in comfortable circumstances with himself* (line 32)
    d. *emitted a collective spirit* (line 38)

(ii) What impression do you receive of the Marshals described?

(iii) Why do you think the author speaks of himself in the third person?

(iv) Mailer's book from which this passage is taken is subtitled *History as a Novel, the Novel as History.* Comment on this extract as a piece of reporting.

    Outside, a truck would arrive every five or ten minutes and some boys and girls would dismount and go to the base of the loading platform to be booked, the boys to enter the bus, the girls to go off to another bus. Still no sign of Lowell or
5 Macdonald. Mailer kept hoping they would appear in the next haul of prisoners. After a while he began to study the Marshals.
    Their faces were considerably worse then he had expected. He had had the fortune to be arrested by a man who was
10 incontestably one of the pleasanter Marshals on duty at the Pentagon, he had next met what must be the toughest Marshal in the place—the two had given him a false spectrum. The gang of Marshals now studied outside the bus were enough to firm up any fading loyalty to his own cause: they had the kind
15 of faces which belong to the bad guys in a Western. Some were fat, some were too thin, but nearly all seemed to have those subtle anomalies of the body which come often to men from small towns who have inherited strong features, but end up, by their own measure, in failure. Some would have
20 powerful chests, but abrupt paunches, the skinny ones would have a knob in the shoulder, or a hitch in their gait, their foreheads would have odd cleaving wrinkles, so that one man might look as if an axe had struck him between the eyes, another paid tithe to ten parallel deep lines rising in ridges
25 above his eye brows. The faces of all too many had a low

cunning mixed with a stroke of rectitude: if the mouth was
slack, the nose was straight and severe; should the lips be
tight, the nostrils showed an outsize greed. Many of them
looked to be ex-First Sergeants, for they liked to stand with
30 the heels of their hands on the top of their hips, or they had
that way of walking, belly forward, which a man will promote
when he is in comfortable circumstances with himself and
packing a revolver in a belt holster. The toes turn out; the
belly struts. They were older men than he might have expected,
35 some in their late thirties, more in their forties, a few looked
to be over fifty, but then that may have been why they were
here to receive prisoners rather than out on the line—in any
case they emitted a collective spirit which, to his mind, spoke of
little which was good, for their eyes were blank and dull, that
40 familiar small-town cast of eye which speaks of apathy rising
to fanaticism only to subside in apathy again. (Mailer had
wondered more than once at that curious demand of small-
town life which leaves something good and bright in the eyes
of some, is so deadening for others—it was his impression
45 that people in small towns had eyes which were generally
livelier or emptier than the more concentrated look of city
vision.)

The following two poems have the same subject—London. They
were written within a few years of each other, but differ dramatically in form and tone. Write a study comparing the two, with
particular reference to the relationship between form and tone in
each.

A.   **Upon Westminster Bridge**

           Earth has not anything to show more fair:
           Dull would he be of soul who could pass by
           A sight so touching in its majesty:
           This city now doth like a garment wear
5   The beauty of the morning; silent, bare,
           Ships, towers, domes, theatres, and temples lie
           Open unto the fields, and to the sky;
           All bright and glittering in the smokeless air.
           Never did sun more beautifully steep
10   In his first splendour valley, rock or hill;
           Ne'er saw I, never felt, a calm so deep!
           The river glideth at his own sweet will:
           Dear God! the very houses seem asleep;
           And all that mighty heart is lying still!

B.   **London**

I wander thro' each chartered street,
Near where the chartered Thames does flow,
And mark in every face I meet
Marks of weakness, marks of woe.

5   In every cry of every man,
In every infant's cry of fear,
In every voice, in every ban,
The mind-forged manacles I hear.

How the chimney-sweeper's cry
10   Every blackening church appalls;
And the hapless soldier's sigh
Runs in blood down palace walls.

But most thro' midnight streets I hear
How the youthful harlot's curse
15   Blasts the new-born infant's tear,
And blights with plagues the marriage hearse.

The Woman at Washington Zoo

The saris go by me from the embassies.
Cloth from the moon. Cloth from another planet.
They look back at the leopard like the leopard.
And I . . . This print of mine, that has kept its colour
5 Alive through so many cleanings; this dull null
Navy I wear to work, and wear from work, and so
To my bed, so to my grave, with no
Complaints, no comment: neither from my chief,
The Deputy Chief Assistant, nor his chief—
10 Only I complain; this serviceable
Body that no sunlight dyes, no hand suffuses
But dome-shadowed, withering among columns,
Wavy beneath fountains—small, far-off, shining
In the eyes of animals, these beings trapped
15 As I am trapped but not, themselves, the trap,
Ageing, but without knowledge of their age,
Kept safe here, knowing not of death, for death
—Oh, bars of my own body, open, open!

The world goes by my cage and never sees me.
20 And there come not to me, as come to these,
The wild beasts, sparrows pecking at the llama's grain,
Pigeons settling on the bears' bread, buzzards
Tearing the meat the flies have clouded . . .
                                        Vulture,
When you come for the white rat that the foxes left,
25 Take off the red helmet of your head, the black
Wings that have shadowed me, and step to me as man,
The wild brother at whose feet the white wolves fawn,
To whose hand of power the great lioness
Stalks, purring . . .
30   You know what I was,
You see what I am: change me, change me!

Write a critical appreciation of this poem. Contemplating the
following questions may help you.
 (i) The speaker is the woman of the title. What do you under-
      stand of her character and her view of her life? In this
      context, what is the significance of Deputy Chief Assistant
      (line 9), of serviceable (line 10), her interrupting herself at
      line 18?

(ii) The poem divides into irregular stanzas; how do these relate to the development of the poem?

(iii) How does the rhythm change at line 19, and to what effect?

(iv) What do the last nine lines disclose about the speaker's feelings about animals?

Read the following passage carefully and then

(i) Discuss the meaning and aptness of:
   a. *capacity for self-deception* (line 9)
   b. *primary creative order* (line 27)
   c. *no masculine aspiring* (line 23)
   d. *piquant twist to what is already accepted* (line 29)

(ii) Comment on the character of the narrator of this passage, as revealed by his interpretation of the facts he selects for presentation.

Myrtle was very feminine, and I have described up to date those of her traits which everyone recognizes as essentially feminine. She was modest, she was submissive, she was sly; she was earthy in its most beautiful sense.

5   In addition to all this, Myrtle was shrewd, she was persistent, and she was determined. At the time I thought she was too young to know what she wanted. Looking back on it I can only reel at the thought of my own absence of insight and capacity for self-deception. She knew what she wanted all

10 right: it is just possible that she was too young to know exactly how to get it.

Myrtle was a commercial artist, employed by a prosperous advertising agency in the town. In my opinion, based on her salary, she was doing well. This much at least I could see. At

15 a hint of the intellectual Myrtle's eyes opened in wonderment, at a hint of the salacious she blushed; and at a hint of business she was thoroughly on the alert.

Myrtle had been trained at the local School of Art. She had talent of a modest order—that is, it was greater than she

20 pretended. Her drawings were quick, lively, observant without being reflective, pretty and quite perceptibly original. I, with her talent, would have been trying to paint like Dufy or somebody: not so, Myrtle. There was no masculine aspiring about her. Trying to paint like Dufy with her talent I should

25 have been a masculine failure. Myrtle with feminine modesty and innocence took to commercial art.

Myrtle's talent was not of the primary creative order that sometimes alarms the public: it was the secondary talent for

giving a piquant twist to what is already accepted. She was
30   made for the world of advertising. And she accepted her
station in life as an artist as readily as she accepted her
salary. My efforts to encourage her to rise above this station,
which would have brought her little but misery, fortunately
made no impression upon her whatsoever.
35   In her business dealings Myrtle showed the same flair. It
was one of her gifts to accept quite readily men's weaknesses.
She was tolerant and down-to-earth about them: she fought
against them much less than many a man does.
Myrtle's employer was a middle-aged man who had intro-
40   duced his mistress into a comparatively important position in the
firm—to the envy and disapprobation of everyone but Myrtle.
Myrtle accepted that such things were likely to happen, made
the best of it, and showed good natured interest in the other
girl. In due course Myrtle found, to her genuine surprise, that
45   the boss began to show much greater appreciation of her work.
So you see that Myrtle was by no means a poor, helpless
girl who had fallen into the clutches of an unscrupulous, lust-
ridden man. I may say that I saw it, plainly, while I sat in the
café with Tom reading his doom-struck newspaper. I was
50   behaving like a cad—admitted. But anyone who thinks behaving like a cad was easy is wrong.

VI

(Dennis Barlow arrives at 'Whispering Glades', an exclusive firm of Californian undertakers.)

Read the passage carefully and then:

(i) Comment on the meaning and effectiveness of the following phrases:
   a. *sterilized and transmuted* (line 24)
   b. *great cumulus of flowers* (line 31)
   c. *in full rig* (line 33)
   d. *some starched and jewelled courtship* (lines 35–36)
   e. *the thick pelt of mobility and intelligence* (lines 50–51)

(ii) Comment on the writer's use of language in the third and fourth paragraphs.
   (You might well look at phrases such as '*poignant sweetness, enchanted stillness, leaded casements*')

(iii) Describe the kind of humour present and explain how it is achieved.

The funeral was fixed for Thursday; Wednesday afternoon was the time for leave-taking in the Slumber Room. That morning Dennis called at Whispering Glades to see that everything was in order.

5   He was shown straight to the Orchid Room. Flowers had arrived in great quantities, mostly from the shop below, mostly in their 'natural beauty'. (After consultation the Cricket Club's fine trophy in the shape of cross bats and wickets had been admitted. Dr Kenworthy had himself given judgement; the
10 trophy was essentially a reminder of life, not of death; that was the crux.) The ante-room was so full of flowers that there seemed no other furniture or decoration; double doors led to the Slumber Room proper.

    Dennis hesitated with his fingers on the handle and was aware
15 of communication with another hand beyond the panels. Thus in a hundred novels had lovers stood. The door opened and Aimée Thanatogenos stood quite close to him; behind her more, many more flowers and all about her a rich hot-house scent and the low voices of a choir discoursing sacred music from the
20 cornice. At the moment of their meeting a treble voice broke out with poignant sweetness: 'Oh for the Wings of a Dove.'

    No breath stirred the enchanted stillness of the two rooms. The leaded casements were screwed tight. The air came, like the boy's voice, from far away, sterilized and transmuted.
25 The temperature was slightly cooler than is usual in American dwellings. The rooms seemed isolated and unnaturally quiet,

160

like a railway coach that has stopped in the night far from any station.

'Come in, Mr Barlow.'

30   Aimée stood aside and now Dennis saw that the centre of the room was filled with a great cumulus of flowers. Dennis was too young ever to have seen an Edwardian conservatory in full rig but he knew the literature of the period and in his imagination had seen such a picture; it was all there, even the
35   gilt chairs disposed in pairs as though for some starched and jewelled courtship.

There was no catafalque. The coffin stood a few inches from the carpet on a base that was hidden in floral enrichments. Half the lid was open. Sir Francis was visible from the
40   waist up. Dennis thought of the wax-work of Marat in his bath.

The shroud had been made to fit admirably. There was a fresh gardenia in the buttonhole and another between the fingers. The hair was snow-white and parted in a straight line from brow to crown revealing the scalp below, colourless and
45   smooth as though the skin had rolled away and the enduring skull already lay exposed. The gold rim of the monocle framed a delicately tinted eyelid.

The complete stillness was more startling than any violent action. The body looked altogether smaller than life-size now
50   that it was, as it were, stripped of the thick pelt of mobility and intelligence. And the face which inclined its blind eyes towards him—the face was entirely horrible; as ageless as a tortoise and as inhuman; a painted and smirking obscene travesty by comparison with which the devil-mask Dennis had
55   found in the noose was a festive adornment, a thing an uncle might don at a Christmas party.

Aimée stood beside her handiwork—the painter at the private view—and heard Dennis draw his breath in sudden emotion.

60   'Is it what you hoped?' she asked.

'More'—and then—'Is he quite hard?'

'Firm.'

'May I touch him?'

'Please not. It leaves a mark.'

65   'Very well.'

Then in accordance with the etiquette of the place, she left him to his reflections.

A critic not normally given to the use of superlatives has said: "If the word great means anything in poetry, this poem is one of the greatest in the English language". What possible grounds are there for such a high evaluation? Do you concur with it? In answering this question, pay close attention to the writer's use of imagery and the effect of the *apparently* simple structure of the poem.

Because I Could Not Stop for Death

Because I could not stop for Death,
He kindly stopped for me;
The carriage held but just ourselves
And Immortality.

5 We slowly drove, he knew no haste,
And I had put away
My labour, and my leisure too,
For his civility.

We passed the school where children played,
10 Their lessons scarcely done;
We passed the fields of grazing grain,
We passed the setting sun.

We paused before a house that seemed
A swelling on the ground;
15 The roof was scarcely visible,
The cornice but a mound.

Since then 'tis centuries; but each
Feels shorter than the day
I first surmised the horses' heads
20 Were toward eternity.

VII

Both of the extracts printed below deal with a group of people on an 'outing' of one sort or another. Extract A was first published in 1815, Extract B in 1973. Read the passages carefully and then:

Extract A
 (i) Comment on the meaning and aptness of the following phrases:
   a. *all the honest pride and complacency* (line 7)
   b. *untainted in blood and understanding* (lines 20–21)
   c. *all her apparatus of happiness* (line 29)
 (ii) The 'alliance' referred to in line 8 is that of marriage. From whose viewpoint do we see the 'Abbey'? What impressions are given of Emma and her future home?
 (iii) Discuss the rhythm and syntax of the sentence:
   'The best fruit in England . . . sit in the shade.' (lines 32–46)
 (iv) What impression do we receive of Mrs. Elton from this extract?

Extract B
 (i) Comment on the irony of:
   a. *then been cleared away themselves* (lines 12–13)
   b. *they could not help giving away their positions* (lines 33–34)
   c. *the poor moaning breathless creature* (lines 44–45)
 (ii) What effects does the author achieve by presenting the facts contained in paragraph one *before* the description of the picnic?
 (iii) What is the attitude of the writer towards his fictional characters in this extract?

Both Extracts
 (i) Describe briefly the kinds of humour present in both extracts and say to what extent the humour depends upon narrative viewpoint.
 (ii) Comment of the style of both passages, paying particular attention to such matters as rhythm, vocabulary, syntax and irony.

A   It was so long since Emma had been at the Abbey, that as soon as she was satisfied of her father's comfort, she was glad to leave him, and look around her; eager to refresh and correct her memory with more particular observation, more exact
5   understanding of a house and grounds which must ever be so interesting to her and all her family.
     She felt all the honest pride and complacency which her alliance with the present and future proprietor could fairly warrant, as she viewed the respectable size and style of the

163

10   building, its suitable, becoming, characteristic situation, low
      and sheltered—its ample gardens stretching down to meadows
      washed by a stream, of which the Abbey, with all the old
      neglect of prospect, had scarcely a sight—and its abundance
      of timber in rows and avenues, which neither fashion nor
15   extravagance had rooted up.—The house was larger than
      Hartfield, and totally unlike it, covering a good deal of ground,
      rambling and irregular, with many comfortable and one or
      two handsome rooms.—It was just what it ought to be, and it
      looked what it was—and Emma felt an increasing respect for
20   it, as the residence of a family of such true gentility, untainted
      in blood and understanding. Some faults of temper John
      Knightley had; but Isabella had connected herself unexcep-
      tionably. She had given them neither men, nor names, nor
      places, that could raise a blush. These were pleasant feelings,
25   and she walked about and indulged them till it was necessary
      to do as the others did, and collect round the strawberry beds.
      —The whole party were assembled, excepting Frank Churchill,
      who was expected every moment from Richmond; and Mrs.
      Elton, in all her apparatus of happiness, her large bonnet and
30   her basket, was very ready to lead the way in gathering,
      accepting, or talking—strawberries, and only strawberries,
      could now be thought or spoken of. 'The best fruit in England—
      everybody's favourite—always wholesome.—These the finest
      beds and finest sorts.—Delightful to gather for one's self—the
35   only way of really enjoying them.—Morning decidedly the best
      time—never tired—every sort good—hautboy infinitely superior
      —no comparison—the others hardly eatable—hautboys very
      scarce—Chili preferred—white wood finest flavour of all—
      price of strawberries in London—abundance about Bristol—
40   Maple Grove—cultivation—beds when to be renewed—garden-
      ers thinking exactly different—no general rule—gardeners
      never to be put out of their way—delicious fruit—only too rich
      to be eaten much of—inferior to cherries—currants more
      refreshing—only objection to gathering strawberries the
45   stooping—glaring sun—tired to death—could bear it no longer
      —must go and sit in the shade.'
          Such, for half an hour, was the conversation—interrupted
      only once by Mrs. Weston, who came out, in her solicitude
      after her son-in-law, to inquire if he were come—and she was
50   a little uneasy.—She had some fears of his horse.
          Seats tolerably in the shade were found; and now Emma was
      obliged to overhear what Mrs. Elton and Jane Fairfax were
      talking of.—A situation, a most desirable situation, was in
      question. Mrs. Elton had received notice of it that morning,

55 and was in raptures. It was not with Mrs. Suckling, it was not
with Mrs. Bragge, but in felicity and splendour it fell short
only of them: it was with a cousin of Mrs. Bragge, an acquaintance of Mrs. Suckling, a lady known at Maple Grove. Delightful, charming, superior, first circles, spheres, lines, ranks,
60 everything—and Mrs. Elton was wild to have the offer closed
with immediately.—On her side, all was warmth, energy, and
triumph—and she positively refused to take her friend's
negative, though Miss Fairfax continued to assure her that she
would not at present engage in any thing, repeating the same
65 motives which she had been heard to urge before.—Still Mrs.
Elton insisted on being authorized to write an acquiescence by
the morrow's post.—How Jane could bear it at all, was
astonishing to Emma.—She did look vexed, she did not speak
pointedly—and at last, with a decision of action unusual to
70 her, proposed a removal.—'Should not they walk?—Would
not Mr. Knightley show them the gardens—all the gardens?—
She wished to see the whole extent.'—The pertinacity of her
friend seemed more than she could bear.

B Hudson added that there had been yet another spot of
bother on the twenty-seventh of February, at Berhampur, a
hundred miles to the north where the 19th Bengal Infantry had
refused to take percussion caps on parade; the absence of any
5 European regiment had made it impossible to deal with this
mutinous act on the spot. . . . Now the defaulting regiment
was slowly being marched down to Barrackpur for disband-
ment. But there was no cause for alarm and, besides, now
that everyone had finished eating, a game of blind man's buff
10 was being called for.
   Everyone cried that this was a splendid idea and in no time
the bearers had cleared the hampers to one side (and then
been cleared away themselves) and the game was ready to
begin. One of the ladies, a plump girl who was already rather
15 hot from laughing so much, had duly been blindfolded and
now she was being turned round three times while everyone
chanted a rhyme that one of the officers, who had decided as
a pastime to study the natives, had learned from the native
children:

20   'Attah of roses and mustard-oil,
            The cat's a-crying the pot's a-boil,
            Look out and fly! the Rajah's thief
            will catch you!'

With that they all darted away and the young lady blundered
about shrieking with laughter until at last her brother, who
was afraid that she might have hysterics, allowed himself to
be caught.

This brother was none other than Lieutenant Cutter, a very
amusing fellow indeed. As he lunged here and there he kept
up a gruff and frightening commentary to the effect that he
was a big bear and that if he caught some pretty lass he
would give her a terrible hug . . . and the ladies were so
alarmed and delighted that they could not help giving away
their positions by their squeals, and they kept only just
escaping in the nick of time.

But soon it became evident that there was something rather
peculiar about Lieutenant Cutter's blunderings. How did it
happen that far from blundering impartially as one would
have expected of a blindfolded man, time and again he
ignored his brother officers and made his frightening gallops in
the direction of a flock of ladies? Perhaps it was simply that he
could locate them by their squeals. But how was it that he so
frequently galloped towards the prettiest of all, that is to say,
towards Louise Dunstaple, and finally caught the poor
moaning, breathless creature and gave her the terrible bear-
hug he had threatened (and how was it, Fleury wondered,
that he had so plainly become animally aroused by this
innocent game?). Lieutenant Cutter had been cheating, the
rascal! He had somehow or other opened a little window in
the folds of the silk handkerchief over his eyes and all this
time he had only been simulating blindness!

And so the merriment continued. What a wonderful time
everyone was having . . . even the ragged natives watching
from the edge of the clearing were probably enjoying the
spectacle . . . and how delightful the weather was! The Indian
winter is the perfect climate, sunny and cool. It was only later
that evening that Fleury remembered that he had wanted to
ask Captain Hudson, who had looked an intelligent fellow, if
he thought any more trouble was to be expected. . . . Because
naturally it would be foolish for himself and Miriam to visit the
Dunstaples in Krishnapur, as they intended, if there was to be
unrest in the country.

The following sonnet demonstrates a high degree of formal organization. It should be read aloud, carefully.

Lucifer in Starlight

On a starred night Prince Lucifer uprose.
Tired of his dark dominion swung the fiend
Above the rolling ball in cloud part screened,
Where sinners hugged their spectre of repose.
5   Poor prey to his hot fit of pride were those.
And now upon his western wing he leaned,
Now his huge bulk o'er Afric's sands careened,
Now the black planet shadowed Arctic snows.
Soaring through wider zones that pricked his scars
10   With memory of the old revolt from Awe,
He reached a middle height, and at the stars,
Which are the brain of heaven, he looked, and sank.
Around the ancient track marched, rank on rank,
The army of unalterable law.

Write an appreciation of the poem. It will be necessary to give careful consideration to the way in which the poet has relied heavily on sound and rhythm for his effect. (Does this reliance diminish the 'concreteness' of his images?)
The following textual questions may give you a starting point.
  (i) All but two lines are end-stopped; to what effect?
 (ii) What is noticeable about the sound of line 5 as compared to the lines preceeding it?
(iii) What is the contribution made by rhyme (particularly in the sestet)?
 (iv) What are the effects of the pauses in lines 10, 11 and 12?
  (v) What is the contribution made by sound and rhythm to the effect of the final line?

VIII

Compare the following two poems, discussing how each develops an attitude towards transformed love.

A. **Kindliness**

When love has changed to kindliness—
Oh, love, our hungry lips, that press
So tight that Time's an old god's dream
Nodding in heaven, and whisper stuff
5   Seven million years were not enough
To think on after, make it seem
Less than the breath of children playing,
A blasphemy scarce worth the saying,
A sorry jest, 'When love has grown
10   To kindliness— to kindliness!' . . .
And yet— the best that either's known
Will change, and wither, and be less,
At last, than comfort, or its own
Remembrance. And when some caress
15   Tendered in habit (once a flame
All heaven sang out to) wakes the shame
Unworded, in the steady eyes
We'll have,—*that* day, what shall we do?
Being so noble, kill the two
20   Who've reached their second-best? Being wise,
Break cleanly off, and get away,
Follow down the windier skies
New lures, alone? Or shall we stay,
Since this is all we've known, content
25   In the lean twilight of such a day,
And not remember, not lament?
That time when all is over, and
Hand never flinches, brushing hand;
And blood lies quiet, for all you're near;
30   And it's but spoken words we hear,
Where trumpets sang; when the mere skies
Are stranger and nobler than your eyes;
And flesh is flesh, was flame before;
And infinite hungers leap no more
35   In the chance swaying of your dress;
And love has changed to kindliness.

B.   **They Flee from Me**

They flee from me, that sometime did me seek
With naked foot, stalking in my chamber.
I have seen them gentle, tame and meek,
That now are wild, and do not remember
5   That sometime they put themself in danger
To take bread at my hand; and now they range
Busily seeking with a continual change.

Thanked be fortune it hath been otherwise
Twenty times better; but once, in special,
10   In thin array, after a pleasant guise,
When her loose gown from her shoulders did fall,
And she caught me in her arms long and small,
Therewith all sweetly did me kiss,
And softly said: "Dear heart, how like you this?"

15   It was no dream: I lay broad waking;
But all is turned, through my gentleness,
Into a strange fashion of forsaking;
And I have leave to go of her goodness:
And she also to use newfangleness.
20   But since that I so kindly am served,
I would fain know what she hath deserved.

Read the following passage very carefully and then:
(i) Comment on the meaning and effectiveness of:
   a. *a blob of jelly* (line 13)
   b. *fears of physical and social consequences* (lines 25–26)
   c. *purchased a renewal* (lines 33–34)
(ii) Examine and discuss the contributions made by the rhythm
    and syntax to the sense of the two sentences:
    Something that had been . . . would read poetry (lines 8–18)
(iii) Examine and discuss the changes of mood and tone that occur
    in this passage.
(iv) What attitudes towards conception and birth do you detect in:
   a. Marjorie?
   b. The narrator?
(v) Choose, and comment upon, two occasions in which irony is
    used.

He gave the final touches to his white tie. From the mirror
her face looked out at him, close beside his own. It was a pale
face and so thin that the down-thrown light of the electric lamp
hanging above them made a shadow in the hollows below the
5   cheek-bones. Her eyes were darkly ringed. Rather too long at

169

the best of times, her straight nose protruded bleakly from the unfleshed face. She looked ugly, tired and ill. Six months from now her baby would be born. Something that had been a single cell, a cluster of cells, a little sac of tissue, a kind of
10 worm, a potential fish with gills, stirred in her womb and would one day become a man—a grown man, suffering and enjoying, loving and hating, thinking, remembering, imagining. And what had been a blob of jelly within her body would invent a god and worship; what had been a kind of fish would
15 create and, having created, would become the battle-ground of disputing good and evil; what had blindly lived in her as a parasitic worm would look at the stars, would listen to music, would read poetry. A thing would grow into a person, a tiny lump of stuff would become a human body, a human mind.
20 The astounding process of creation was going on within her; but Marjorie was conscious only of sickness and lassitude; the mystery for her meant nothing but fatigue and ugliness and a chronic anxiety about the future, pain of the mind as well as discomfort of the body. She had been glad, or at least she
25 had tried to be glad, in spite of her haunting fears of physical and social consequences, when she first recognized the symptoms of her pregnancy. The child, she believed, would bring Walter closer; (he had begun to fade away from her even then). It would arouse in him new feelings which would
30 make up for whatever element it was that seemed to be lacking in his love for her. She dreaded the pain, she dreaded the inevitable difficulties and embarrassments. But the pains, the difficulties would have been worth while if they purchased a renewal, a strengthening of Walter's attachment. In spite of
35 everything, she was glad. And at first her previsions had seemed to be justified. The news that she was going to have a child had quickened his tenderness. For two or three weeks she was happy, she was reconciled to the pains and discomforts. Then, from one day to another, everything was
40 changed; Walter had met that woman. He still did his best, in the intervals of running after Lucy, to keep up a show of solicitude. But she could feel that the solicitude was resentful, that he was tender and attentive out of a sense of duty, that he hated the child for compelling him to be so considerate to
45 its mother. And because he hated it, she too began to hate it. No longer overlaid by happiness, her fears came to the surface, filled her mind. Pain and discomfort—that was all the future held. And meanwhile ugliness, sickness, fatigue. How could she fight her battle when she was in this state?
50   'Do you love me, Walter?' she suddenly asked.
170

Read carefully the two passages below, and then answer the questions which follow.

A.   We think that, as civilization advances, poetry almost necessarily declines. Therefore, though we fervently admire those great works of imagination which have appeared in dark ages, we do not admire them the more because they have appeared
5   in dark ages. On the contrary, we hold that the most wonderful and splendid proof of genius is a great poem produced in a civilized age. We cannot understand why those who believe in that most orthodox article of literary faith, that the earliest poets are generally the best, should wonder at the
10   rule as if it were the exception. Surely the uniformity of the phenomenon indicates a corresponding uniformity in the cause.
     The fact is, that common observers reason from the progress of the experimental sciences to that of imitative
15   arts. The improvement of the former is gradual and slow. Ages are spent in collecting materials, ages more in separating and combining them. Even when a system has been formed, there is still something to add, to alter, or to reject. Every generation enjoys the use of a vast hoard bequeathed to
20   it by antiquity, and transmits that hoard, augmented by fresh acquisitions, to future ages. In these pursuits, therefore, the first speculators lie under great disadvantages, and, even when they fail, are entitled to praise. Their pupils, with far inferior intellectual powers, speedily surpass them in actual
25   attainments. Every girl who has read Mrs. Marcet's little dialogues on Political Economy could teach Montague or Walpole many lessons in finance. Any intelligent man may now, by resolutely applying himself for a few years to mathematics, learn more than the great Newton knew after
30   half a century of study and meditation.
     But it is not thus with music, with painting, or with sculpture. Still less is it thus with poetry. The progress of refinement rarely supplies these arts with better objects of imitation. It may indeed improve the instruments which are
35   necessary to the mechanical operations of the musician, the sculptor, and the painter. But language, the machine of the poet, is best fitted for his purpose in its rudest state. Nations, like individuals, first perceive, and then abstract. They advance from particular images to general terms. Hence the

40   vocabulary of an enlightened society is philosophical, that of a
half-civilized people is poetical.

B.   The reference of all production at last to an Aboriginal
Power explains the traits common to all works of the highest
art,—that they are universally intelligible, that they restore to
us the simplest states of mind, and are religious. Since what
5   skill is therein shewn is the reappearance of the original soul,
a jet of pure light, it should produce a similar impression to
that made by natural objects. In happy hours nature appears
to us one with art; art perfected,—the work of genius. And
the individual in whom simple tastes, and susceptibility to all
10   the great human influences, overpower the accidents of a
local and special culture, is the best critic of art. Though we
travel the world over to find the beautiful, we must carry it
with us, or we find it not. The best of beauty is a finer charm
than skill in surfaces, in outlines, or rules of art can ever
15   teach, namely, a radiation, from the work of art, of human
character,—a wonderful expression, through stone or canvas
or musical sound, of the deepest and simplest attributes of our
nature, and therefore most intelligible at last to those souls
which have these attributes. In the sculptures of the Greeks, in
20   the masonry of the Romans, and in the pictures of the Tuscan
and Venetian masters, the highest charm is the universal language they speak. A confession of moral nature, of purity, love,
and hope, breathes from them all. That which we carry to them,
the same we bring back more fairly illustrated in the memory.
25   The traveller who visits the Vatican, and passes from chamber
to chamber through galleries of statues, vases, sarcophagi,
and candelabra, through all forms of beauty, cut in the richest
materials, is in danger of forgetting the simplicity of the
principles out of which they all sprung, and that they had
30   their origin from thoughts and laws in his own breast. He
studies the technical rules on these wonderful remains, but
forgets that these works were not always thus constellated;
that they are the contributions of many ages and many
countries; that each came out of the solitary workshop of one
35   artist, who toiled perhaps in ignorance of the existence of
other sculpture, created his work without other model save
life, household life, and the sweet and smart of personal
relations, of beating hearts, and meeting eyes, of poverty, and
necessity, and hope, and fear. These were the inspirations,
40   and these are the effects he carries home to your heart and
mind.

172

From passage A.
  (i) Explain what the writer means by
      a. *that most orthodox article of literary faith* (line 8)
      b. *a vast hoard* (line 19)
      c. *the progress of refinement* (lines 32–33)
 (ii) Explain in your own words why, according to the author, a
      civilized society is not a prerequisite of great poetry.
From passage B:
  (i) Comment on the meaning or meanings of
      a. *Aboriginal Power* (lines 1–2)
      b. *the accidents of a local and special culture* (lines 10–11)
      c. *constellated* (line 32)
      d. *solitary workshop* (line 34)
 (ii) Does the writer convince you that the 'highest art' restores to
      us 'the simplest states of mind'? If so, how does he, and if not,
      why not?
From both passages:
  (i) Compare, briefly, the way each writer presents his argument,
      the way each uses language.
 (ii) Are there ways in which these writers complement or
      illuminate each other? How do their ideas differ?

Write a study of the following poem, perhaps using as a point of
departure the questions you will find below.

Low Barometer

> The south-wind strengthens to a gale,
> Across the moon the clouds fly fast,
> The house is smitten as with a flail,
> The chimney shudders to the blast.
>
> 5   On such a night, when Air has loosed
> Its guardian grasp on blood and brain,
> Old terrors then of god or ghost
> Creep from their caves to life again;
>
> And Reason kens he herits in
> 10   A haunted house. Tenants unknown
> Assert their squalid lease of sin
> With earlier title than his own.
>
> Unbodied presences, the pack'd
> Pollution and remorse of Time,
> 15   Slipp'd in from oblivion reenact
> The horrors of unhouseld crime.

Some men would quell the thing with prayer
Whose sightless footsteps pad the floor,
Whose fearful trespass mounts the stair
20   Or bursts the lock'd forbidden door.

Some have seen corpses long interr'd
Escape from hallowing control,
Pale charnel forms—nay ev'n have heard
The shrilling of a troubled soul,

25   That wanders till the dawn hath cross'd
The dolorous dark, or Earth hath wound
Closer her storm-spredd cloke, and thrust
The baleful phantoms under ground.

 (i) How, and to what effects, has the poet achieved a great deal
     of movement within the regular stanza form as it is established
     by the first four lines?
 (ii) Why, do you think, has the poet made much use of archaic
      language and spelling (e.g. lines 9, 16, 27)? Does this establish
      some relation with a particular literary genre?
(iii) At what point does it become apparent that the house and
      other images have meanings other than literal?
(iv) Why are certain words capitalized?

Write an appreciation of the following poem, giving consideration to its two main 'lines' of imagery (from this point of view it would be profitable to contrast it with W. R. Rodgers' *White Christmas*, page 88).

First Snow in Alsace

The snow came down last night like moths
Burned on the moon; it fell till dawn,
Covered the town with simple cloths.

Absolute snow lies rumpled on
5   What shellbursts scattered and deranged,
Entangled railways, crevassed lawn.

As if it did not know they'd changed,
Snow smoothly clasps the roofs of homes
Fear-gutted, trustless and estranged.

10   The ration stacks are milky domes;
Across the ammunition pile
The snow has climbed in sparkling combs.

You think: beyond the town a mile
Or two, this snowfall fills the eyes
15   Of soldiers dead a little while.

Persons and persons in disguise,
Walking the new air white and fine,
Trade glances quick with shared surprise.

At children's windows, heaped, benign,
20   As always, winter shines the most,
And frost makes marvellous designs.

The night-guard coming from his post,
Ten first-snows back in thought, walks slow
And warms him with a boyish boast:

25   He was the first to see the snow.

Read the following passage carefully and then:
  (i) Comment on the irony present in:
      a. *unabundant brown hair* (lines 16–17)
      b. *savage power* (line 19)
      c. *the lines of black dots* (line 25)
      d. *some Brahms rubbish* (lines 28–29)
 (ii) Examine and discuss the syntax of the sentence
      'He looked over at Margaret . . . to himself and her'. (Lines
      44–50)
(iii) How are the characters Dixon and Welch revealed by their
      use of language?

      'Of course, this sort of music's not intended for an audience,
    you see,' Welch said as he handed the copies round. 'The
    fun's all in the singing. Everybody's got a real tune to sing—a
    real tune,' he repeated violently. 'You could say, really, that
5   polyphony got to its highest point, its peak, at that period, and
    has been on the decline ever since. You've only got to look at
    the part-writing in things like, well, *Onward, Christian
    Soldiers*, the hymn, which is a typical . . . a typical. . . .'
      'We're all waiting, Ned,' Mrs Welch said from the piano.
10 She played a slow arpeggio, sustaining it with the pedal. 'All
    right, everybody?'
      A soporific droning filled the air round Dixon as the singers
    hummed their notes to one another. Mrs. Welch rejoined them
    on the low platform that had been built at one end of the
15 music-room, taking up her stand by Margaret, the other
    soprano. A small bullied-looking woman with unabundant
    brown hair was the only contralto. Next to Dixon was Cecil
    Goldsmith, a colleague of his in the College History Depart-
    ment, whose tenor voice held enough savage power, especially
20 above middle C, to obliterate whatever noises Dixon might feel
    himself impelled to make. Behind him and to one side were
    three basses, one a local composer, another an amateur
    violinist occasionally summoned at need by the city orchestra,
    the third Evan Johns.
25   Dixon ran his eye along the lines of black dots, which
    seemed to go up and down a good deal, and was able to
    assure himself that everyone was going to have to sing all the
    time. He'd had a bad setback twenty minutes ago in some
    Brahms rubbish which began with ten seconds or so of
30 unsupported tenor—more accurately, of unsupported Gold-
    smith, who'd twice dried up in face of a tricky interval and
    left him opening and shutting his mouth in silence. He now
    cautiously reproduced the note Goldsmith was humming and

found the effect pleasing rather than the reverse. Why hadn't
35 they had the decency to ask him if he'd like to join in, instead
of driving him up on to this platform arrangement and forcing
sheets of paper into his hand?

The madrigal began at the bidding of Welch's arthritic
forefinger. Dixon kept his head down, moved his mouth as
40 little as possible consistent with being unmistakably seen to
move it, and looked through the words the others were
singing. 'When from my love I looked for love, and kind
affections due,' he read, 'too well I found her vows to prove
most faithless and untrue. But when I did ask her why. . . ' He
45 looked over at Margaret, who was singing away happily
enough—she turned out regularly during the winter with the
choir of the local Conservative Association—and wondered
what changes in their circumstances and temperaments would
be necessary to make the words of the madrigal apply,
50 however remotely, to himself and her. She'd made vows to
him, or avowals anyway, which was perhaps all the writer
had meant. But if he'd meant what he seemed to mean by
'kind affections due', then Dixon had never 'looked for' any of
these from Margaret. Perhaps he should: after all, people
55 were doing it all the time. It was a pity she wasn't a bit better-
looking. One of these days, though, he would try, and see
what happened.

'Yet, by and by, they'll arl, deny, arnd say 'twas *bart* in jast,'
Goldsmith sang tremendously and very loudly. It was the last
60 phrase; Dixon kept his mouth open while Welch's finger
remained aloft, then shut it with a little flick of the head he'd
seen singers use as the finger swept sideways. All seemed
pleased with the performance and anxious for another of the
same sort. 'Yes, well, this next one's what they called a ballet.
65 Of course, they didn't mean what we mean by the similar. . . .
Rather a well-known one, this. It's called *Now is the Month of
Maying*. Now if you'll all just. . . .'

A man revisits a place he has not seen for twelve years. He hopes
for a meaningful experience of some sort, but nothing like that
seems to happen. Irritated, he decides to return to the town.
Read the passage below with care, and then:

(i) Comment on the meaning and effectiveness of
   a. *dragging its grey broken columns* (lines 5–6)
   b. *eye-corner* (line 11)
   c. *plastering beat* (line 25)
   d. *the chilly sheet lead of his suit became a tight, warm mould*
   (lines 54–55)
   e. *bringing dwarfs and continents and animals out of its
   scurfy bark* (lines 64–65)
(ii) What impression are we given of this man's character, and
   what might be the significance of the horse for him?
(iii) How strong a sense of the locality and the weather has the
   writer created?
(iv) Discuss the syntax, rhythm and general effect of the following
   sentences:
   a. *But the thought . . . deterred him* (lines 2–4)
   b. *Down this front . . . a fallow field* (lines 35–36)
   c. *At the wood top . . . watching him* (lines 84–86)
(v) *The Rain Horse*—the story from which this extract is taken—
   has often been called 'mysterious' or 'puzzling'. On the
   evidence of this passage, are you able to suggest why this is?

It would be quicker to go straight forward to the farm a mile
away in the valley and behind which the road looped. But the
thought of meeting the farmer—to be embarrassingly remembered or shouted at as a trespasser—deterred him. He saw
5 the rain pulling up out of the distance, dragging its grey
broken columns, smudging the trees and the farms.

A wave of anger went over him: anger against himself for
blundering into this mud-trap and anger against the land that
made him feel so outcast, so old and stiff and stupid. He
10 wanted nothing but to get away from it as quickly as possible.
But as he turned, something moved in his eye-corner. All his
senses startled alert. He stopped.

Over to his right a thin, black horse was running across the
ploughland towards the hill, its head down, neck stretched
15 out. It seemed to be running on its toes like a cat, like a dog up
to no good.

From the high point on which he stood the hill dipped

slightly and rose to another crested point fringed with the tops
of trees, three hundred yards to his right. As he watched it,
20   the horse ran up that crest, showed against the sky—for a
moment like a nightmarish leopard—and disappeared over the
other side.

For several seconds he stared at the skyline, stunned by the
unpleasantly strange impression the horse had made on him.
25   Then the plastering beat of icy rain on his bare skull brought
him to himself. The distance had vanished in a wall of grey.
All around him the fields were jumping and streaming.

Holding his collar close and tucking his chin down into it he
ran back over the hilltop towards the town-side, the lee-side,
30   his feet sucking and splashing, at every stride plunging to the
ankle.

This hill was shaped like a wave, a gently rounded back
lifting out of the valley to a sharply crested, almost concave
front hanging over the river meadows towards the town.
35   Down this front, from the crest, hung two small woods
separated by a fallow field. The near wood was nothing more
than a quarry, circular, full of stones and bracken, with a few
thorns and nondescript saplings, foxholes and rabbit holes.
The other was rectangular, mainly a planting of scrub oak
40   trees. Beyond the river smouldered the town like a great heap
of blue cinders.

He ran along the top of the first wood and finding no shelter
but the thin, leafless thorns of the hedge, dipped below the
crest out of the wind and jogged along through thick grass to
45   the wood of oaks. In blinding rain he lunged through the
barricade of brambles at the wood's edge. The little crippled
trees were small choice in the way of shelter, but at a sudden
fierce thickening of the rain he took one at random and
crouched down under the leaning trunk.
50   Still panting from his run, drawing his knees up tightly, he
watched the bleak lines of rain, grey as hail, slanting through
the boughs into the clumps of bracken and bramble. He felt
hidden and safe. The sound of the rain as it rushed and lulled
in the wood seemed to seal him in. Soon the chilly sheet lead
55   of his suit became a tight, warm mould, and gradually he sank
into a state of comfort that was all but trance, though the
rain beat steadily on his exposed shoulders and trickled down
the oak trunk on to his neck.

All around him the boughs angled down, glistening, black as
60   iron. From their tips and elbows the drops hurried steadily,
and the channels of the bark pulsed and gleamed. For a time
he amused himself calculating the variation in rainfall by

179

the variations in a dribble of water from a trembling twig-end
two feet in front of his nose. He studied the twig, bringing
65 dwarfs and continents and animals out of its scurfy bark.
Beyond the boughs the blue shoal of the town was rising and
falling, and darkening and fading again, in the pale, swaying
backdrop of rain.

He wanted this rain to go on forever. Whenever it seemed to
70 be drawing off he listened anxiously until it closed in again.
As long as it lasted he was suspended from life and time. He
didn't want to return to his sodden shoes and his possibly
ruined suit and the walk back over that land of mud.

All at once he shivered. He hugged his knees to keep out the
75 cold and found himself thinking of the horse. The hair on the
nape of his neck prickled slightly. He remembered how it had
run up to the crest and showed against the sky.

He tried to dismiss the thought. Horses wander about the
countryside often enough. But the image of the horse as it had
80 appeared against the sky stuck in his mind. It must have come
over the crest just above the wood in which he was now
sitting. To clear his mind, he twisted around and looked up the
wood between the tree stems, to his left.

At the wood top, with the silvered grey light coming in
85 behind it, the black horse was standing under the oaks, its
head high and alert, its ears pricked, watching him.

An Open Air Performance of 'As You Like It'

Art is unmade
To nature and the wild again
On the scythed grass before
A lime and a skeletal ash
5 And the wall, solid with flowering,
Of longer unmown grass
Fumy with parsley flowers,
A level mist rising;
Where the young actors, barefoot,
10 Warm in their exhultation
Burn in the evening's chill.

The art the poet won
From wilderness dissolves again,

15   Unformed upon this formless stage
        Confluent with all earth's air;
        For infiltrating winds,
        Laughter, mid-distant trains
        Steal the speech from their voices,
20   Being amateur, unsure,
        And moths bemuse their faces,
        And our attention loses
        Stragglers to cloud and star.

        Envoys of life
25   At their set hour the swifts fly over,
        Possess the air above us
        And fish-tailed, fast as sight,
        Play in their foamy margins,
        Their intertidal light;
30   While the flood lamps yet hardly
        Sophisticate the earth's colours,
        And we half ride with the birds
        Over our audience faces
        Over the reckless words.

35   And when 'If you have been . . .'
        Orlando cries, 'If ever been
        Where bells have knolled to church . . .'
        And sweet upon his words
        The Christ Church evening bell
40   Answers the homesick youth
        Like rhyme confirming verse,
        Evidence crowning truth,
        It seems to our delight
        As though the poet's earth
        And ours lay in one night;
45
        As though we had heard
        The bell before the words were made
        With him. Therefore I love
        All loose ends, distractions
50   At such performances,
        All their imperfections;
        And if we bring our children,
        Their soft and stubborn questions
        Threading the marble words;
55   And art delivered up
        To nature and the wild again.

Write an appreciation of this poem which includes answers to the following questions:

What are the meanings and functions of these words and phrases: *Confluent* (15); *our attention loses/Stragglers to cloud and star* (21-22); *Envoys of life* (23); *Sophisticate* (30); *reckless* (33); *lay in one night* (44); *marble* (53).

How does the poet use rhyme?

In the first stanza, art is *unmade to nature*; in the second art *dissolves*; in the fifth art is *delivered up* to nature. How might these changes in phraseology indicate a progression in the poet's ideas about the relationship between art and nature?

The poet claims to love all loose ends (lines 47-48); are there any in the poem itself?

What is the significance of the swifts in the third stanza and of 'our children' in the fifth?

XII

The two poems which follow are both *prayers*, in that each is
addressed to God and each ends with a plea. Further, they are
similar in that both poets are struggling to maintain their belief in
divine justice. On a first reading, therefore, these poems may
appear to be very much alike in both form and intention, but they
do in fact differ in subtle but crucial ways. Write a study which
brings out these differences. You will need to pay very close
attention to the way each poet uses linguistic devices in order to
achieve strong emotional impact. Sound-effects are extremely
significant in both poems. Consider, for example, the use of
end-rhyme in poem A: almost every rhyme has a *semantic*
significance in excess of the words' syntactical functions. *Immortal
us/envious/heinous/glorious* is in itself almost a sequence of ideas.
Equal importance should be attached to rhythmical variations (this
is where scansion comes in useful) since they serve to dramatize
the emotional development of both poems.

A   **If Poisonous Minerals**

If poisonous minerals, and if that tree
Whose fruit threw death on else immortal us,
If lecherous goats, if serpents envious
Cannot be damned, Alas! why should I be?
5   Why should intent or reason, born in me,
Make sins, else equal, in me more heinous?
And mercy being easy, and glorious
To God, in his stern wrath why threatens he?
But who am I, that dare dispute with thee,
10   O God? O! of thine only worthy blood,
And my tears, make a heavenly Lethean flood,
And drown in it my sin's black memory;
That thou remember them, some claim as debt,
I think it mercy, if thou wilt forget.

B   **Thou Art Indeed Just, Lord**

Thou art indeed just, Lord, if I contend
With thee; but, Sir, so what I plead is just.
Why do sinners' ways prosper? And why must
Disappointment all I endeavour end?
5   Wert thou my enemy, O thou my friend,
How wouldst thou worse, I wonder, than thou dost

CE–C*

Defeat, thwart me? Oh, the sots and thralls of lust
Do in spare hours more thrive than that I spend,
Sir, life upon thy cause. See, banks and brakes
10   Now, leavèd how thick! lacèd they are again
With fretty chervil, look, and fresh wind shakes
Them; birds build—but not I build; no, but strain,
Time's eunuch, and not breed one work that wakes.
Mine, O thou lord of life, send my roots rain.

Carefully read the passage below and then answer the questions which follow.

(Lydgate, a doctor, has just told the scholar and clergyman Casaubon that he has a fatal disease.)

Lydgate, certain that his patient wished to be alone, soon left him; and the black figure with hands behind and head bent forward continued to pace the walk where the dark yew-trees gave him a mute companionship in melancholy, and the little
5   shadows of bird or leaf that fleeted across the isles of sunlight, stole along in silence as if in the presence of a sorrow. Here was a man who now for the first time found himself looking into the eyes of death—who was passing through one of those rare moments of experience when we feel
10 the truth of a commonplace, which is as different from what we call knowing it, as the vision of the waters upon the earth is different from the delirious vision of the water which cannot be had to cool the burning tongue. When the commonplace 'We must all die' transforms itself suddenly into the acute
15 consciousness of 'I must die—and soon,' then death grapples us, and his fingers are cruel; afterwards he may come to fold us in his arms as our mother did, and our last moments of dim earthly discerning may be like the first. To Mr. Casaubon now, it was as if he suddenly found himself on the dark river-
20 brink and heard the splash of the oncoming oar, not discerning the forms, but expecting the summons. In such an hour the mind does not change its lifelong bias, but carries it onward in imagination to the other side of death, gazing backward— perhaps with the divine calm of beneficence, perhaps with
25 the petty anxieties of self-assertion. What was Mr. Casaubon's bias his acts will give us a clue to. He held himself to be, with some private scholarly reservations, a believing Christian, as to estimates of the present and hopes of the future. But what we strive to gratify, though we may call it a distant hope, is an

30 immediate desire; the future estate for which men drudge up
city alleys exists already in their imagination and love. And
Mr. Casaubon's immediate desire was not for a divine
communion and light divested of earthly conditions; his
passionate longings, poor man, clung low and mist-like in very
35 shady places.

Dorothea had been aware when Lydgate had ridden away,
and she had stepped into the garden, with the impulse to go at
once to her husband. But she hesitated, fearing to offend him
by obtruding herself; for her ardour, continually repulsed,
40 served, with her intense memory, to heighten her dread, as
thwarted energy subsides into a shudder; and she wandered
slowly round the nearer clumps of trees until she saw him
advancing. Then she went towards him, and might have
represented a heaven-sent angel coming with a promise that
45 the short hours remaining should yet be filled with that
faithful love which clings the closer to a comprehended grief.
His glance in reply to hers was so chill that she felt her timidity
increased; yet she turned and passed her hand through his
arm.
50 Mr Casaubon kept his hands behind him and allowed her
pliant arm to cling with difficulty against his rigid arm.

(i) Comment on the meaning and effectiveness of the following
phrases:
a. *mute companionship in melancholy* (line 4)
b. *isles of sunlight* (lines 5-6)
c. *death grapples us* (line 15)
d. *as thwarted energy subsides into a shudder* (line 41)
e. *her pliant arm* (lines 50-51)
(ii) What, according to the author, is Casaubon's reaction to the
news of his illness? What impression do you receive of his
character?
(iii) Describe and analyze the way the writer moves the reader
from externals to the interior of the minds of the characters.
What tone does the author adopt when talking directly to the
reader?

XIII

The following extract is from the beginning of a novel. Read it carefully and then:

(i) Comment on the meaning and effectiveness of the following phrases:
   a. *steady creaking* (line 1)
   b. *soft feathery feeling* (lines 4-5)
   c. *humped over the big dyke* (line 16)
(ii) What effects are obtained by the syntax of the following sentences:
   a. *It was a warm . . . floated.* (2nd paragraph)
   b. *Curiously . . . patch* (2nd paragraph)
(iii) Comment on the contributions made to the meaning of the passage by the rhythm of the first three paragraphs.
(iv) What mood or moods do you think the author wishes to create in the first section? (1–18) How does the author emphasize the horrific facts of line 27?
(v) Examine this passage as the opening paragraphs of a novel. How successful do you consider it to be?

Only the steady creaking of a flight of swans disturbed the silence, labouring low overhead with outstretched necks towards the sea.

It was a warm, wet, windless afternoon with a soft feathery
5   feeling in the air: rain, yet so fine it could scarcely fall but rather floated. It clung to everything it touched; the rushes in the deep choked ditches of the sea-marsh were bowed down with it, the small black cattle looked cobwebbed with it, their horns jewelled with it. Curiously stumpy too these cattle
10   looked, the whole herd sunk nearly to the knees in a soft patch.

This sea-marsh stretched for miles. Seaward, a greyish merging into sky had altogether rubbed out the line of dunes which bounded it that way: inland, another and darker blurred greyness was all you could see of the solid Welsh hills. But
15   near by loomed a solitary gate, where the path crossed a footbridge and humped over the big dyke; and here in a sodden tangle of brambles the scent of a fox hung, too heavy today to rise or dissipate.

The gate clicked sharply and shed its cascade as two men
20   passed through. Both were heavily loaded in oilskins. The elder and more tattered one carried two shotguns, negligently, and a brace of golden plover were tied to the bit of old rope he wore knotted round his middle: glimpses of a sharp-featured

weather-beaten face showed from within his bonneted sou'-
25 wester, but mouth and even chin were hidden in a long
weeping moustache. The younger man was springy and tall
and well-built and carried over his shoulder the body of a
dead child. Her thin muddy legs dangled against his chest,
her head and arms hung down his back; and at his heels
30 walked a black dog—disciplined, saturated and eager.
   Suddenly the older man blew through the curtain of his
moustache as if to clear it of water before speaking, but he
thought better of it after a quick glance round at his companion. There was no personal grief in the young man's face
35 but it was awe-struck.

Nightingales

Beautiful must be the mountains whence ye come,
And bright in the fruitful valleys the streams wherefrom
   Ye learn your song:
Where are those starry woods? O might I wander there,
5   Among the flowers, which in that heavenly air
      Bloom the year long!

Nay, barren are those mountains and spent the streams:
Our song is the voice of desire, that haunts our dreams,
   A throe of the heart,
10 Whose pining visions dim, forbidden hopes profound,
      No dying cadence nor long sigh can sound,
      For all our art.

Alone, aloud in the raptured ear of men
We pour our dark nocturnal secret; and then,
15   As night is withdrawn
From these sweet-springing meads and bursting boughs of May,
      Dream, while the innumerable choir of day
      Welcome the dawn.

   There are two speakers in this poem: the first stanza is the
poet's assumption as he expresses it to the nightingales; the second
and third are the nightingales' reply. In writing a study of this
poem, discuss the concept of beauty and poetry ("song") conveyed
by this reply. What is implied about the original impulse for art?
What is the role of symbolism in this poem? Discuss also the rather
complicated stanza form, and the complexity of the poet's syntax;
what is the effect of these structural phenomena?

XIV

For light relief, our last 'paper' offers two poems and a prose extract all involving unkind thoughts, satire and downright rudeness.

Which of these poems do you think the more effective? Is it more effective because it is funnier? Which do you think is better from a more critical point of view, and why?

A   **The Statesman**

I knew a man who used to say,
Not once but twenty times a day,
That in the turmoil and the strife
(His very words) of Public Life
5   The thing of ultimate effect
Was Character—not Intellect.
He therefore was at pains
To atrophy his puny brains
And registered success in this
10   Beyond the dreams of avarice,
Till, when he had at last become
Blind, paralytic, deaf and dumb,
Insensible and cretinous,
He was admitted ONE OF US.
15   They, therefore (meaning Them by 'They')
His colleagues of the N.C.A.,
The T.U.C., the I.L.P.,
Appointed him triumphantly
To bleed the taxes of a clear
20   200,000 Francs a year
(Swiss), as the necessary man
For conferences at Lausanne,
Geneva, Basle, Locarno, Berne:
A salary which he will earn,
25   Yes—*earn* I say—until he Pops,
Croaks, passes in his checks and Stops:—
When he will be remembered for
A week, a month, or even more.

B   **Chloe**

'Yet Chloe sure was formed without a spot'—
Nature in her then erred not, but forgot.
'With every pleasing, every prudent part,
Say, what can Chloe want?' She wants a heart.

She speaks, behaves, and acts just as she ought;
But never, never, reached one generous thought.
Virtue she finds too painful an endeavour,
Content to dwell in decencies forever.
So very reasonable, so unmoved,
As never yet to love, or to be loved.
She, while her lover pants upon her breast,
Can mark the figures on an Indian chest;
And when she sees her friend in deep despair,
Observes how much chintz exceeds mohair.
Forbid it Heaven, a favour or a debt
She e'er should cancel—but she may forget.
Safe is your secret still in Chloe's ear;
But none of Chloe's shall you ever hear.
Of all her Dears she slandered never one,
But cares not if a thousand are undone.
Would Chloe know if you're alive or dead?
She bids her footman put it in her head.
Chloe is prudent—would you too be wise?
Then never break your heart when Chloe dies.

Read the following extract and then:
  (i) Comment on the meaning and aptness of
    a. *strict but well-tailored . . . garb* (lines 4–5)
    b. *wearisomely common doctrinal confusion* (lines 23–24)
    c. *his relations with the Omnipotent* (lines 59–60)
  (ii) What impressions do you gather of (a) Father Colgate, (b) Roger?
  (iii) Describe the kind of humour present and show how it is achieved by the writer. (You might like to look at such things as the 'reliability' of Roger's account of the meeting, the use of dialogue, the vocabulary and syntax.)

  'This is Father Colgate.'
    Oh, what nonsense, how can it be? was Roger's thought as a flamboyantly handsome and muscular man of thirty, dressed up for some unfathomable reason of his own in strict but
5 well-tailored clerical garb, shook his hand and told him he was very glad to know him. And how could he know him after five seconds' acquaintance? Still, by the same token Roger could not very well accuse the fellow immediately of masquerading, and until he knew more he decided to follow his
10 usual policy towards actual priests, a show of cordial respect and interest. The normal response to a few minutes of this was the query whether Roger himself was not of the faith. Roger

would say yes, with the silent qualification that he was of the
faith chiefly in the sense that the church he currently did not
15 attend was Catholic, and would go on to be fairly daring and
original about Arianism. It was intrinsically worth while to be
seen to be in with the priesthood, as well as going down well
with the women he always saw to it were about. Even so, he
could not help leaning sarcastically on the last word when he
20 now asked: 'Are your duties connected with the College,
Father?'

'No, they are not,' the man replied with a touch of
impatience, as if rebuking some wearisomely common doctrinal
confusion. 'Budweiser is a Protestant foundation, as might be
25 expected in this part of the country. There was no substantial number of communicants here until ten or fifteen
years ago.'

'And now?'

'Pardon me?'

30 'The number of communicants nowadays?'

'Substantial,' the supposed divine said, and inhaled his
cigarette in such a way as to cause a ball of smoke to come
into being for an instant above the back of his tongue before
vanishing with a hiss. 'Substantial,' he added, nodding.

35 'Oh, how frightfully agreeable.'

'Yes, right now there's plenty of God's grace around in
these parts.'

This was unsatisfactory. Even an impersonator should be
able to do better. 'Do you really think so?' Roger asked
40 incredulously.

'These are happy people. Certainly they have their problems
—who doesn't?—but they do their best to help one another
with them and they have charity. If that's not a heavenly gift
I'd like to know what is. Are you yourself of any religious
45 communion, sir?'

Now this, again, had come too soon to be altogether
welcome. 'It so happens that I am—of the Roman Catholic
Church, actually.'

'Uh-huh.' The ecclesiastic showed no interest or even
50 evidence of recognition, let alone pleasure. Perhaps he
belonged to some appalling sort of local High Anglican thing.
Just as likely he had been christened Father, did football-
stadium revivalism and enjoyed dressing-up. Well, as far as
the last part went he would be squarely in the line of
55 Church tradition. One of Roger's chronic difficulties was
reconciling his belief in the importance of priests and the
Church with his antipathy towards most of the former and

190

aversion from most of the doctrines and practices of the latter, a conflict also to be seen in his relations with the Omnipotent. Accepting a fresh drink from an anonymous hand, he tried to suppress all that for the moment and give this black-clad clown his last fair chance by listening to some of what he was saying.

60

Bibliography

Anthologies:

The New Oxford Book of English Verse ed. Helen Gardner (1972)
The Oxford Book of Twentieth Century English Verse ed. Philip
Larkin (1973)
A rather out-of-the-ordinary 'anthology' of prose, verse, ideas and
aphorisms is A Certain World by W. H. Auden (Faber, 1971)

Works of Criticism:

I. A. Richards: Practical Criticism
                 Principles of Literary Criticism
F. R. Leavis: Revaluation
                 The Common Pursuit
      (ed.):   Determinations
These are the legs upon which stand Established Criticism.
They are not for idle reading; they are undoubtedly important
and infinitely useful. Practical Criticism is based upon an
experiment in which Richards issued unidentified poems to a
number of readers whose critical responses to each he would
collect. The first part of the book reprints the poems and
discusses the responses. Advanced level students who are
future victims of the Unseen might well find this first section of
interest.

Cleanth Brooks and
Robert Penn Warren: Understanding Poetry (3rd edition, New
      York 1960). Written in 1938, but there doesn't seem to be an
      English edition. Very well worth hunting down. Large and
      good selection of verse under discussion, and an illuminating
      chapter on 'How Poems Come About'.

Christopher Butler and
Alistair Fowler: *Topics in Criticism* (Longman 1971). A simple idea nicely executed. Butler and Fowler have collected a hoard of snippets from fiction, poetry and criticism and arranged them—without editorial comment—under various headings: 'Unity', 'Genre and Mode', 'Moral Influence', etc. The reader makes his own connections between the quotations. A readable wealth of ideas, and attractive to look at.

H. Coombes: *Literature and Criticism* (Pelican 1963). A book often seen around sixth-form classrooms. Dryish, but to the point on such topics as Rhythm, Diction, Feeling, etc. Coombes makes his points by examining passages of poetry, seldom indulging in discussion of critical ideas. 'By *image*, in this chapter, we mean figure of speech', he says, and off he goes. . . .

James Scully (ed.): *Modern Poets on Modern Poetry.* (Fontana 1966). A collection of essays, etc., by poets including Yeats and Eliot, Dylan Thomas and e. e. cummings.

Winifred Nowottny: *The Language Poets Use* (London 1961). Hard but intelligent; very good on metaphorical language.

Robin Skelton: *The Practice of Poetry* (Heinemann 1971): Not many poets have had the neck to write books advising on how to write poetry. This one is quite convincing, with useful sections on technical matters, and in the chapter 'Approaches to Form' the development of a poem (by Thomas Kinsella) is traced from its original twinkle in the poet's eye to finished form. One can only recommend this book, since it is morally incumbent upon any would-be critic to try to write poetry first.

Josef Malof: *A Manual of English Meters* (sic) (Indiana 1970)

G. N. Leech: *A Linguistic Guide to English Poetry* (Longman 1969).

Two books which deal in detail with technical linguistic matters. Malof's book is basically a scansion handbook, and pretty comprehensive (although some of the terminology is peculiarly American—*slacks* for unstressed syllables, and suchlike). Leech discusses a wider range of matters: metre, ambiguity, poetic licence, verbal repetition. His concern is the 'surface texture' of language, but the surface turns out to be quite deep.

Robert Millar and Ian Currie: *The Language of Prose* (Heinemann Educational Books 1972). An excellent book: well written and clearly organized. It deals in more depth with many of the topics examined in the chapter on prose in this book.

Marjorie Boulton: *The Anatomy of Prose* (Routledge and Kegan Paul 1954). A very thorough book which also attempts to explore prose in terms of such categories as 'Realism', 'Romance' and 'Unreality'. The chapter on prose rhythm is fascinating but perhaps eccentric.

Herbert Read: *English Prose Style* (G. Bell & Sons Ltd. 1928 [Revised 1952]). Although originally published some time ago, this is still a very readable and interesting book. It is very thorough, and, at times, idiosyncratic; a book to look at after Millar and Currie.

For those students who are interested in the study of language as such, there are many books available. The authors have found these books interesting and helpful:

Simeon Potter: *Our Language* (Pelican 1950). A basic, clear and well written paperback.

G. L. Brook: *A History of the English Language* (The Language Library, Deutsch 1958). One of the standard works on the English language. A scholarly work: students might well find the chapters on 'The development of English' and 'Semantics' interesting.

J. A. Sheard: *The Words We Use* (The Language Library, Deutsch 1954). Another standard and scholarly work on how we make words and where they come from.

Anthony Burgess: *Joysprick* (The Language Library, Deutsch 1973). A witty, fascinating and often irreverent study and loving appraisal of the language of the author James Joyce. For devotees.

Books on irony as such, seem relatively rare, although, of course, there are many hundreds that explore the use of irony made by such individual authors as Swift, Austen, Dickens and Twain and so on. The best approach to this subject might well be to read the ironists themselves rather than books of criticism.

195

D. C. Mueke: *The Compass of Irony* (London 1969). A very thorough and scholarly work on the various kinds of irony. It is especially interesting (though demanding) on the subject of 'Romantic' irony.

Wayne C. Booth: *The Rhetoric of Fiction* (University of Chicago Press 1961). An excellent and now standard work on the narrative methods employed by various novelists, a study which also naturally involves the examination of the ironic viewpoint.

M. Hodgart: *Satire* (London 1969). Perhaps the best (clearest and most useful as an introduction) book on the subject of satire that the authors have come across.

J. Sutherland: *English Satire* (Cambridge 1958). Originally the Clark lectures; a broad survey, often very illuminating.

Arthur Pollard: *Satire* (*The Critical Idiom*, Methuen 1970). A thorough introduction, especially useful on satiric poetry.

One book that authors have found invaluable is:

D. C. Mueke: *Irony* (*The Critical Idiom*, Methuen 1970). It is one of the few books we have come across which attempts to make useful and relevant connections between terms like 'Dramatic' and 'Tragic' irony. The chapter headed 'A Note on Meaning, Irony and Tone in Prose' in this book is indebted to many of the suggestions made by Mueke in his chapter 'The Nature of Irony'.

Glossary

Many of the definitions and descriptions given here are necessarily simplifications of rather complex matters. For this reason several entries refer you to books in which you will find more detailed accounts of the topic in question.

Words in capitals indicate that they are terms defined elsewhere in the glossary.

Abstract Form. 'Abstract' and 'organic' are terms used by Sir Herbert Read in an attempt to group literary forms into two main categories. His definitions are a little vague. Organic form, he says, is 'when a work of art has its own inherent laws, originating with its very invention and fusing in one vital unity both structure and content.' Abstract form occurs 'when an organic form is stabilized and repeated as a pattern, and the intention of the artist is no longer related to the inherent dynamism of an inventive act, but seeks to adapt content to a predetermined structure.' The difficulty in applying these definitions to particular literary forms is perhaps demonstrated by the fact that Sir Herbert chooses to illustrate his two types of form by referring, not to literature, but to primitive forms of decorative metalwork. The idea seems to be that an organic form is evolved when a writer develops a form with its own unique 'rules' because no form already in existence is capable of expressing that writer's vision, whereas abstract form is 'conventional'. Yet it is extremely difficult to point to undisputed examples. Is James Joyce's *Ulysses* organic, while, say, Jane Austen's *Emma* is abstract? Or T. S. Eliot's *The Waste Land* organic while Shakespeare's *Sonnets* are abstract? Although there is unlikely to be agreement on which literary works can be assigned to which category, the idea of 'abstract' and 'organic' form is in itself interesting, and it is

197

useful in that it concentrates our attention on the closeness or looseness of the relationship between form and content.
See Sir Herbert Read's *Collected Essays In Literary Criticism* (Faber 1938 & 1954) Part I

Accent. We have used this word to mean 'stress' or 'emphasis', although some writers distinguish between 'stress', meaning *metrical stress*, and 'accent', meaning the emphases of natural speech. See **metre**.

Accentual Verse. See **Stress-Verse** and page 31.

Alexandrine. A metrical line of six two-syllable feet. The name comes from an Old French romance on Alexander the Great in which this metre is used. The most familiar example is the second line of this couplet by (inevitably) Pope:

> A needless Alexandrine ends the song,
> That, like | a wound | ed snake, | drags its | slow length | along.

Allegory. Basically, an extended metaphor; that is, a work in which the characters, events, locations, etc, represent or symbolize other things, often abstractions. In the best known English allegory—Bunyan's *Pilgrim's Progress*—life is presented as a hazardous pilgrimage, Vanity and Despair are places, Sin is a heavy pack on Christian's back, and so forth. Thus allegories make systematic use of **personification** and **symbolism**. Allegories tend to be *didactic*. Works which are not, strictly speaking, allegories may have conspicuous allegorical elements if certain symbols are developed in the narrative—as in, for examples, Coleridge's *The Rime of the Ancient Mariner*, Melville's *Moby Dick*, Golding's *Pincher Martin*.

Alliteration. (Sometimes called 'initial rhyme').
The repetition of initial consonant sounds. See Page 23.

Amphibrach. See **Metrical Feet.**

Anapaest. See **Metrical Feet** and page 25.

Anthropomorphization. Literally, 'the giving of human form'—either ascribing human characteristics to God or the gods, or, in poetry, attaching human characteristics to abstract or inanimate things. (An extended example is Shelley's *To Night*, page 131).

198

Antithetical Balance. See Page 63.

Apostrophe. See **Rhetorical Devices.**

Approximate Rhyme. Near, half or slant rhyme. See Page 23.

Assonance. The repetition of a vowel sound through a passage. See Page 23.

Ballad. Folk Ballads are narrative verses, songs composed for musical accompaniment. Often anonymous and of ancient origin, they are likely to undergo adaption and alteration over the generations. They usually tell of a legendary incident, a battle, a folk hero such as Robin Hood, or some traditional romantic episode, making much use of repetition or refrains, and simple rhymes. Within this rough definition, the form of ballads varies, but by the **ballad stanza** we commonly mean a four line verse, rhyming ABCB, with the first and third lines as tetrameters and the second and fourth lines trimeters, e.g.,

> The King sits in Dunfermline town,
> Drinking the blood-red wine:
> 'O where will I get a good sailor,
> To sail this ship of mine?'

It is usual for a ballad to have an iambic metre, but there are plenty of exceptions. Ballads are often written in COMMON MEASURE. **Literary Ballads** are, obviously, poets' imitations or adaptations of folk ballads. Some stick close to the traditional form (e.g. Keats' *La Belle Dame Sans Merci*) while others entail considerable deviation. (Perhaps because the ballad form is quite easy to memorize, ballads have often been written with a political or satirical content.) Modern practitioners and adapters of the ballad include Auden and Dylan Thomas.

Ballade. Generally, a poem consisting of three eight-line stanzas (with a strict rhyme scheme based on very few different rhymes—usually three) plus a concluding **Envoy.** The Envoy is a dedication or direct address to a particular person (e.g. the poet's lover) or to a personification, or to God or Christ. The Envoy is shorter than the stanza, normally by half. Needless to say, there are many variations.

Bathos. The Greek word for 'depth', it has come to mean an unintentional or ludicrous descent from what is meant to be grand or noble sentiment into the trivial or mundane. The *intentional* use of bathos is a stock-in-trade of the satirist. **Anticlimax** is often used as a synonym for bathos.

Blank Verse. Simply, unrhyming iambic pentameter verse as used, for instance, by Shakespeare and Milton. See **verse paragraph**.

Cadence. See **Caesura**.

Caesura. The main pause in a line of verse. Its position may be determined by the demands of natural speech, or grammar, or by **Cadence**. It is often marked by a punctuation of some sort, but this is by no means a general rule. The positioning of the caesura is one way a poet can achieve **Metrical Variation**. We discuss this in the 'Note on Rhythm and Rhyme' pages 28 to 31, and again, with reference to a stanza by Auden, on page 128.

Common Measure. (often abbreviated as C.M.)
The quatrain of the **Ballad Stanza**, but stricter in its iambic metre and rhymes, which are usually ABAB.
It is the form of many English hymns, and is therefore also called the **Hymnal Stanza**.

> Ŏ Gód|oŭr hélp|iň ág|ĕs pást,
> Oŭr hópe|fŏr yeárs|tŏ cóme,
> Oŭr shel|tĕr fróm|thĕ stór|mў blást
> Aňd oúr| ĕ tér|năl hóme.

Conceit. Originally meaning an idea, concept or image, it is now commonly used in a derogatory sense to signify an image or metaphor in which the dissimilarity between the things compared is more striking than their similarity. In this sense, the word suggests *incongruity*, as in Crashaw's image (referred to on page 95) of weeping eyes as 'Two walking baths . . .' Conceit is used in a non-derogatory, neutral, sense, however, particularly when it refers to the imagery of Metaphysical poetry. A well-known **metaphysical conceit** is to be found in Donne's *A Valediction: Forbidding Mourning* where he compares the souls of himself and his lover with the twin legs of a draughtsman's compasses.

Consonance.   The repetition of a sequence of consonants with a change of intervening vowels. Wilfred Owen is noted for his use of this technique, and lines from his poem *Exposure* are often quoted by way of example:

> Our brains ache, in the merciless iced east winds that
>   *knive us* . . .
> Wearied we keep awake because the night is *silent* . . .
> Low, drooping flares confuse our memory of the *salient* . . .
> Worried by silence, sentries whisper, curious, *nervous*,
> But nothing happens.

This stanza is also rich in ASSONANCE.

Couplet.   Two consecutive lines of verse, usually united by the same metre or by rhyme or both.

Dactyl.   See **Metrical Feet** and Page 25.

Elegy.   A poem of lament or mourning. The Classical elegy was composed in a special elegiac metre, but in present critical use the word involves no particular formal conventions, as can be demonstrated by comparing the forms of the most famous elegies in English—Milton's *Lycidas*, Gray's *Elegy in a Country Churchyard*, and Tennyson's *In Memoriam*. Auden's *In Memory of W. B. Yeats* employs FREE VERSE (see pages 127 to 129).

Elision.   The omission of an unstressed syllable in order that the line be made to conform to a metrical scheme. Noticeable in such words as o'er (over) and e'en (even).

End-Rhyme.   Rhymes falling at the ends of lines.

Enjambment (Also called **Run-on**).   Enjambment occurs when the end of a line does not coincide with a normal pause dictated by sense, logic or punctuation:

> My faint spirit was sitting in the light
> of thy looks, my love;

When pauses do coincide with line-endings, these lines are **end-stopped**. An **open couplet** is one in which there is an enjambment on the second line which requires the first line of the next couplet to complete the meaning.

201

Epithalamion. A poem written to celebrate a marriage. Spenser's *Epithalamion* (1595) is the most famous English poem of this sort.

Even Accent. More than one syllable in a word is stressed, e.g. mankind, brainstorm.

Fancy. Fancy has come to signify a mental activity inferior to imagination, in that it merely elaborates or embroiders sensory experiences while the imagination (ideally) orders, unifies and reassesses them. Thus 'fanciful' now has derogatory implications. Using both words in their modern sense, a CONCEIT is a product of fancy. Coleridge's distinction between Imagination and Fancy is famous; see I. A. Richards' *Coleridge on Imagination* (1934).

Feminine Ending. See **Metre** and **Metrical Feet**.

Foot-Verse. Metrical verse. See pages 28 to 31.

Free Verse. Verse not built upon metrical feet or regular stress-patterns. See pages 31 to 32.

Georgianism. A term usually applied to the work of a group of poets writing during the reign of George V (1910-36). Their poetry, collected in four anthologies by Edward Marsh (the first published in 1912), is not now highly esteemed, generally. It is traditional in form and technique, refined and craftsman-like rather than passionate or adventurous, and its subject-matter is predominately rural. Even Marsh referred to its 'lack of inspiration.' Despite the fact that Georgian verse is looked upon with some condescension, a number of very good poets are identified or associated with the movement—Edward Thomas, Thomas Hardy and Wilfred Owen, for example—although A. E. Housman, John Masefield and W. H. Davies are more commonly cited as 'typical' Georgian Poets. Georgianism is representative of the kind of poetry against which the 'radical' poets, such as Pound, Eliot and the IMAGISTS, reacted. (See pages 31 and 123).
Georgian Verse, ed. James Reeves, 1962.

Gothic Novel. 'Gothic' originally denoted the Goths, that Germanic tribe who so ungenteely participated in the destruction of Rome. The term then came to mean 'mediaeval', and describes fiction which employs pseudo-mediaeval trappings—castles, towers, dungeons, and general dankness—and which enjoyed much popularity during the latter part of the eighteenth century and through the nineteenth. The vogue began with Horace Walpole's *Castle of Otranto, a Gothic Story* (1764); other famous examples are Beckford's *Vathek* (1786), Mrs. Radcliffe's *The Mysteries of Udolpho* (1794) and Lewis' *The Monk* (1797). Gothic novels are intended to evoke terror, and do so by means of ghosts, nightmarish violence, premature burials, various sinister secret passageways and tunnels, and widespread nastiness. They deal, in other words, with morbid psychological states and the irrational, and they often conceal a rather perverse eroticism. Melodrama is their mode. Gothic elements are to be found in Dickens, and the taste lingers on in 'Horror' cinema. In the United States, Gothic literature is identified with the South, where the menacing Black man is added to the terrifying repertoire. Edgar Allen Poe is the nineteenth-century American Gothicist *par excellence*, and in the twentieth century the word is in some ways applicable to the work of such Southern writers as William Faulkner, Carson McCullers and Truman Capote. Gothic writing may be seen as 'the dark underside of Romanticism.'

Three Gothic Novels Ed. P. Fairclough, Penguin Books (1968);
Montagu Summers, *The Gothic Quest* (1968);
Pastoral and Romance ed. Eleanor T. Lincoln. (1969).

Haiku. (or Hokku). A Japanese poetic form which presents a vivid and precise image which has philosophical or spiritual significance. The Haiku has three lines, of which the first and third have five syllables and the second seven. See IMAGISM and page 99.

Hyperbole. See also 'A Note on Meaning, Irony and Tone in Prose' (chapter 7). Hyperbole is the Greek word for 'overthrow' or 'overshoot'; it signifies, in literature, a deliberate exaggeration or overstatement. The *Shorter Oxford Dictionary* quotes Deuteronomy, Ch. 6: ' . . . cities great and fenced up to Heaven.' Marlowe's plays show a fondness for hyperbole, and a well-known Shakespearian hyperbole is Macbeth's cry that his bloodstained hand would dye the ocean red:

> . . .this my hand will rather
> The multitudinous seas incarnadine,
> Making the green one red.

The technique is often used for comic or ironic effects. The opposite device is MEIOSIS, or **Understatement**. In serious use, meiosis can intensify feeling by conveying strong emotion in utterly simple language. A somewhat chilling use of it in a satirical context is Swift's: 'Last week I saw a woman flayed, and you will hardly believe how much it altered her appearance for the worse.' Meiosis resembles, in this respect, **Litotes**, which understates a positive assertion by affirming the negative: 'He was not altogether polite', meaning 'He was extremely rude.'

Iamb.   A metrical foot of one unstressed syllable followed by a stressed syllable. See page 25.

Idyl.   A form of PASTORAL, the idyl is specifically a short poem giving an idealized picture of rural life.

Image.   See 'A Note on Imagery.'

Imagism.   That poetic movement which flourished in England during the second decade of this century, associated with Ezra Pound, T. E. Hulme, 'H.D.' et. al. Its criterion was the freshness, economy and purity of the image, which must be liberated from sentimentality, fuzziness and loose allusiveness. One model for these poets was the HAIKU. The characteristic Imagist poem is short and in free verse. The movement has been influential; its effect can be detected in Yeats and a great deal of subsequent American poetry. See Pages 98 to 100.
Stanley T. Coffman *Imagism* (1921)
Imagist Poetry (Penguin 1972) ed. Jones.

Implied Author.   See **Persona.**

Internal Rhyme.   Rhymes within a line. See Page 23.

Irony.   See 'A Note on Meaning, Irony and Tone in Prose' (chapter 7).

Italian Sonnet. (Petrarchan Sonnet). See **Sonnet.**

Lay, or **Lai.**   A term applied to certain mediaeval French poems, some of which were LYRICS, while others were composed in rhyming tetrameter couplets; both kinds can be sung to musical accompaniment. Traditionally, their subject matter is legend, particularly Arthurian legend. Scott's *Lay of the Last Minstrel* is perhaps the best known example in English.

Lyric.   The term originally signified a poem to be accompanied by music played on the lyre. The current use of the word need not signify a song, but is applied generally to a fairly short, non-narrative poem intended to express a personal feeling or state of mind or response. The poet often speaks in the first person, but the 'I' may well be a consciously adopted PERSONA. By this loose definition, the lyric is the commonest form in modern poetry.

Masculine Ending.   See **Metrical Foot.**

Masculine Rhyme.   See **Rhyme.**

Meiosis.   See **Hyperbole.**

Metaphor.   See 'A Note on Imagery' (chapter 9).
Our above-mentioned chapter is in large part a discussion of metaphor, so we shall restrict ourselves here to additional information. A metaphor, in that it is a mode of comparison, necessarily has at least two elements. I. A. Richards named these two elements **Tenor** and **Vehicle,** and these two terms have passed into the modern critical vocabulary. The **Tenor** is the subject, the thing being characterized, while the **Vehicle** is the means by which it is characterized, the *figure* which makes the comparison. In the metaphorical phrase 'the cataract of sunshine', the tenor is 'sunshine', and 'cataract' is the vehicle. In 'We must not make a scarecrow of the Law', 'Law' is tenor and 'scarecrow' vehicle. In the following lines from *Hamlet,* the tenor is the dawn, and the vehicle is an approaching woman dressed in a reddish cloak:

> But look, the morn in russet mantle clad
> Walks o'er the dew on yon high eastern hill. . . .

It is very often the case that the tenor of a metaphor is only implied; one might say therefore, that an ALLEGORY is an extended metaphor with the tenor left implicit while the vehicle is developed into a narrative.
A **Subdued Metaphor** is one which implicity underlies a sequence of images, as when in *Macbeth* Duncan says to Banquo:

I have begun to plant thee, and will labour
to make thee full of growing. . . .

where the subdued metaphor is of Banquo as a sapling or
young plant which, when full grown, will 'yield a harvest' of
the qualities needed in a ruler.

A **Mixed Metaphor** is one in which over-complexity or incongruity
destroy any effectiveness; the suggested resemblance between
dissimilars is false. In her *Cold Comfort Farm*, Stella Gibbons
wrings many comic effects out of mixed metaphors:

> Huddled in the hollow like an exhausted brute, the frosted
> roofs of Howling, crisp and purple as broccoli leaves,
> were like beasts about to spring.

A **Simile** is a metaphor in which the tenor and vehicle are
identified, and their relationship specified by the word 'like'
or 'as': 'a memory like a sieve', 'a heart heavy as lead', etc.

Metonymy. Use of the name of one attribute of a thing instead of
naming the thing itself. e.g. 'hand' for worker, 'crown' for
king, 'head' for person. A similar device is SYNECDOCHE,
where the part stands for the whole, e.g. 'the printed word'
for all books, a 'bite' for a meal etc.

Metre. See pages 24 to 30.
The patterns of a poem's rhythms when they are formally
organized. A metrical line divides into more or less equal
units (METRICAL FEET) of stressed and unstressed syllables.
These regulate the speed at which verse may be read, and a
metrical foot is therefore a measurement of *time*.
Metres are named according to the number of feet to a line:

Monometer: One foot   **Hexameter:** Six feet
Dimeter: Two feet   (see **Alexandrine**)
Trimeter: Three feet   **Heptameter:** Seven feet
Tetrameter: Four feet   **Octameter:** Eight feet
Pentameter: Five feet

(lines of more than six feet tend to break up into two lines of
say, trimeter and tetrameter.)

Metrical Foot. In the 'Note on Rhythm and Rhyme' we have
already defined four metrical feet: the iamb, trochée, the

206

anapaest and the dactyl. There are one or two further terms which describe fairly common metrical phenomena, and which are useful in SCANSION:

A **Spondée** is a foot of two more or less equal stresses. Shakespeare's epitaph begins with a Spondaic foot:

Goód fríend, | Fŏr Jés | ŭs' sáke | fŏrbéar
To dig the dust enclosed here . . .

A **Pyrrhic** is a foot of two short or unstressed syllables, as in the third foot of:

Sée, thĕ|líght ĭs|ăt thĕ|wíndŏw.

It is possible, however, to argue that, strictly speaking, the pyrrhic does not exist. An important point in metrics is that the prevalent metre can persuade the reader to give stress to syllables which in normal speech would not be stressed. The dominant trochaic metre in the above line imposes some slight emphasis upon 'at', and therefore that third foot is not a 'true' pyrrhic.

The most common forms of **metrical variation** are

i) **Catalexis**, the dropping of an unstressed syllable from a line. This happens most frequently in trochaic metres:

Tígĕr, |Tígĕr, | búrnĭng |bríght
Iń thĕ |fórĕst | óf thĕ | níght

when the last syllable of the line is omitted.

ii) **Substitution**, i.e. of one kind of foot for another. The commonest substitution is that of a trochée for the first iamb in iambic pentameters. There are hundreds of examples. It occurs in the first of these two lines:

Fáde făr|ăwáy,|dĭssólve,|ăńd quíte|fŏrǵet
Whăt thóu|amóng|thĕ leáves|hăs név|eŕ knówn.

Lines such as the last four quoted have **Masculine Endings**— they close with a stressed syllable; while lines ending with an unstressed syllable have **Feminine Endings**. The first line of Keats' *Endymion* has a feminine ending:

Ă thíng|ŏf beáu|tў ís|ă jóy|fŏr é|vĕr

(If you now turn to page 128, you will see, in Auden's quatrain from *In Memory of W. B. Yeats*, a clear example of catalexis and feminine ending used for dramatic effect.)

See Karl Shapiro and Robert Beum: *A Prosody Handbook* (1965).
Joseph Malof: *A Manual of English Metres*. (1970)
Harvey Gross (ed): *The Structure Of Verse*. (1966)

Octave. An eight-line poem or stanza, or the first part of a sonnet.

Ode. A long lyric poem, the subject and style of which is serious, elevated and elaborate. The **Pindaric Ode** (also called the **Regular Ode**) is an imitation of the odes of the Greek poet Pindar, who based his ode-structure on the songs sung by the chorus in Greek Drama. Pindar's odes were written to eulogize and glorify winners of the Olympic games and Pindaric odes in English often retain this commemorative or adulatory purpose, whether directed to a person, an abstraction (e.g. Wordsworth's *Ode to Duty*) or some natural phenomenon (e.g. Shelley's *Ode to the West Wind*). The **Irregular Ode**, which abandons the formal structure of the Pindaric Ode, is more common in English poetry; it allows for changes in mood and subject and is generally more flexible. Wordsworth's *Ode: Intimations of Immortality* . . . is one impressive example.

The **Horation Ode** differs from the Pindaric in two respects: its tone is one of meditativeness, rather than eulogy, and its structure is a single repeated stanza form. The best known instance is Keats' *Ode on a Grecian Urn*.

Perhaps because of the intense meditativeness associated with it, the ode form in English reached its acme with the Romantic poets; its form and tone have not appealed greatly to twentieth-century writers. Such modern odes as do exist (e.g. versions by Auden and Allen Tate) tend to be ironic.

Onomatopoeia. Strictly, an onomatopoeic word resembles, in its pronunciation, the thing it signifies: 'hiss', 'cuckoo', 'buzz', and so forth. In a rather less precise way, these much-quoted lines by Tennyson are onomatopoeic:

> The moan of doves in immemorial elms,
> And murmuring of innumerable bees.

In its more general, looser, sense, the concept of onomatopoeia raises fundamental questions about language as imitation. It

208

seems certain, anyway, that certain sounds have particular effects. Low, rounded vowel sounds suggest heaviness, depth —'doom', 'labour', 'cave'—while others suggest darkness, or lightness, or sharpness. (All this, of course, is more or less subjective.)

The meaning of onomatopoeia is often expanded to include the parallelism of rhythmic effects and subject matter, or, say, the use of sharp stressed consonants when describing fierce emotion or violence. Pope, who wrote that 'The sound must seem an echo to the sense,' was adept in this 'onomatopoeic' technique.

Oxymoron and **Paradox.** A phrase, statement or idea which seems absurd or self-contradictory and thus impossible, but which might, in fact, express a new truth, or an original view of an orthodox idea, or a meaning valid in some way. The Metaphysicals were fond of punning paradoxes; John Donne, in writing of the unfaithfulness of women, observes that:

> For as Philosophy teacheth us, that light things do always tend upwards and heavy things decline downward; Experience teacheth us otherwise, that the disposition of a *light* woman is to fall . . .

Andrew Marvell's *The Definition of Love* is full of clever paradoxes which culminate in his lament that the harmony between he and his lover actually keeps them apart; their lives are 'so truly parallel' that, like parallel lines, they may be infinitely long but can never meet.

An **Oxymoron** is a conjunction of two terms which are ordinarily contradictory: 'a wise fool', 'a cheerful pessimist', 'living death'. Because it involves a discrepancy between language and meaning, paradox may be considered an aspect of *Irony*.

Pastoral. The word comes from the Latin *Pastor*, a shepherd. The Pastoral, as developed by the classical poets, was a poem which idealized the 'innocence' of country life. The standard trappings will be familiar: shepherds playing pipes, eternal summer, conversations with visiting goddesses, and so on.

Christian pastoralists, employing the symbolism of Christ the shepherd, added a religious and allegorical dimension to the conventional pastoral.

Over the centuries, of course, the credibility of the idyllic pastoral world lessened; by 1800 Pastoral had been parodied to death. Modern usage of the term is more generalized. William Empson (in *Some Versions of Pastoral*, 1950) applies it to widely differing works of literature whose common theme is an admiration or celebration of a simple life-style and an implicit or explicit attack on sophisticated and dehumanizing social organization.

Pathos. Deep feeling. The word is now usually applied to poems, scenes, etc., intended to kindle feelings of a sorrowful or pitying kind. Excessive pathos tends to turn into sentimentality.

Persona and **Tone of Voice.** See also 'A Note on Meaning, Irony and Tone in Prose'.

This is a subtle and complicated business. The word **Persona** means, literally, 'a mask'; applied to literature, it means the 'filter' through which the writer addresses his audience. This 'filter' may take the form of an actual *character* who is the 'author' of the book, which is written in the first person. This **Narrator** may have a good deal in common with the real author, or he may have characteristics, circumstances and beliefs very different from those of his creator, as is the case in Swift's *Gulliver's Travels*. Sometimes the author may speak through more than one such narrator, and the personalities and viewpoints of these personae may differ greatly. William Faulkner uses this technique in *The Sound and The Fury*, and again in *As I Lay Dying*, in which the members of a family each in their turn address the reader directly. The most obvious advantage of such a method is that it allows the reader to see the same sequence of events from more than one point of view.

In the works we have mentioned so far, the narrating persona is a more-or-less fully realized character; that is, he tells us about himself, his life, his feelings, his part in the events which take place. (We know, for instance, Gulliver's age, his family background, his education; we know he wears spectacles, that he is gullible and that in the end he goes mad.) Such a character participates in the action—indeed, is, often, the central character, the protagonist. But there are many books in which the narrating persona, although speaking 'from experience' as a participant in the action, is not the central character. Our attention is not focussed on his or her adventures or attitudes. This kind of narrator is somewhat detached; he reports what he witnessed rather than what he felt. This creates the impression that the narrative is more 'objective', and the reader is thus more easily persuaded to accept the narrator's version of what happened. This is an important rhetorical device; see **Rhetoric**. (This 'objectivity' is, of course, illusory; we are still subject to one point of view.) Examples of this use of persona are Chaucer's *Canterbury Tales*, in which the narrator is one of the pilgrims but does not, in the *Prologue*, describe himself; Melville's *Moby-Dick*, which begins with the words 'Call me Ishmael', but our attention is centred not on Ishmael but on Captain Ahab; and Conrad's *Lord Jim*, in which the misadventures of the protagonist are presented as an after-dinner anecdote delivered by 'Marlow'. The practical advantages of using a narrator who is not a fully-realized character should be fairly obvious. The author does not need to maintain the *consistency* of the narrator's character—we can 'forget' that we are seeing from one point of view, and this enables the author to include scenes the narrator cannot have witnessed, or to convey feelings the narrator is unlikely to have experienced; the constant use of 'I' is unnecessary. In other words, the narrator who is not a 'rounded' character can be used more flexibly.

The narrator-persona who is not really a character functions as a **Voice**, or **Implied Author**. The tone of voice indicates not only the narrator's attitude towards the characters and situations he describes but also his attitude towards us, his readers. As readers of *Lord Jim* we are made, so to speak, honorary guests of Marlow; we join a select group of colonial expatriates on his veranda, light our imaginary cigars and watch the Oriental night. Marlow speaks to us as members of this group and his tone invites a rather melancholy meditativeness; he assumes that, like him, we have a wise but troubled awareness of human nature; we are invited to contemplate and relish his experiences.

Chaucer's use of his Pilgrim-Narrator demonstrates the flexibility of the Implied Author. This Narrator is often naive and impressionable, as when he speaks admiringly of the Monk as a 'fine example' of the Brotherhood when he is, in fact, an example of the decadence of the mediaeval monastic orders. What happens here is that the Narrator's foolish praise draws our attention to the Monk's corruption; both Monk and Narrator are being satirized. In this instance, Chaucer is clearly using a persona whose point of view is different from his own; but at other points in the *Prologue*, such as the eulogy of the simple country parson and the savage portrait of the Pardoner, we sense that this persona is partly or altogether dropped; the voice seems to be Chaucer's own, rather than the Narrator's.

A similar inconsistency occurs in the main body of the *Tales*. When it is the Pilgrim-Narrator's turn to tell a story, he begins one which is so dreadful and boring that the Host is compelled to put a stop to it; the verse is so 'drasty' (lovely word) that it is 'not worth a turd.' Yet there has been nothing 'drasty' about the Narrator's verse so far—quite the reverse, in fact. These inconsistencies do not disturb the reader. We are prepared to grant Chaucer a free hand in achieving his ironic effects; we are amused by switches in tone, attitude and character which in real life would perhaps perplex or annoy us. (To wonder why this is so, why we are so ready to suspend our disbelief and be seduced into a fictitious world, would lead us into speculations of a psychological or philosophical kind which are outside the limits of this book.)

So far, we have discussed personae and implied authors who are, to a greater or lesser extent, participating characters. Let us turn now to the implied author who is characterized *only* by his tone of voice. The classic example is The Author of Fielding's *Tom Jones*. (From now on, when we write The Author—capitalized—we mean this narrating voice, as distinct from the author, the *actual* writer of the book.) In *Tom Jones*, The Author—as he calls himself—is a distinct presence. He addresses us directly as 'Dear Reader'; he interrupts the action to make comments, to apologize for presenting un-savoury incidents, to answer critics, to digress into discussions of love and reflect upon his writing. At one point The Author makes an apologetic appearance on the 'stage' in order to say something which he 'could not prevail on any of my actors to speak.' (One effect of this is to remind the reader that the book is an artifice, a game in which the reader is participating. An even nicer example of the technique is to be found in Sterne's *Tristram Shandy*, in which, rather than risk describing Widow Wadman, Sterne leaves a blank page upon which the reader may draw her.) The Author gives us no biographical information about himself; his character we deduce from his tone and manner, which are ironic but basically benevolent, extremely polite yet playful, sly and knowing but at times ostentatiously naive. The Author is god-like; we might call him the 'Organizing Intelligence'. His attitude toward the world he has created conditions *our* attitude towards it; more importantly, perhaps, he conditions our attitude towards the *real* world, in so far as it resembles the world of *Tom Jones*. The point to remember is that The Author is a voice *adopted* by Fielding for his purposes. We cannot say simply that The Author is Henry Fielding.

Finally, a word about the 'I' we encounter in poems. When we read 'I meditate upon a swallow's flight,' we ought not merely to assume that 'I' is the poet William Butler Yeats, aged 74, of Thoor Ballylee, Galway, Ireland. Or that the 'I' that 'wandered lonely as a cloud' is William Wordsworth, 1770–1850. It may be as well to consider the first person singular of a poem as a type of persona, in that the man who writes a poem is adopting a special attitude towards his personal experience, and the 'I' in the poem is therefore a rôle, a particular stance which the poet does not usually adopt for the purposes of his day-to-day living. A 'heightened consciousness', if you like.

Generally, the concept of persona counteracts the tendency to interpret a writer's work in terms of his or her life experience. Fiction and poetry are not autobiography. When discussing an individual poem which is written in the first person it is better to refer to 'the poet' rather than 'Blake' or 'Keats' or 'Eliot' or whoever.

See: Wayne C. Booth's *The Rhetoric of Fiction* (1961)
J. O. Perry's *Approaches to the Poem* (1965)

Prosody.   The rules or principles which govern a verse structure. Prosody involves such things as metres, rhythms, stanza forms, etc. The word may be used to indicate the principles of a species of poetry—so that the technicalities of STRESS VERSE are collectively known as **stress prosody**; or it may be applied to the poetic techniques of an individual writer—as in Robert Bridges's book *Milton's Prosody*.

Quantitative Verse (Also called **Classical Prosody**).
The classical poets of Greece and Rome employed a system of metrics which was not based on stress, but upon the length of syllables. A long syllable took twice as long to pronounce as a short one. Metre was therefore a matter of the quantities of time allowed to syllables, and therefore it has come to be called quantitive verse. English does not lend itself readily to quantitive verse, although some Elizabethan poets practised it, as did Coleridge and Tennyson. English poets have, however, written a good deal of **Syllabic Verse**, is which the lines are dictated not by metre or stress-pattern but by the *number* of syllables. Milton and Pope wrote verses in ten-syllable lines.

Quatrain.   See Also **Stanza forms** and **Common Measure**.
A four line stanza.

Rhetoric. Simply put, rhetoric is the art of persuasion, the art of presenting an argument. To list and demonstrate the techniques of the art of rhetoric as it was developed by Aristotle and later classical writers would require at least a full-length essay. We will limit ourselves here to a few observations.

The classical rhetoricians divided the rhetorical process into three stages: *invention* (the conceiving of an argument and its conclusion or proof); *disposition* (the arrangement of the argument); and *style* (the selection of words, images, speech-rhythms, and so forth, which would express the ideas most effectively). These divisions clearly correspond to elements of imaginative literature. Style obviously does; *invention* corresponds to the 'theme', 'idea', 'belief' or 'inspiration' the poet or novelist want to convey, and *disposition* to the plot of a novel or play, or a narrative generally. Although Aristotle makes a distinction between the methods of rhetoric and poetry, the closeness of the relationship between the two was a preoccupation of critics and writers up to the end of the eighteenth century. (This may help us to understand how it was that writers such as Dryden, Addison and Pope could propose 'rules' and 'models' for literature in a way that seems so 'scientific' to a modern reader.) With the arrival of nineteenth-century Romanticism, interest in the mechanics of rhetoric diminished; a literary work was seen more as an expression of the artist's soul and brain; it was personal and individual, it need not conform to the rules of rhetoric or anything else.

In recent years the interest of some critics has shifted away from the idea of literature as personal expression, and has refocussed on the ways in which writers affect their readers. The effectiveness of a writer depends on how well he can *persuade* his readers to feel what he wants them to feel, or imagine what he wants them to imagine. This interest in a writer's 'methods of persuasion' has led to a revival of interest in rhetoric. One result of all this is the current emphasis on the PERSONA as a rhetorical device in literature, and this has certainly increased our understanding of certain writers— Swift, for one. Generally speaking, the more *didactic* a piece of work is, the more rhetorical it is likely to be.

Certain poetic forms are by nature more rhetorical than others; the PINDARIC ODE, for example, or the SONNET.

Rhetorical Devices. Of these the best known is the **Rhetorical Question**, which is a question posed in order to make a point, not to obtain an answer, the answer being inevitable: 'Do you

214

want to be a seven-stone weakling?' Milton's *Epitaph on Shakespeare* demonstrates this device:

> What needs my Shakespeare for his honoured bones
> The labour of an age in piled stones,
> Or that his hallowed relics should be hid
> Under a starry-pointing pyramid?
> Dear Son of Memory, great heir of fame
> What need'st thou such weak witness of thy name?

An **Apostrophe** is an interruption of a narrative or poem in order that the poet make a *direct address* to a person (alive or dead, absent or present) or to an abstract or symbolic thing. Chaucer makes much use of the apostrophe; his merchant, for example, several times interrupts his tale to deliver apostrophes on marriage, or infidelity, or jealousy. Keats' *To Autumn* is apostrophic, since the poem 'speaks' to that season directly:

> who has not seen thee oft amid thy store?

A **Zeugma** is a device which *joins* (the word derives from the Greek word meaning 'to yoke'); in particular it joins two incongruous things together by means applying one verb to both, with comic effect e.g.:

> She came in a flood of tears and a bath chair

or

> To stain her honour, or her new brocade.

Many other figures of speech, such as HYPERBOLE, PARADOX, UNDERSTATEMENT, ANTITHESIS etc., may be used for rhetorical effects.
Wayne C. Booth: *The Rhetoric of Fiction* (1961)
George Kennedy: *The Art of Persuasion in Greece* (1963)

Rhyme. See pages 23 to 30.

Rhyme-Scheme. The pattern of end-rhymes in a stanza or poem. A rhyme-scheme is expressed by labelling each line with a letter of the alphabet, using the same letter for lines which rhyme with each other. The rhyme-scheme of the following stanza can thus be written as AAABCBDEEDC.

This is the hidden place that hiders *know.*
This is where the hiders *go.*
Step softly, the snow that falls here is different *snow,*
The rain has a different *sting.*
Step softly, step like a cloud, step softly as the *least*
Whisper of air against the beating *wing,*
And let your eyes be *sealed*
With two blue *muscadines*
Stolen from the secret *vines*
Or you will never find, in the lost *field*
The table spread, the signs of the hidden *feast.*

Certain kinds of stanza have characteristic rhyme-schemes; see STANZA FORMS and SONNET.

Rhythm. See A Note on Rhythm and Rhyme.

Scansion. The analysis of the metrical pattern of a line of verse. See: **Metre** and **Metrical Foot;** and A Note on Rhythm and Rhyme (section 3, pages 24 to 27).

Sestet. A poem, or a stanza, of six lines; also the second 'section' of a sonnet.

Sight-Rhyme. See Page 23.

Sonnet. See also 'A Note on Form and Structure', pages 116 to 118. A single-stanza poem of 14 iambic pentameter lines, which may usually be divided into two groups, one of eight lines (the OCTAVE) followed by one of six lines (the SESTET). This division is either implicit, or made explicit by the rhyme-scheme and/or by an actual space left on the page between the eight and ninth lines.

There are many varieties of sonnet, which are identified by their RHYME-SCHEMES; the best-known are those named after their most famous practitioners.

The **Petrarchan** (or **Italian**) **Sonnet,** is named after Petrarch, the fourteenth-century Italian poet. Its octave has two rhymes arranged ABBAABBA, and its sestet either two or three rhymes capable of a variety of arrangements—CDDCDC, CDECDE, etc. The following sonnet by Wordsworth is Petrarchan; it is also about the discipline of the sonnet form:

Nuns fret not at their convent's narrow room;
And hermits are contented with their cells;
And students with their pensive citadels;
Maids at the wheel, the weaver at his loom,
Sit blithe and happy; bees that soar for bloom,
High as the highest peak of Furness-fells,
Will murmur by the hour in foxglove bells;
In truth the prison, unto which we doom
Ourselves, no prison is: and hence for me,
In sundry moods, 'twas pastime to be bound
Within the Sonnet's scanty plot of ground;
Pleased if some Souls (for such there needs must be)
Who have felt the weight of too much liberty,
Should find brief solace there, as I have found.

The Italian language is richer in rhymes than is English, and consequently English poets have made alterations to the Italian sonnet form. (There are signs of strain in Wordsworth's sonnet—he resorts to the archaic word 'doom', meaning 'sentence', and the parenthesis in line twelve is a bit feeble.) The **Shakespearian Sonnet** divides the 14 lines into three quatrains with a concluding rhyming couplet. Each quatrain has a different pair of rhymes, as does the couplet. The basic octave/sestet division is implicit. The rhyme-scheme is therefore ABAB CDCD EFEF GG:

Shall I compare thee to a summer's day?
Thou art more lovely and more temperate.
Rough winds do shake the darling buds of May,
And summer's lease hath all too short a date.
Sometime too hot the eye of heaven shines,
And often is his gold complexion dimmed;
And every fair from fair sometime declines
By chance, or nature's changing course, untrimmed;
But thy eternal summer shall not fade,
Nor lose possession of that fair thou ow'st,
Nor shall Death brag thou wand'rest in his shade,
When in eternal lines to time thou grow'st.
   So long as men can breathe or eyes can see,
   So long lives this, and this gives life to thee.

The **Spenserian Sonnet** has a rhyme-scheme which unites the three quatrains, but again concludes with an independently rhyming couplet; the rhyme-scheme is ABAB BCBC CDCD EE.
   We have already considered some aspects of the sonnet in

Chapter 11. A few more comments of a general nature may help you in writing appreciations.

As we remarked in our 'Note on Form and Structure', the sonnet has had a very long lease of life in European literature, and even the most 'experimental' poets have employed the form. To some extent this may be explained by the fact that, in purely quantitative terms, love—sexual and spiritual—has been the greatest preoccupation of poetry, and for a long time the sonnet was held to be the perfect poetic vehicle for love. But it is the sonnet's *formal qualities* which have continuously attracted poets, not its amorous associations. What are these formal qualities?

First of all, its length. The sonnet is just long enough to allow for a quite complex 'train of thought' and an accompanying intricacy in imagery, but it is short enough to be 'taken in whole' by the reader; this relative brevity obliges the poet to be coherent and tightly-knit in his use of language. Then the very fact that the sonnet form is quite rigidly prescribed is a challenge to the poet's ingenuity, his craftsmanship. This same conventionality emphasizes that poetry is an *artifice*, and we could therefore argue that highly-stylized language, or use of CONCEITS, is more acceptable in a sonnet than in more organic forms. As we suggested on page 121, the 'rules' of the sonnet can impose a discipline upon an unruly imagination, and without such formal discipline imagination cannot find expression. Or as Wordsworth's sonnet suggests, it is 'Solace' for those 'who have felt the weight of too much liberty.'

Because the sonnet imposes certain limitations upon the poet it is arguable that there might even be some objective standard by which to evaluate particular sonnets. One might analyze several sonnets and be able to say that one is better than all the rest because the poet has been most successful in coming to terms with the form's discipline, and using that discipline to the greatest possible effect. Theoretically, you could perhaps analyze *all* sonnets to this purpose (you would have to be rather mad, of course). So, just feasibly, poets have been tempted by the possibility that *the* perfect sonnet exists. A sort of poetic Holy Grail. In any case, at least one critic has claimed that one particular sonnet (by Swinburne) is "the most perfect in the language."

The sonnet—particularly the Shakespearian variety—has a rather rhetorical structure. Several of Shakespeare's sonnets pursue what we could loosely call an argument. The one quoted on page 116 (sonnet 130) does so by going through a series of propositions which take the form of comparisons (all of which are dismissed as invalid). Sonnet 18, quoted above, begins with a *proposition* ('Shall I compare thee to a summer's day?') and then corrects this proposed simile by a number of what a rhetorician would call *exempla* (proofs by example). The sestet begins with the word 'But' which introduces an *assertion* in opposition to the original proposed simile; the final couplet is a *resolution* of the argument—his mistress' beauty cannot die while 'this' (i.e. the poem) exists to com-memorate it. This sonnet is thus 'rhetorical' in that it follows a logical (or pseudo-logical) progression.

Not all critics at all times have admired the sonnet. In his *Introduction to Shakespeare's Sonnets*, Auden quotes from an eighteenth-century commentator:

> Quaintness, obscurity and tautology are to be
> regarded as the constituent parts of this
> exotic species of composition. . . .I am one
> of those who should have wished it to have
> expired in the country where it was born. . . .
> (A sonnet) is composed in the highest strain
> of affectation, pedantry, circumlocution and
> nonsense.

Stanza. Stanzas are the groups of lines into which a poem is divided. We use the word, normally, to indicate a group which is repeated in a regular pattern, but **Irregular Stanzas** are not unusual. A stanza is identified by one or all of the following:
  a) the metre of its lines
  b) its rhyme-scheme
  c) the number of its lines.

Certain stanza-forms have special names (see below), but generally two-line stanzas are **Couplets,** three-line stanzas are **Triplets** or **Tercets,** four-line stanzas are **Quatrains,** five-line stanzas are **Quintains,** six-line stanzas are **Sestets,** seven-line stanzas are **Septets,** and eight-line stanzas are **Octaves.** (Octaves are frequently a combination of two Quatrains.) There is a shorthand with which to express a stanza, which consists of the notation for a RHYME-SCHEME (i.e. labelling with the same alphabetical letter lines which rhyme together) and a numeral above each letter to indicate the number of feet or stresses in that line. The following stanza (we've marked the stresses) can be expressed as A^3 B^4 A^3 B^4 :

Stand not uttering sedately
Trite oblivious praise above her!
Rather say you saw her lately
Lightly kissing her last lover.

Stanza Forms. See: **Ballad Stanza, Ballade, Common Measure, Couplet, Sonnet**. Other named stanza forms include:

The **Heroic Couplet,** a rhyming iambic pentameter couplet used, for example, by Chaucer throughout most of *The Canterbury Tales,* and by Pope, extensively.

Terza Rima is a series of tercets interlinked by rhyme in the pattern ABA, BCB, CDC etc. Shelley's *Ode to the West Wind* is probably the most famous example in English:

Thou on whose stream, mid the steep sky's commotion,
Loose clouds like earth's decaying leaves are shed,
Shook from the tangled boughs of Heaven and Ocean,

Angels of rain and lightning; there are spread
On the blue surface of thine aery surge,
Like the bright hair uplifted from her head . . .

Ottava Rima is an eight-line iambic pentameter group rhyming ABABABCC. The best-known instance is Byron's *Don Juan*.

Rhyme Royal is a seven-line iambic pentameter stanza. Because Chaucer used it for his *Troilus and Criseyde* it is also known as the **Troilus Stanza.** If rhymes ABABBCC.

For his *The Faerie Queene* Spenser devised a rather difficult nine-line stanza—the **Spenserian Stanza,** as we now call it—which consists of eight iambic pentameters and a concluding ALEXANDRINE. The rhyme-scheme runs ABABBCBCC. As well as being difficult, this stanza form is very satisfying, being rounded, harmonious and leisurely. It has been used by Byron, Keats, Shelley and Tennyson.

Stress Verse (Strong-Stress Metres) See page 31.
The rhythm of stress-verse is determined by the *number* of strong stresses to a line. Whereas in foot-verse metre is a matter of *feet* consisting of stressed and unstressed syllables grouped together, stress-verse discounts light and unstressed syllables, which can vary in number from line to line.

In Anglo-Saxon and Old English verse, the unity of a line was created by alliteration (**Alliterative Verse**). One sees this in *Beowulf*. The line did not rhyme. In Middle English poetry alliteration is still the basic formal device, but the synchronization of alliterated syllables and stresses is more systematized, and there are usually four stresses, or 'beats' to the line. There is a main pause, or CAESURA, at the middle of each line. A couplet from *Sir Gawain and the Green Knight* gives you some idea of the form:

> Mony klyf he overclambe · in contrayes straunge,
> Fer floten fro his frendes · fremedly he rydes.

Another fourteenth-century poem, Langland's *Piers Plowman*, opens with this lovely line in a similar pattern, but with beats and alliterations falling together:

> In somer seson whan soft was the sonne.

The four-stress metre—with the caesura dividing the line in half—is the basic rhythm of most stress verse. In modern usage, the number of beats per line varies in some regular pattern (see page 30), and alliteration is far less important as a formal device. Ezra Pound has written a very fine version of an Anglo-Saxon poem, *The Seafarer*. This brief extract demonstrates his use of stress-verse rhythms:

> Drear all this excellence, delights unendurable!
> Waneth the watch, but the world holdeth.
> Tomb hideth trouble. The blade is layed low.
> Earthly glory ageth and seareth.

Symbol. See Pages 100 to 102.

Synecdoche. See **Metonymy**.

Tenor. See **Metaphor**.

Terza Rima. See **Stanza Forms**.

Verse Paragraph. A group of lines of verse, usually BLANK VERSE, which form a 'unit of sense' similar to a prose paragraph. There are no general 'rules' as to the length of a verse paragraph.

Versification.   The technical aspects of poetry—metrics, and so forth—as they are involved in the practice, rather than the theory, of writing. See **Prosody**.

Villanelle.   A sophisticated but surprisingly adaptable French form which consists of nineteen lines arranged in five tercets and a final quatrain. There are only two rhymes throughout, the tercets being ABA, the quatrain ABBA. The first and third lines of the first tercet alternate as the last line of all the other tercets, and they are also the last two lines of the quatrain. If that sounds complicated, perhaps the first two tercets and the quatrain of William Empson's *Missing Dates* will clarify it a little:

> Slowly the poison the whole blood stream fills.
> It is not the effort nor the failure tires.
> The waste remains, the waste remains and kills.
>
> It is not your system or clear sight that mills
> Down small to the consequence a life requires;
> Slowly the poison the whole blood stream fills.
>
> It is the poems you have lost, the ills
> From missing dates, at which the heart expires.
> Slowly the poison the whole blood stream fills.
> The waste remains, the waste remains and kills.

Another very well-known modern villanelle is Dylan Thomas' *Do Not Go Gentle Into That Goodnight*.

Zeugma.   See **Rhetorical Devices.**

AUTHORSHIP OF POEMS AND PASSAGES NOT IDENTIFIED
IN THE TEXT

Chapter 4: A: from *Felix Holt the Radical* by George Eliot
(1819-1880)
B: from *Tono Bungay* by H. G. Wells (1866-1946)

Chapter 6: from an essay by Dr. Samuel Johnson (1709-1784)

Chapter 11: *To Night* by P. B. Shelley (1792-1822)
The Visitant by Theodore Roethke (1908-1963)

Practice Exercises:

I: *On the Dowager Countess of Pembroke* by William Browne
of Tavistock (1591-1643?)
Epitaph on the Lady Mary Villiers by Thomas Carew
(1598-1639?)
Extract from *Growing Up* by Joyce Cary (1888-1957)

II: *An Elementary School Classroom in a Slum* by Stephen
Spender (1909-   )
Extract from *A Hanging* by George Orwell (1903-1950)

III: Passage A from *Nottingham and the Mining Country* by
D. H. Lawrence (1885-1930)
Passage B from *Hard Times* by Charles Dickens (1812-
1870)
The Survivor by R. S. Thomas (1913-   )

IV: Extract from *The Armies of the Night* by Norman Mailer
(1968)
Upon Westminster Bridge by William Wordsworth (1770-1850)
London by William Blake (1757-1827)

V: *The Woman at Washington Zoo* by Randall Jarrell
(1914-1965)
Extract from *Scenes of Provincial Life* by William Cooper
(1910-   )

VI: Extract from *The Loved One* by Evelyn Waugh (1903-1966)
Because I Could Not Stop for Death by Emily Dickinson
(1830-1886)

VII: Extract A from *Emma* by Jane Austen (1775-1817)
B from *The Siege of Krishnapur* by J. G. Farrell
(1935-   )
Lucifer in Starlight by George Meredith (1828-1909)

VIII: *They Flee from Me* by Sir Thomas Wyatt (c. 1503-1542)
Kindliness by Rupert Brooke (1887-1915)
Extract from *Point Counterpoint* by Aldous Huxley (1894-
1963)